Who Wants What?

Why do some people support redistributive policies such as a generous welfare state, social policy, or protections for the poor, and others do not? The (often implicit) model behind much of comparative politics and political economy starts with redistribution preferences. These affect how individuals behave politically, and their behavior in turn affects the strategies of political parties and the policies of governments. This book challenges some influential interpretations of the political consequences of inequality. Rueda and Stegmueller provide a novel explanation of how the demand for redistribution is the result of expected future income, the negative externalities of inequality, and the relationship between altruism and population heterogeneity. This innovative and timely volume will be of great interest to readers interested in the political causes and consequences of inequality.

David Rueda is Professor of Comparative Politics at the Department of Politics and IR and Professorial Fellow at Nuffield College, Oxford University. He is the author of *Social Democracy Inside Out* (2007) and has received numerous research awards, including a British Academy Research Development Award (2008–2010). He has held visiting positions at the Centre d'Études Européennes (Sciences Po, Paris), Yale University, Princeton University, and Stanford University.

Daniel Stegmueller is an associate professor in the Department of Political Science at Duke University. He is also a Fellow at Nuffield College, Oxford University. His research has appeared in the *Annual Review of Political Science*, *American Journal of Political Science*, the *Journal of Politics*, *Political Analysis*, *Public Opinion Quarterly*, and the *Quarterly Journal of Political Science*.

Cambridge Studies in Comparative Politics

General Editors

Kathleen Thelen   *Massachusetts Institute of Technology*
Erik Wibbels   *Duke University*

Associate Editors

Catherine Boone   *London School of Economics*
Thad Dunning   *University of California, Berkeley*
Anna Grzymala-Busse   *Stanford University*
Torben Iversen   *Harvard University*
Stathis Kalyvas   *Yale University*
Margaret Levi   *Stanford University*
Helen Milner   *Princeton University*
Frances Rosenbluth   *Yale University*
Susan Stokes   *Yale University*
Tariq Thachil   *Vanderbilt University*

Series Founder

Peter Lange   *Duke University*

Other Books in the Series

Christopher Adolph, *Bankers, Bureaucrats, and Central Bank Politics: The Myth of Neutrality*

Michael Albertus, *Autocracy and Redistribution: The Politics of Land Reform*

Santiago Anria, *When Movements Become Parties: The Bolivian MAS in Comparative Perspective*

Ben W. Ansell, *From the Ballot to the Blackboard: The Redistributive Political Economy of Education*

Ben W. Ansell and David J. Samuels, *Inequality and Democratization: An Elite-Competition Approach*

Ana Arjona, *Rebelocracy: Social Order in the Colombian Civil War*

Leonardo R. Arriola, *Multi-Ethnic Coalitions in Africa: Business Financing of Opposition Election Campaigns*

David Austen-Smith, Jeffry A. Frieden, Miriam A. Golden, Karl Ove Moene, and Adam Przeworski, eds., *Selected Works of Michael Wallerstein: The Political Economy of Inequality, Unions, and Social Democracy*

S. Erdem Aytaç and Susan C. Stokes *Why Bother? Rethinking Participation in Elections and Protests*

Andy Baker, *The Market and the Masses in Latin America: Policy Reform and Consumption in Liberalizing Economies*

Laia Balcells, *Rivalry and Revenge: The Politics of Violence during Civil War*

Lisa Baldez, *Why Women Protest? Women's Movements in Chile*

Kate Baldwin, *The Paradox of Traditional Chiefs in Democratic Africa*

(continued after Index)

Who Wants What?

Redistribution Preferences in Comparative Perspective

DAVID RUEDA

University of Oxford

DANIEL STEGMUELLER

Duke University

CAMBRIDGE
UNIVERSITY PRESS

CAMBRIDGE
UNIVERSITY PRESS

University Printing House, Cambridge CB2 8BS, United Kingdom

One Liberty Plaza, 20th Floor, New York, NY 10006, USA

477 Williamstown Road, Port Melbourne, VIC 3207, Australia

314–321, 3rd Floor, Plot 3, Splendor Forum, Jasola District Centre, New Delhi – 110025, India

79 Anson Road, #06–04/06, Singapore 079906

Cambridge University Press is part of the University of Cambridge.

It furthers the University's mission by disseminating knowledge in the pursuit of education, learning, and research at the highest international levels of excellence.

www.cambridge.org
Information on this title: www.cambridge.org/9781108484626
DOI: 10.1017/9781108681339

© David Rueda and Daniel Stegmueller 2019

First published 2019

Printed in Singapore by Markono Print Media Pte Ltd

A catalogue record for this publication is available from the British Library.

Library of Congress Cataloging-in-Publication Data
NAMES: Rueda, David, author. | Stegmueller, Daniel, 1981– author.
TITLE: Who wants what? : redistribution preferences in comparative perspective / David Rueda, Daniel Stegmueller.
DESCRIPTION: Cambridge, United Kingdom ; New York, NY : Cambridge University Press, [2019] | Series: Cambridge studies in comparative politics | Includes bibliographical references and index.
IDENTIFIERS: LCCN 2018060513 | ISBN 9781108484626 (hardback) | ISBN 9781108723435 (paperback)
SUBJECTS: LCSH: Income distribution. | Income distribution–Political aspects. | BISAC: POLITICAL SCIENCE / General.
CLASSIFICATION: LCC HB523 .R84 2019 | DDC 339.2/2–dc23
LC record available at https://lccn.loc.gov/2018060513

ISBN 978-1-108-48462-6 Hardback
ISBN 978-1-108-72343-5 Paperback

Contents

Figures

Tables

Acknowledgments

We started this project a number of years ago, when the decline of the Left, the rise of populism, Brexit, and Trump were yet not part of our consciousness. At that time, David was a Professor at the Department of Politics and International Relations and a Fellow at Merton College and Daniel a Postdoctoral Prize Research Fellow at Nuffield College, Oxford University. In a way perhaps related to later political developments, we were both concerned about the causes and consequences of inequality and interested in exploring the main individual assumptions of political economy models about redistribution. We were both dissatisfied with these assumptions and thought that they needed to be complemented with arguments that would help us understand why some individuals support redistribution while other do not. Almost ten years (and several professional and geographic moves) later, this book represents our attempt to illuminate these issues.

The project, its related papers, articles, and book manuscript versions, have taken longer than most. And our list of acknowledgments is therefore also longer than most. First, we want to thank a number of colleagues and friends who have been influential with comments, suggestions, support, and encouragement from the very beginning of this project. We owe our greatest debt of gratitude to Pablo Beramendi, Desmond King, Jonas Pontusson, and Sue Stokes. We then presented related portions of the book in so many different forums that we are bound to forget or overlook some of the people who provided comments, suggestions and advice along the way. If so, we apologize. In these meetings, we were lucky to receive a great number of reactions that very much influenced the book we ended up writing. Special thanks go to Jim Alt,

Christopher Anderson, Ben Ansell, Cesc Amat, Lucy Barnes, Larry Bartels, Michael Becher, Carles Boix, Brian Burgoon, Marius Busemeyer, Andrea Campbell, Charlotte Cavaille, Adam Dean, Matt Dimmick, Alexandre Debs, Michael Donnelly, Ray Duch, Rob Franzese, Jane Gingrich, Bernard Grofman, Thomas Gschwend, Peter Hall, Silja Häusermann, Tim Hicks, John Huber, Torben Iversen, Larry Jacobs, Michael Jones-Correa, Mark Kayser, Orit Kedar, Hyeok Yong Kwon, Johannes Lindvall, Noam Lupu, Philip Manow, Isabela Mares, Yotam Margalit, John Marshall, Nolan McCarty, Anja Neundorf, David Nickerson, Bruno Palier, Clara Park, Thomas Pluemper, Sergi Pardos Prado, Carlo Prato, Philipp Rehm, Frances McCall Rosenbluth, Ron Rogowski, Ken Scheve, Martin Seeleib-Kaiser, Michael Shalev, Ian Shapiro, Katri Sieberg, David Soskice, Jeremy Spater, Lukas Stoetzer, Milan Svolik, Richard Traunmueller, Vera Troeger, Chris Way, and Erik Wibbels. At Cambridge University Press, Robert Dreesen and two anonymous reviewers really helped with the final push.

In the fall of 2015, Kathy Thelen organized a book workshop at MIT. The great comments from Pablo Beramendi, Andrea Campbell, James Conran, Jeremy Ferwerda, Torben Iversen, Kathy Thelen, and Andreas Wiedemann directed our editing and rewriting for more than a year afterwards.

In addition to the support of Duke University, University of Essex, University of Mannheim, Nuffield College, and the University of Oxford, several institutions made working on this book possible. David spent a productive year at the beginning of the project as a Visiting Senior Research Scholar at the Center for the Study of Democratic Politics (Princeton University) and one as we started to write the final version of the book manuscript as a Visiting Professor in Political Science and Senior Fellow at the MacMillan Center's Program on Democracy (Yale University). Discussions with colleagues and friends during these two periods were invaluable.

David and Daniel have taught a graduate seminar on the Political Economy of Inequality at different times and in different places since 2011. Successive cohorts of Essex, Oxford, and Mannheim graduate students (as well as some at Yale and Pompeu Fabra) have therefore contributed to our thinking about the politics of redistribution. Conversations with Cesc Amat, Lucie Cerna, Love Christensen, Verena Fetscher, Tim Hicks, Gerda Hooijer, Timo Idema, Ignacio Jurado, Karl Kahn, and Julia du Pont de Romemont were particularly helpful.

Finally, and most importantly, we would like to thank both our families. Without their support, we would not have even started, let alone finished, this project. We dedicate this book to them.

Introduction

This is a book about the demand for redistribution of income through taxes and transfers. It is also a book about how our main intuition about what affects individual preferences for redistribution (whether a person is rich or poor) needs to be complemented with the consideration of other factors. Income will take us some ways into understanding whether a person supports redistribution and whether that support affects her political behavior (we will show later that the poor do support redistribution more than the rich and that their votes follow their preferences). But a fuller explanation of the demand for redistribution will require developing three complementary arguments: one considering the effects of expected future income, a second one about the negative externalities associated to inequality, and a final one emphasizing the consequences of population heterogeneity in a society. We dedicate the rest of the book to work through these propositions, but we begin by offering three illustrations of how we think these factors influence the political outcomes we are interested in exploring.

The Power of Expected Income

Whether because of Brexit in the United Kingdom, the election of Donald Trump in the United States or the increased (but eventually short-lived) popularity of Marine Le Pen in France's most recent presidential election, the resurgence of populism has been a frequent topic in the mainstream media since the summer of 2016. When looking for common threads uniting the success of populist alternatives in such diverse circumstances, it is difficult not to notice an underlying theme about future expectations.

On April 21, 2017, the *Financial Times* asked its readers why Marine Le Pen was the choice of "unhappy France."[1] The article reported research by SciencesPo and Cepremap exploring support for different candidates in the impending first round of the 2017 French presidential election (which was held on April 23). When asked about their expectations for the future, the FT article declared, the individuais who were most pessimistic were those most likely to vote for Le Pen (the candidate for the National Front) or Jean-Luc Mélenchon (the far-left candidate). Respondents most satisfied with their future prospects, were more likely to vote for Emmanuel Macron (the eventual president, elected after a run-off second-round election held on May 7). The article noted that "a sense of deteriorating wellbeing is one of the main explanations for rising support for the FN in Sunday's first round of the French presidential election, cutting across most boundaries of age, education or economic status and sapping support for mainstream parties."

A similar set of conclusions can be reached when looking at the relationship between economic prospects and the likelihood to vote for Trump or for Alternative for Germany (AfD). In a survey conducted in August of 2016, the Pew Research Center found clear differences between the supporters of the two main presidential candidates. As reported by *The Washington Post*, when asked whether the next generation could expect life in the United States to be better or worse, "a plurality of supporters of Hillary Clinton said better" while "a majority – two-thirds – of Donald Trump supporters said worse."[2] On September 20, 2017, days before the election that saw Alternative for Germany celebrate a historic third place with 13 percent of the vote, the *Financial Times* reported research by the German Institute for Economic Research (DIW) and the Hans Böckler Foundation. It showed that AfD supporters were more likely to be "dissatisfied with, and concerned about, their financial future, and to worry about downward social mobility" (Stabe and Maier-Borst, 2017).

Clearly, many factors affect the recent rise of populism in some industrialized democracies, and it would be injudicious to believe that only material self-interested future income matters to the events outlined earlier. Nevertheless, these stylized facts do point to the importance of an often-underemphasized set of economic considerations involving expectations

[1] See https://tinyurl.com/waxz3dk.
[2] See http://tinyurl.com/y8aynnmo.

about the future (to complement generally accepted arguments about the effects of present economic circumstances).

The Negative Externalities of Inequality

In his *The Condition of the Working Class in England*, written from 1844 to 1845, Friedrich Engels presents an intuitive argument about the relationship between inequality and crime when he observes of the poor working man:

> He is poor, life offers him no charm, almost every enjoyment is denied him, the penalties of the law have no further terrors for him; why should he restrain his desires, why leave to the rich the enjoyment of his birthright, why not seize a part of it for himself? What inducement has the proletarian not to steal? It is all very pretty and very agreeable to the ear of the bourgeois to hear the "sacredness of property" asserted; but for him who has none, the sacredness of property dies out of itself. (Engels, 1993)

But we don't need a Marxist analysis, or one going back to the 1840s, for evidence about the negative externalities of inequality. Research led by the University of York and funded by the Economic and Social Research Council illustrates the connection between levels of inequality and its crime-related negative externalities in the United Kingdom. The research is based on semistructured interviews with policy-makers, focus groups with frontline welfare practitioners, and repeated qualitative longitudinal interviews with a diverse sample of 480 welfare recipients.[3] The five-year study will not conclude until 2018, but its preliminary findings, as reported by *The Guardian*, show that increases in inequality (promoted by benefit sanctions) "are leaving people almost destitute, with some individuals being pushed toward 'survival crime' in order to eat."[4]

Do rich people understand this relationship? The affluent's concern about crime is easy to illustrate. A large number of newspaper stories could be mentioned, but a 2005 story in *The Independent* is worth quoting. "On London's streets neighbours cower behind barred and bolted doors – watched over by CCTV cameras – while former soldiers pound the pavements with guard dogs, ready to respond within minutes of a panic button being pushed," the journalist writes. "This is not an inner-city sink estate, however, nor a futuristic vision of a lawless city," the story continues "but wealthy enclaves such as Kensington and Chelsea,

[3] For more information, see http://tinyurl.com/ybzqrjjn.
[4] See http://tinyurl.com/yctmms3r.

Belgravia and St John's Wood, where the well-heeled are willing to part with £1,000 a year for private security patrols, such is their fear of crime."[5]

The radical Jacksonians of the early American labor movement in the nineteenth century argued against building prisons because redistribution and public education would make crime unnecessary and the punishment of criminals superfluous (Greenberg, 2010: 1). The rich in more recent times, although not as radical, also see social policy as mitigating the influence of poverty on crime. In the rest of the book, we will show that, in the right circumstances, the affluent perceive crime as a negative externality of inequality and, more importantly, support redistribution as a solution to it.

Population Heterogeneity and Support for Redistribution

On April 28, 2010, after the last of the prime ministerial debates in the United Kingdom, there was hope in the Labour Party. A resurgent Conservative Party and, more importantly, the increased popularity of the Liberal Democrats were certainly significant concerns. But Labour had won the previous three general elections, and Gordon Brown (Chancellor of the Exchequer under Tony Blair and Prime Minister after his resignation) had shown a mastery of economic issues (despite being in the middle of the Great Recession) not matched by his opponents. This was all to change, however, in an unscripted interaction with a pensioner in Rochdale.

According to *The Telegraph*, Gillian Duffy, a sixty-five-year-old pensioner and former council worker, "had been talking to reporters at the back of a crowd observing Mr Brown's visit to a community pay back scheme, where offenders were picking up litter, when Sue Nye, his long-term aide and 'gatekeeper' summoned her over to discuss her concerns with the Prime Minister." Mrs. Duffy expressed strong views about immigrants receiving welfare, and Mr. Brown responded with some general statements about the benefits of immigration.

That could have been the end of this episode. Again according to *The Telegraph*, after the conversation with the Prime Minister, "Mrs Duffy had said that she had been happy with Mr Brown's responses and would be voting for him. She said their conversation had been 'very good,' adding: 'seems a nice man.'" Gordon Brown, however, had got into his car and, unaware that he still had his microphone on, could be heard telling an

---

[5] See http://tinyurl.com/y7a7p4fb.

aide: "That was a disaster. Should never have put me with that woman. Whose idea was that?" The aide asked what Mrs. Duffy had said, and Mr. Brown replied: "Everything. She's just a sort of bigoted woman who says she used to be Labour. I mean it's just ridiculous."[6]

As well-known political commentator Andrew Rawnsley wrote for *The Observer* on Sunday May 2, 2010: "In the wake of his self-inflicted humiliation on a Rochdale housing estate, this prime minister looks like a boxer who has been hit once too often." The importance of Brown's Rochdale moment is difficult to quantify, but even five years later, as the United Kingdom got ready for another general election, Gillian Duffy was referred to as "the pensioner who helped torpedo Gordon Brown's re-election chances" (*The Observer*, Sunday February 22, 2015). The 2015 election of a new Labour leader after another electoral defeat prompted the following assessment in the editorial response in *The Observer*: "Nothing better crystallises Labour's problem with this [i.e., immigration] than Gordon Brown's comments about Gillian Duffy in 2010. Labour has never shaken off its image as a party of the London liberal elite that simply doesn't get the stresses and strains – economic, but also cultural – that have come with globalisation, the changing structure of our labour market and immigration" (July 19, 2015).

Gordon Brown's electoral defeat in 2010, and his inevitable resignation as the leader of the Labour Party, did in fact promote a new perspective on immigration and the welfare state. Inspired by the work of Maurice Glasman, Ed Miliband's new leadership turned the party toward "Blue Labour." Lord Glasman was part of what was described then as Ed Miliband's "long-term strategy group"[7] and advocated deemphasizing the focus on the traditional welfare state while adopting more restrictive positions regarding immigration. While the particularities of Brown's Rochdale moment and Blue Labour are perhaps specific to the United Kingdom, they represent a general set of concerns affecting politics (and particularly the strategies of Left parties) everywhere. More importantly, the episode summarized earlier illustrates the political relevance of one of this book's central themes: the importance of redistribution to politics, and the relationship between immigration (and ethnic diversity) and the demand for redistribution.

---

[6] The transcript of the conversation between Brown and Duffy and the subsequent conversation between Brown and the aide in the car can be found here: http://tinyurl .com/ybfwdxrd.

[7] See, for example, the *New Stateman* of July 20, 2011.

1.1 WHY REDISTRIBUTION PREFERENCES?

Distributional issues have been at the core of political science for a long time. Yet over the last two decades the study of the political origins and consequences of inequality has taken center stage. This resurgence is shedding new light on many themes central to the discipline. Deeply connected to topics such as the origins of democracy, political behavior, partisan alignments or political representation, inequality is attracting the attention of economists, sociologists, political scientists, and economic historians alike.

Many politicians, the popular media, and most casual observers of politics would agree that an individual's relative income (i.e., whether she is rich or poor) affects her political behavior. This book addresses one of the assumptions underlying most arguments about the importance of economic circumstances to political outcomes. If income matters to individual political behavior, it seems reasonable to assume that it does so through its influence on redistribution and social policy preferences. These redistribution preferences may (or may not) then be reflected on party positions and, eventually, government policy. To begin at the beginning, the determinants of redistribution preferences is a topic in need of closer study.

The importance of income as a determinant of redistribution preferences is highly variable. While it is the case that the rich support redistribution less than the poor almost everywhere in industrialized democracies, the strength of this relationship is hardly consistent (very significant in the United States, for example, quite weak in Portugal).[8] We dedicate most of this book to develop four main points. First, we propose that one of the reasons for the inconsistent effects in the literature has to do with a general lack of attention to the nature of material self-interest. The idea that material self-interest determines redistribution preferences should not be limited to a measure of present income, but should also include expectations of future income. Second, we contend that there exists a fundamental asymmetry in preferences between rich and poor. The preferences of the rich are highly dependent on the macrolevel of inequality, while those of the poor are not. The reason for this effect is not related to immediate tax and transfer considerations but to a negative externality of inequality: crime. We show that the rich in more unequal regions are more supportive of redistribution than the rich in more equal regions because of their concern with crime. Third, we argue that altruism is an important

---

[8] See Dion (2010), Dion and Birchfield (2010), and Beramendi and Rehm (2016).

omitted variable in much of the political economy literature and that it significantly influences redistribution preferences. Other-regarding concerns, moreover, are subject to the same fundamental asymmetry as affects the negative externalities of inequality. They matter most to those in less material need, and they are conditional on the identity of the poor. We show that while the poor are, once again, uniformly in favor of redistribution, the support of the rich is much higher when population homogeneity is high. And fourth, we finally ask why we should care about redistribution preferences in the first place. In this section of the book, we focus on perhaps the most momentous potential consequence of redistribution preferences: voting. We argue that redistribution preferences are indeed a most significant determinant of voting. The poor, those who expect to be poor, those who are concerned about the negative externalities of inequality, and those whose altruism is affected by population homogeneity are more supportive of redistribution, and, we contend, these redistribution preferences make them significantly more likely to vote for redistributive parties.

We spend most of the following pages exploring these four different but connected issues. But why is it so important to get this question about the determinants of redistribution preferences right? In a practical sense, as suggested by the events sketched in the previous section, the importance of redistributive preferences to politics is obvious. It would not be difficult to find other examples of how the demand for redistribution influences: how people vote, what politicians talk about, what governments do, etc. For the analysis of comparative politics (and political science in general), we would like to argue, the reasons are equally clear. The (often implicit) model behind much of comparative politics and political economy starts with redistribution preferences as given. After all, in Dahl's seminal work, the key characteristic of democracy is "the continuing responsiveness of the government to the preferences of its citizens" (1973: 1). Taking Anderson and Beramendi (2008a: 12) as inspiration, one can think about this model as being represented by Figure 1.1.

In this figure, the starting point is a set of redistribution preferences that affect how individuals behave politically. Their political behavior (whether it is voting or other less conventional forms of political participation) then affects, and is in turn affected by, the actions of political parties (and other political agents). Political parties then affect (and, again, are themselves affected) by the nature of institutions. The literature on comparative politics and political economy often focuses on political (the electoral and party systems, the relationship between legislatures and executives, the nature of government, etc.) or economic

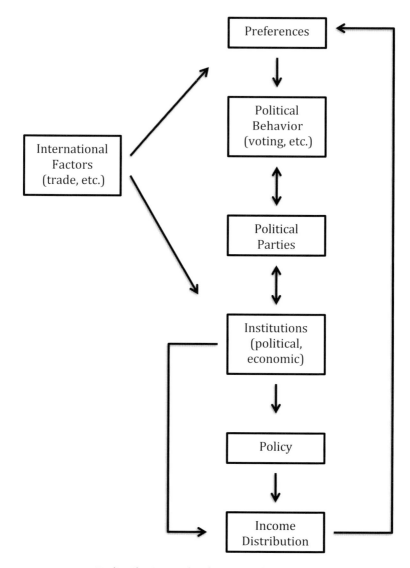

FIGURE 1.1 Redistribution and politics in industrialized democracies

(the nature of labor markets, welfare state regimes, etc.) institutions. These institutional arrangements are often understood to constrain political agents in their ability to design and implement policy, which then will affect the income distribution within a society and also (going back to the beginning of this causal chain) the redistribution preferences of individuals. At different points in the causal chain, finally, a number of international factors can intervene: globalization (or immigration) may affect redistribution preferences, trade openness may affect the nature of labor market institutions, or European integration may limit the autonomy of partisan economic policy.

It is clear that different approaches to the analysis of comparative politics and political economy choose to emphasize different elements in the conceptual causal chain illustrated in Figure 1.1. We would argue, however, that much of this literature depends on this implicit model. This is clearly the case with arguments related to the fourth argument in this book. We have in mind work about, to use the words of Lipset, the "social bases of politics" (1983) and more specifically contributions proposing that pocketbook issues (Downs, 1957; Key, 1966; Fiorina, 1981) and class (Lipset, 1983; Brooks and Manza, 1997; Evans, 1999), both strongly related to income, influence vote choice. The main insight of the economic voting literature is that individuals will vote following a comparison of what they gain or lose from the policies proposed by each party. Whether economic voting takes the form of *sanctioning* (Key, 1966; Kramer, 1971; Fiorina, 1981) or *selection* (Downs, 1957; Stigler, 1973; Meltzer and Richard, 1981), these approaches can easily be integrated into the structure presented in Figure 1.1 and are therefore essential to the arguments we present in the rest of the book.

A similar argument could be made about the influential work on the welfare state in the comparative political economy literature. Redistribution preferences are the implicit but essential building block for both the "power resources" approach that emphasized the role played by Left governments and working-class mobilization (Stephens, 1979; Korpi, 1983) and for the class-coalition approaches that focus either on the influence of a political alliance between the working class and agrarian interests for the emergence of social democratic welfare states (Esping-Andersen, 1990) or on the importance of social insurance and risk (Baldwin, 1990; Mares, 2003). It is also the point of departure for the "logic of industrialism" approach arguing that economic development and its demographic, social, and economic consequences explains variation in the nature of the welfare state (Cutright, 1965; Wilensky, 1975).

The relationships outlined in Figure 1.1, moreover, underpin the most influential comparative conceptions of the relationship between government partisanship and policy. The nature of the demand for redistribution influences what we could call the "traditional partisanship school." Its authors – Alt (1985) and Hibbs (1977) being the most cited examples –

believe that Left governments will promote the interests of labor (and be more likely to promote policies against unemployment), while conservative ones will satisfy the demands of upscale groups (and be more likely to promote policies curbing inflation). More generally, an extensive comparative literature explores how the partisan nature of government affects redistributive policies, whether these take the form of compensation against unemployment/inflation, against inequality (see Rueda and Pontusson, 2000; Pontusson et al., 2002), or in favor of labor market insiders (as in Rueda, 2005, 2006, 2007).

In this vein, a significant literature relevant to the relationships described in Figure 1.1 argues that social policy's most significant role is as compensation in favor of losers from globalization and international trade. As a long line of work suggests, this compensatory approach to market risks plays a prominent role in work on the development of the welfare state in Northern Europe. Whether the welfare state is seen as an efficient compromise in the face of open markets (Cameron, 1978; Katzenstein, 1985; Garrett, 1998; Rodrik, 1998; Adsera and Boix, 2002) or a reflection of varieties of capitalism (Hall and Soskice, 2001; Iversen, 2005; Iversen and Soskice, 2010), social policy compensation, we are told, provides the linchpin between welfare state politics and globalization.

Finally, the importance of redistribution preferences as part of the causal chain depicted in Figure 1.1 is essential to an influential literature exploring the relationship between inequality and democracy. The significance to democracy of the distribution of wealth has been the focus of political science for centuries (from Aristotle's *Politics* to Alexis de Tocqueville's *Democracy in America*). More recently, it is the starting point for a number of prominent contributions to comparative politics. Whether democracy prevails when either economic equality or capital mobility are high in a given country (Boix, 2003), high inequality and land-based wealth make democracy threatening to elites (Acemoglu and Robinson, 2005), or when rising but politically disenfranchised groups demand more influence (Ansell and Samuels, 2014), the distributional consequences of different political regimes are closely related to issues emphasized in Figure 1.1 (and, more specifically, the Meltzer and Richard framework we adopt as our baseline in this book).

1.2 WHO WANTS WHAT?

In the much quoted words of Harold Lasswell (1950), politics is all about who gets what, when, and how. And, as shown in the previous section, redistribution preferences (who wants what?) matter a great deal to our understanding of comparative politics and political economy. What do we have to say about them in this book? As we mentioned earlier, we make three distinct but related arguments.

First, most distributive theories in political economy understand individuals to be motivated by material self-interest, often approximated by their current positions in the income distribution. In the initial section of the book, we challenge this traditional view and argue that there are two significant determinants of preferences: redistribution (related to an individual's present income) and insurance (related to expectations of future income). Based on the labor economics literature on life-cycle profiles, we propose a simple way of estimating the present value of an individual's expected future income as the result of the interplay between age and experience. We believe that many of the existing approaches in comparative political economy (emphasizing concepts as diverse as risk or mobility) are best understood both theoretically and empirically by being integrated into this model of expected life income.

Second, moving beyond income, we show that the difference in redistribution preferences between the rich and the poor is very high in some countries and very low in others. In this section of the book, we argue that this has a lot to do with the rich and very little to do with the poor. We contend that while there is a general relative income effect on redistribution preferences, the preferences of the rich are highly dependent on the macrolevel of inequality. The reason for this effect is not related to immediate tax and transfer considerations but to a negative externality of inequality: crime. We show that the rich in more unequal regions are more supportive of redistribution than the rich in more equal regions because of their concern with crime.

Third, and related to the previous arguments, we propose that altruism is an important determinant of redistribution preferences that has not received enough attention in much of the political economy literature. While material self-interest is the base of most approaches to redistribution (first affecting preferences and then politics and policy), there is a paucity of research on inequality aversion. We propose that other-regarding concerns influence redistribution preferences and that they matter most to those in less material need and are conditional on the identity of the poor. In this section of the book, we propose that population heterogeneity (ethnic, national, or religious diversity) affects the willingness of the rich, and not the poor, to support redistribution. Altruism is most relevant to the rich (because the poor have shorter-term

motivations), and it is most influential when the recipients of benefits are
similar to those financing them.

We are not the first scholars interested in exploring the reasons why
some people support redistribution and others do not. While most argu
ments in political economy take an uncomplicated (and often unspec-
ified) Meltzer and Richard (1981) approach as their starting point, a
number of other possibilities have been examined in the literature. As
we will explain in more detail in the chapters that follow, there are arguments emphasizing social insurance and risk (as in Sinn, 1995; Iversen
and Soskice, 2001; Mares, 2003; Moene and Wallerstein, 2003; Rehm,
2009), and social mobility and life-cycle profiles (Benabou and Ok, 2001;
Haider and Solon, 2006; Alesina and Giuliano, 2011). There are those
focusing on religiosity as an intermediary between individual insurance
considerations and demand for redistribution (Pergament, 1997; Scheve
and Stasavage, 2006). And there is an increasingly important literature
on how other-regarding concerns influence redistribution preferences (see,
e.g., Shayo, 2009; Lupu and Pontusson, 2011; Cavaillé and Trump, 2015).
In economics, arguments have been presented to emphasize the influence
of beliefs about fairness (Alesina et al., 2001; Benabou and Tirole, 2006),
of perceptions of inequality as the result of "luck" or "effort" (Alesina and
Glaeser, 2004; Alesina and Angeletos, 2005), or of the desire to obtain a
higher social standing (Corneo and Grüner, 2002).

What differentiates our approach is, first, our goal to integrate mate-
rial/economic and noneconomic motivations into a coherent explanation
of redistribution preferences. We do not present a formal treatment of
this issue in these pages, but what we have in mind in conceptual terms
is a reconsideration of the usual utility function determining redistribution preferences to accommodate four distinct parts: (i) the usual present
income element, (ii) our expected income term (which we describe in
detail in Chapter 2) and is meant to capture present redistribution as
potential future insurance, (iii) a macro-inequality term that is separable
from relative income (as well as expected income) and reflects concerns
for negative externalities like crime (see Chapter 4), and (iv) a population heterogeneity effect that would capture the importance of in-group
altruism (see Chapter 6).

The second argument distinguishing our approach concerns the distinction between the rich and the poor. An ongoing theme throughout the
second and third parts of the book is that noneconomic factors (defined as
those not directly affecting the income/tax/transfer nexus) affect the poor
and the rich differently. We conceive of both the negative externalities of

inequality and the moral benefits of altruism as affected by time-horizon and stakes factors. Like some other authors (examining, for example, investments in human capital or retirement), we argue that the poor have shorter-term motivations than the rich, and we propose that the relative importance of receiving benefits is greater for the poor than the relative importance of paying taxes is for the rich. We expect that, as the stakes of redistribution decline, longer-term considerations related to inequality and population heterogeneity will increase. We therefore argue that longer time horizons and lower stakes (in relation to current tax and transfer considerations) mean that the negative externalities of inequality and the benefits of altruism will be more important to the rich.

It is important to emphasize that we propose the effects of expected income (in Part I of this book) not to be dependent on present income. While we argue in Parts II and III that negative externalities and parochial altruism are income-dependent (more important to the affluent, less relevant to the poor), we agree with other insurance-related material interest arguments (like Iversen and Soskice, 2001 and Rehm, 2009, 2016) that expected income (like risk or mobility) is important regardless of an individual's level of income. In this sense, we make a distinction between the tax and transfer side of our argument (dominated by material interests having to do with present and expected income) and the negative externality and heterogeneity ones. We will show in the following chapters that tax and transfer considerations are significant to the poor and the rich alike. We will also show that the negative externalities of inequality and the moral benefits of parochial altruism are income-dependent (and become more relevant to those with higher levels of income).

One of the important challenges for the political economy literature focusing on the demand for redistribution has been separating "economic" (taken here to mean income, tax, and transfers) from "noneconomic" motivations. This is particularly the case because of the difficulty distinguishing between insurance and other-regarding considerations.[9] The same could be said about motivations related to the negative externalities of inequality. This is the reason why the arguments that we present later need to start with an analysis of the relationship between redistribution and insurance. We propose a way to capture insurance motivations: redistribution today is related to present income but, to the

---

[9] See (Dimick et al., 2016) for a more detailed explanation of how insurance-based arguments about risk aversion and altruism-based arguments about inequality aversion have similar implications.

extent that expected income matters to individuals, redistribution today is also insurance (against future expected income losses). Once we capture directly the influence of these expected future income motivations, we can be confident that the effects of negative externalities or altruism are not affected by insurance considerations.

The logic summarized earlier results in a figure that underpins our theoretical expectations in Parts II and III of this book. We introduce it here, but reproduce it in Chapters 4 and 6. The main idea is represented in Figure 1.2. We expect both inequality and population homogeneity to be associated with more support for redistribution. Because we argue that for the poor altruism and longer-term externalities are trumped by material incentives (whether related to present income or insurance), redistribution preferences converge regardless of macro-inequality or group homogeneity as income declines. We expect macro-inequality to promote concern for negative externalities and group homogeneity to promote altruism only for the rich. In Figure 1.2, the redistribution preferences of an individual with low income v_i in a low inequality/homogeneity region w_r, denoted $R(v_i, w_r)$, and in a high inequality/homogeneity region $R(v_i, w_r')$ do not differ by much. In contrast, we expect more inequality/homogeneity to promote externality and altruistic concerns only for the rich, so that the redistribution preferences of a rich individual in a low inequality/homogeneity region $R(v_i', w_r)$ differ starkly from those in high inequality/homogeneity regions $R(v_i', w_r')$.

We should also emphasize at this point an important caveat to the arguments and analyses in this book. As we mentioned when discussing Figure 1.1, we conceive of comparative politics and political economy models as starting from redistribution preferences that then move through a causal chain culminating in policy. Another way to think of this is, as commonly noted (e.g., McCarty and Pontusson, 2009; Alesina and Giuliano, 2011), to argue that the Meltzer–Richard model involves two separate propositions: a "demand-side" proposition, concerning the preferences of voters in general and the median voter in particular ("distance to the mean determines demand for redistribution") and a "supply-side" proposition, concerning the aggregation of preferences and their translation into redistribution policy ("the preferences of the median voter will prevail"). This book focuses on the first proposition (who wants what?) and its connection to voting. It leaves for future research the task of following these preferences and voting choices through the causal chain in Figure 1.1 that eventually results in policy.

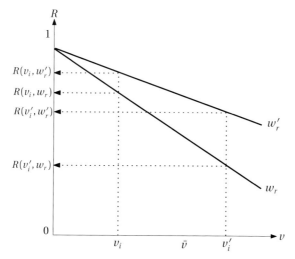

FIGURE 1.2 The relationship between inequality/homogeneity (w), income (v), and support for redistribution (R)

As mentioned earlier, the one link that we explicitly return to in Part IV of this book is the one uniting preferences and voting. We argue that assumptions about what determines redistribution preferences are essential to most approaches in political economy, but, ultimately, we care about political outcomes. In other words, we want to know how these preferences are translated into political behavior. Perhaps the most momentous outcome of interest is voting. A significant and influential literature in comparative politics, starting as early as Almond and Verba's *The Civic Culture*, has been dedicated to the question of whether income influences voting. In the "resource" model of participation, it is argued that high income is associated with more resources (whether material or other) and therefore linked to more participation in politics (see, for example, Leighley, 1995; Verba et al., 1995; Anderson and Beramendi, 2008b). The evidence for this relationship, however, has not been unambiguous.[10] In Part IV we explore the effects on voting of the causally complex relationships emphasized in the rest of the book.

---

[10] See, for example, Chapman and Palda (1983) and some of the evidence in Verba et al. (1995).

1.3 ANALYTICAL STRATEGIES

Our preceding discussion makes clear that the book's empirical strategy will rely on both variation across individuals and across contexts. Thus our basic design involves comparisons. On the one hand, we will conduct comparisons between units, for example comparing regions of varying levels of population homogeneity. On the other hand, we will compare the same units over time, for example by comparing the levels of population homogeneity in US states at different points in time, or by comparing the levels of expected income of an individual over time. The type of comparison employed will depend on the specific research question asked in different parts of the book.

Part 1 of this book develops the argument that income expectations shape individuals' redistribution preferences. The mechanism underlying our argument operates solely at the individual level: both the formation of expectations and preferences happen *within* an individual. We test our hypothesis using a large cross-national survey data set covering Western European countries, as well as household panel data sets covering Germany and the United Kingdom. Our use of cross-national data is driven by our desire to subject our hypothesis to a test involving a large number of individuals living in varying contexts, characterized by differing political cultures and economic institutions (King et al., 1994: 24). We are not interested in modeling the influence of institutions or culture, rather we want to focus on individual level processes while keeping these possibly confounding country-level factors constant. Furthermore, evidence relying on a broad set of countries underscores that our theoretical argument is not confined to a particular subset of countries, but applies (in principle) to advanced industrialized societies.

We further test our income expectation hypothesis in analyses relying on household panel data from Germany and the United Kingdom. These data are obviously much more limited in scope compared to a multicountry survey. However, their strength is that they follow the same set of individuals over time. Thus our analysis shifts from testing our hypothesis in different contexts to testing it with different individuals. It is sometimes said that "each individual in panel data is his own best control" (Hausman and Wise, 1979: 455). This means that the comparison we perform is with the same individual over time, and that we therefore can hold constant unobserved individual characteristics that might affect preferences. This is impossible in a purely cross-sectional design, where one has to rely on a (often limited) set of "control variables" meant to capture systematic differences across individuals.

Parts II and III of this book develop arguments that link macrolevel inequality and heterogeneity to individual-level preferences. We test our hypothesis using a large cross-national survey data set covering Western European countries, a long-running survey covering three decades in the United States, as well as household panel data covering the United Kingdom. Our use of cross-national data follows straightforwardly from our research questions, which involve differences in inequality and heterogeneity. Using information on individuals collected in different contexts allows us to link variation in contextual characteristics to variation at the individual level. As Heinz Eulau once put it: "The accent in micro-macro thinking is on the hyphen, for the hyphen is the bond" (Eulau, 1986: 113). The "bond" in our design is the link between variation in macrolevels of, say, inequality, to the variation in the effect of income on preferences. We will use both variation across individuals (we observe individuals with different preferences at different points in the distribution of income) and variation across contexts (we observe different regions in Europe with different levels of inequality) to examine how contexts affect individual-level relationships. Thus we follow calls for a tighter integration of contextual characteristics and individual or group behavior in comparative politics and political economy (e.g., Kedar and Shively, 2005; Anderson and Singer, 2008).

Parts II and III of this book propose that macrolevels of inequality and heterogeneity matter to the relationship between income and redistributive preferences. Higher inequality or population homogeneity make the rich more likely to support redistribution. These arguments therefore assume the existence of cognitive linkages that connect personal experiences to evaluations of inequality and immigration (in the first instance) and to preferences about redistribution and voting behavior.[11] What level of aggregation should be the focus for our macrovariables is therefore an important issue in these sections of the book. We justify our choice by referring to the theoretical intuitions guiding our empirical analysis.[12] In Part II, our theoretical argument proposes that the importance of inequal-

---

[11] For a similar approach, see, for example, Citrin et al. (1997).

[12] We accept that context can be both objective and subjective (Wong, 2010), that different contextual units may be constructed by individuals (Wong et al., 2012), and that the geographic focus for inequality or population heterogeneity is itself politicized (Hopkins, 2010). But we sidestep these issues here.

ity emerges from its relationship to crime as a negative externality. This implies that the relevant level of macro-inequality should be one at which a visible connection to crime could be made by individuals. In Part III, we contend that there are "moral" benefits attached to the promotion of equality within in-group members that are most relevant to the rich. We consider the appropriate macrolevel to be one where immigration or racial diversity are plausibly linked to individual attitudes about the benefits of redistribution. In both cases, we therefore move away from national data and use regional levels of inequality and heterogeneity.[13] In Part II, inequality is measured in 37 NUTS2 regions when we analyze household panel data in the United Kingdom and in 129 regions in 14 countries when we analyze European Social Survey data. In Part III, we use the same regional level for the European analysis and measure heterogeneity at the state level when analyzing General Social Survey data in the United States between 1976 and 2008.

We argue that, unlike more aggregate levels, regional or state levels of inequality and homogeneity are visible and proximate and that it is plausible to assume that they would be related to fear of crime or parochial altruism by rich individuals. Critics, however, could point out that it would be good to use even more disaggregated units (like neighborhoods, as in some crime research). Our first response is that the availability of the data at our disposal limits what we can do. But, more importantly, while working with subregional or substate units (such as counties) would be desirable, it is not clear that going ever smaller is better for our analysis. The intuition behind wanting to resist the temptation to disaggregate much further is once again related to our theoretical arguments. While it is true that there is heterogeneity in levels of inequality, immigration, or racial diversity within our regions, it is not self-evident that very small geographic units would be more appropriate to test our hypotheses. Would income dispersion in an individual's street, for example, matter more to a desire to limit the potential negative consequences of inequality than income dispersion in a region?[14] We lack strong theoretical reasons that would

---

[13] In related work, however, we have shown some of our main hypotheses to be corroborated by national data. See Dimick et al. (2018) or Rueda (2018).

[14] Note that this issue is distinct from (and arises in addition to) the modifiable areal unit problem (Openshaw, 1983) where differences in effects arise from the mere act of aggregating spatial units. The concern here is that an analysis of contexts "too local" to an individual estimates different behavioral parameters. For example, when studying the contextual importance of racial diversity, Wong et al. (2012: 1155) point out that "because individuals rarely live and work in the same census tract – and the effects of

help us identify the exact level of disaggregation most appropriate for our argument. Our intuition, however, is that the regional level used in the rest of the book is both theoretically reasonable and politically meaningful. Larger or smaller geographic units, we feel, could entail benefits but also significant costs.

On balance, our approach in this book taps into two strengths of observational data: coverage and generality. By *coverage* we mean both the spatial and temporal extent covered by our evidence. Our data spans both Western Europe and the United States. Because the domain of our theoretical arguments is advanced industrialized societies, we need this geographical coverage to subject our hypotheses to plausible empirical scrutiny. Investigations using data from, say, Sweden and Norway alone (even if they were of higher quality) would not satisfy this research objective. In some cases we test our hypotheses using comparisons over time involving spans of more than two decades. This temporal coverage lends credence to our assertions that the relationships we document are not just "flukes" occurring at a very specific and unusual point in time (e.g., during periods of upheaval in financial markets). By *generality* we mean having access to data that approximate an equiprobable random sample from a population, and which allows us to draw conclusions that are generalizable to our population of interest (the individuals that make up advanced industrialized society) instead of just a local subpopulation.

Where there is light, there must be shadow. The virtues of large-scale observational data come at the cost of various threats to the validity of causal inferences drawn from them. The biggest threat comes from the possibility of endogeneity at both the individual and contextual level. On the individual level, endogeneity may be caused by processes of selection, omitted variables, or simply measurement error in covariates. While we can deal with the latter using more sophisticated models, the first two are difficult (and sometimes impossible) to address. If individuals with, say, high ability invest in different types of job-specific skills and in turn prefer less redistribution, the fact that we do not have measures of ability in our survey data will pose a clear threat to the inferences we draw. On the contextual level, endogeneity issues result from sorting of individuals into geographical units, for example, if individuals move into a high-income, high inequality region because of their political beliefs.

racial context in one's life overall, not just one's neighborhood, may have political effects – county may be the ideal contextual unit of analysis despite its extreme heterogeneity."

While we cannot argue away the shortcomings of an observational research design, we can increase the reliability and confidence in our results by subjecting them to stringent robustness tests. The core idea of robustness tests is that there is never only one correct model specification in observational data analysis. Save for the simplest randomized experiments, statistical modeling always involves subjective judgments of model specification. We regard two aspects as especially consequential: (i) the details of the statistical model used and (ii) the set of covariates, intended to "control" for heterogeneity across units, that are included in a model. In order to make the influence of these decisions transparent, robustness tests need to address both issues. Throughout this book we therefore present robustness tests, which explore how sensitive our results are to the inclusion of theoretically relevant alternative covariates, how sensitive our results are to changes in model assumptions, and how sensitive our results are to changes in the composition of our sample. The question remains of what it means for findings to be "robust." Given the limits of observational studies discussed earlier it is illusory to expect to find identical numerical results in each robustness test. We rather opt for a substantive definition of robustness, where we require that the direction of effects does not change and that they remain statistically distinguishable from zero. Nonetheless, when a robustness test results in a substantively different effect, we will address it in our discussions.

1.4 DATA SOURCES AND COVERAGE

As discussed in the previous section, we rely both on comparisons across different individuals in regions (and states) as well as on changes for the same individuals over time. Thus we utilize two principal data sources: cross-sectional survey data and household panel data. In this section we describe each data set's basic features and design. The actual samples used in the analysis chapters might be slightly different, as demanded by the theoretical arguments and data needs. However, a common feature of each constructed sample is that we limit it to working-age individuals. The reason for this is straightforward. The arguments in this book concern the redistributive role of government policy as a determinant of income equality. A number of authors have noted that pensions play a major role in overall income redistribution in OECD countries.[15] The arguments

---

[15] See, for example, Mahler and Jesuit (2006).

about the demand for redistribution summarized earlier are hypothesized to apply particularly to the working-age population, and including pensioners would potentially distort the analysis.

European Social Survey

The data source we use for our cross-national analyses is the European Social Survey (ESS). It is a large-scale multicountry survey administered biannually in European countries starting in 2002.[16] Its target population is all individuals age 15 or over, residing in private households (regardless of nationality, language, citizenship, or legal status). Interviews are conducted face-to-face. While the number of participating countries varies between years, a core set of Western European countries is represented in most survey rounds. As a lowest common denominator in all our analyses relying on the ESS, we select countries who participated in at least two rounds (to obtain usable regional sample sizes) and which provided consistent regional identifiers (discussed later) over time. There are three key strengths that make the ESS the most adequate choice for our book. First, the ESS is a truly comparative survey. Already in the design phase of each survey round, issues of cross-national comparability (such as question wording and translation, definition of target populations, and survey sampling) take center stage (Stoop et al., 2010). Second, the ESS provides consistent regional-level identifiers following a harmonized classification established by the European Union, the NUTS system of territorial classification (Eurostat, 2007). This allows us to match each respondent to his or her corresponding regional characteristics such as unemployment rates, inequality, or population heterogeneity. Third, the ESS provides a measure of income that is applied consistently over countries and survey waves, and which provides enough detail for us to construct a usable measure of an individual's income distance to the national mean (*the* core ingredient of most models of redistribution preferences). It is these characteristics that lead us to favor the European Social Survey over other widely used surveys.[17]

---

[16] For more information see www.europeansocialsurvey.org.

[17] An obvious competitor are surveys from the International Social Survey Programme (ISSP), which cover a longer time period than ESS surveys and include the United States and other non-European advanced capitalist countries of interest. However, income measures reported by the ISSP vary not only across countries within each wave, but also, for many countries, between waves. Furthermore, some ISSP surveys we would have to rely on are only harmonized ex post and not in their design stage. Finally, regional level identifiers are not consistently available.

General Social Survey

The American equivalent to the ESS (or maybe one of its venerable forefathers) is the General Social Survey (GSS: Davis and Smith, 1994).[18] It has been conducted since 1972, first annually (until 1994) and then biannually. Its target population are all individuals age 18 or over living in private residential households.[19] Until 2006, the GSS only sampled English-speaking respondents (adding Spanish in 2006). Interviews are conducted face-to-face. The GSS provides regional identifiers (each respondent's state of residence), a measure of redistribution preferences via a widely used item, and a measure of income that is detailed enough to provide information on respondents' income distance (discussed later).

British Household Panel Study

So far the data described are repeated cross sections, that is, surveys repeated in the same country but with a new sample of individuals. The British Household Panel Survey (BHPS) provides repeated measures of income and preferences for the same individuals over time. It is an annual survey of occupants of British households that began in 1991 and ended in 2008.[20] The BHPS is a household panel. It starts with a representative sample of households and then interviews every adult member of that household in successive waves. If individuals move out and form their own household they (and their new household) are interviewed too. Thus its target population are individuals age 16 and over living in residential households. Interviews are conducted face-to-face.[21] We use the original ("Essex") sample of the BHPS, which is designed to be representative of the private household population of Great Britain south of the Caledonian Canal.[22] As in our other analyses, we limit our sample to working-age individuals.

One of the advantages of household panel data is the availability of high-quality income data, information on work history and unemployment spells, as well as detailed background information (such as parental education). However, while the household-following rules of the BHPS

---

[18] For more information see www3.norc.org/Gss+website.

[19] As in the ESS this means that individuals living in "group quarters" – college dorms, military quarters, nursing homes, and long-term care facilities – are not represented.

[20] For more information see www.iser.essex.ac.uk/bhps.

[21] The exception are sensitive questions, such as the General Health Questionnaire, which are collected using self-completion questionnaires.

[22] This means that we do not include "refreshment samples" for Scotland, Wales, and Northern Ireland drawn in the mid to late nineties.

ensure the basic representativeness of the sample over time, every long-running panel study suffers from attrition. Panel attrition might occur for "natural" reasons (death, moving abroad) or because individuals or complete household leave the study either temporarily or forever. This is not a problem as long as sample members drop out "randomly" (i.e., the attrition process is ignorable). However, dropout usually occurs selectively for those with low income or education, among the young (16–24), and those in unemployment (cf. Lynn, 2006). While this is the case in the BHPS, the extent to which dropout affects the sample is relatively modest. Lynn concludes that "although under-representation of these groups is statistically significant, the actual magnitude of under-representation is generally small" (Lynn, 2006: 67).

German Socio-Economic Panel Study

Similar to the BHPS, the German Socio-Economic Panel Study (SOEP) is a unique representative panel survey of residential households in Germany.[23] The study started in 1984 with a sample of (West-) German households, where the head of household was either German, Turkish, Italian, Spanish, Greek, or from the former Yugoslavia. Following German unification in 1990 a refreshment sample of households from the former GDR was added. Two further refreshment samples (random samples from the full population) were added in 1998 and 2000 to maintain the overall representativeness of the panel.[24] No other panel study with political variables encompasses such a long time span. SOEP sampling started using a representative sample of households and interviews every eligible member in successive waves. Its target population are individuals 16 years and older living in private households in Germany. Interviews are conducted face-to-face.

1.5 MEASURING REDISTRIBUTION PREFERENCES

The central concept of this book are redistribution preferences. Using different data sources, with their respective strengths and weaknesses, means we will have different empirical measurements for the same concept.

---

[23] For more information on the GSOEP contents and structure see Haisken-DeNew and Frick (2005) and Wagner et al. (2007).

[24] We use these samples (in GSOEP terminology: A, B, C, E, and F), and exclude oversamples of immigrants (D) and high incomes (G).

TABLE I.I *Redistribution preferences in Western Europe*

Strongly disagree	Disagree	Neither agree nor disagree	Agree	Strongly agree
2.9	13.4	14.7	43.0	26.1

Note: Average percentages per category. ESS, Rounds 1-5. N = 100,756.

In the ESS, our preferred measure of redistribution preferences is an item commonly used in individual level research on preferences (e.g., Rehm, 2009). It elicits a respondent's support for the statement "the government should take measures to reduce differences in income levels" measured on a five-point agree–disagree scale with labeled answer categories ("Strongly agree" to "Strongly disagree"). Table 1.1 shows percentages for our pooled European sample. Here, as well as in all following analyses, we reverse the scale such that higher values represent support for redistribution. In some of the analyses in the book, we will group those who strongly disagree or disagree with those who express "middle-of-the-road" preferences ("neither agree not disagree"), because one could interpret it as another, less overt, expression of opposition.[25] Table 1.1 shows that Western Europe is characterized by a rather high level of popular support for redistribution. More than two thirds of ESS respondents either agree or strongly agree with the statement that the government should take measures to reduce income differences. Explicit opposition is much less widespread.

However, behind these aggregate numbers lies considerable cross-national (and regional) variation, which we will exploit in our analyses. Figure 1.3 shows country-by-country preferences collapsed into "agree," "neither nor," and "disagree" categories. The existence of high levels of support for redistribution in each country (represented by light gray bars) is immediately apparent. When focusing on explicit opposition (the dark gray bars), one finds interesting cross-national variation. Explicit opposition is high in countries such as Luxembourg, the Netherlands, and Denmark, while it is far less common in countries such as Portugal, Spain, and Finland.

When turning to the American case a somewhat different picture emerges. In our analysis of GSS data we capture redistribution preferences with a commonly used measure (e.g., Alesina and Angeletos, 2005),

---

[25] Note that specifications that keep this "neutral" option do not lead to different results.

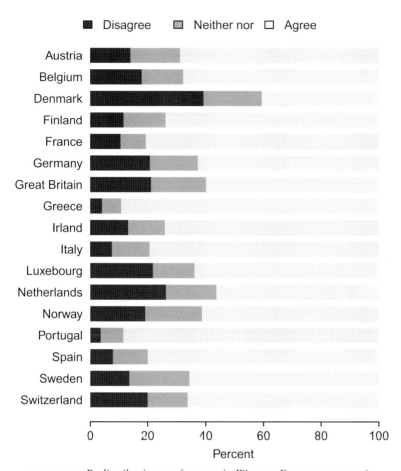

FIGURE 1.3 Redistribution preferences in Western European countries

available over time. It presents respondents with the following statement: "the government should reduce income differences between the rich and the poor, perhaps by raising the taxes of wealthy families or by giving income assistance to the poor." Answers are recorded on a seven-point scale, with labeled endpoints "1 = should" and "7 = should not", which, again, we reverse for ease of interpretation. Table 1.2 shows the distribution of responses in our sample (aggregated over time). It is apparent that opposition to redistribution is more widespread in the United States than in Western Europe. Even if we only take the lowest two response categories as indicating opposition, we find that more than 20 percent of Americans clearly oppose redistributive policy as opposed

TABLE 1.2 *Redistribution preferences in the United States, 1978–2010*

Should government reduce income difference between rich and poor?

No						Yes
1	2	3	4	5	6	7
12.8	7.8	12.8	19.5	17.9	10.5	18.7

Note: Average percentages per category. GSS. N = 21,704.

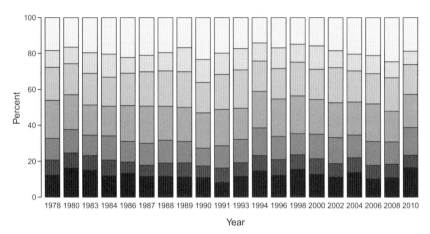

FIGURE 1.4 Distribution of redistribution preferences in the United States, 1978–2010

to 16 percent of Europeans. Table 1.2 also shows that clear support for redistribution (now taken as the two highest categories) does exist as well, with almost one third of Americans agreeing. It goes without saying that the aggregate percentages in Table 1.2 mask considerable variation both across states and over time. Figure 1.4 plots histograms of response categories (ranging from 1 to 7) from 1978 to 2010 and makes clear that there has been variation over time. But we must remember that these are aggregate numbers and do not necessarily reflect the within-state variation to be emphasized later. In chapter 6 we will describe state variation in preferences in more detail.

When using the British Household Panel Study we have information on the redistribution preferences of the *same* individuals over time. The measure we use is available in seven waves and covers almost the full length of the panel. It was asked first at the beginning of the BHPS in 1991 and last in 2007, one year before its end. Our measure is support for active

TABLE 1.3 *Redistribution preferences in the United Kingdom 1991–2008*

Strongly disagree	Disagree	Neither agree nor disagree	Agree	Strongly agree
5.4	34.3	18.3	35.9	6.1

Note: Average percentages per category. BHPS, waves A, C, E, G, J, N, and Q. N respondents 6,324.

economic policy, more specifically stated support for the government's active role in implementing a "full-employment policy" (Ansell, 2014: 17). Answers to the survey question, "It is the government's responsibility to provide a job for everyone who wants one" were recorded on a five-point agree–disagree scale with labeled categories. In keeping with the rest of the book, we reverse this scale such that higher values indicate agreement with redistributive policy.[26] While we recognize that this question could be argued not to be as clearly connected to redistribution preferences as the previous ones, we follow previous work using it as an appropriate proxy for redistribution demand.[27] Table 1.3 shows percentages of respondents choosing each category averaged over time. Compared to our American sample, respondents in the United Kingdom are less likely to choose response categories indicating "strong" agreement or disagreement. However, we find a similar picture of polarized opinion. On the issue of government job creation the sample is divided in high levels of support (42 percent) and opposition (about 40 percent).

Behind these aggregated figures lies considerable change over time. In Figure 1.5 we combine both "agree" categories and plot the proportion of individuals who support government activity over the length of the panel. We find that support for redistributive policy, which started at a fairly high level in the early 1990s, declined slightly toward the end of the decade stabilizing at around 43 percent. With the beginning of the new century preferences for government intervention declined further toward 35 percent.

In our analysis using German data we employ a measure similar to the one in the BHPS, which probes respondents' views on government intervention in the market in order to secure employment. The survey presents

---

[26] This item is available in waves A, C, E, G, J, N, and Q.
[27] See Ansell (2014), who uses BHPS data, and Ashok et al. (2015), who use ANES data, asking respondents whether the government in Washington should see to it that every person has a job and a good standard of living.

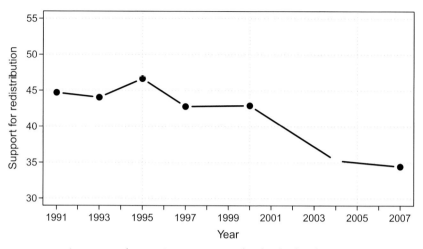

FIGURE 1.5 Aggregate changes in percentage of individuals who support redistribution, UK

respondents with the following statement: "At present a multitude of social services are provided not only by the state but also by private freemarket enterprises, organizations, associations, or private citizens. What is your opinion on this?" It then continues to ask who should be responsible for "job creation measures" offering response options ranging from "only private forces" to "only the state," as displayed in Table 1.4.[28] Given the broad nature of the question it is probably not surprising that few respondents choose to indicate that only the market or "private forces" should address job creation, and many instead opt for the somewhat ambiguous middle category. Nonetheless, there is a clear group of individuals who hold strong redistributive preferences answering in the topmost category.

1.6 MEASURING INCOME

The measures of income described here are based on respondents' household income after taxes and transfers. Household income is also the basis for the calculation of the measure of income distance used through Parts II, III, and IV of this book. In Part I, where we examine

---

[28] In this descriptive summary we use a sample from the full population. In our analysis of income dynamics and preferences in Chapter 3 we use a sample of males. The distribution of responses is similar, with a 2.7 percentage point higher response in the two lowest categories for males.

TABLE 1.4 *Redistribution preferences in Germany,* 2002

Only private	Mostly private	Both private and state	Mostly state	Only state
1.3	7.2	48.9	26.3	14.9

Note: Average percentages per category. SOEP, full sample wave S. N = 8,039.

income expectations, our measure of income is restricted to a respondents' income from labor.

When analyzing ESS data, our measure of net household income is constructed using respondents' answers to the following survey question: "Using this card, if you add up the income from all sources, which letter describes your household's total net income? If you don't know the exact figure, please give an estimate. Use the part of the card that you know best: weekly, monthly or annual income."[29] Respondents are presented with a show-card, which contains several labeled categories representing income ranges.[30] This scheme poses several challenges for our purposes. The income bands used cover very different income ranges. For example, category "R" contains a range comprising €2,400 (€1,800 to €3,600), while the range for category "U" is €30,000 (€90,000 to €120,000). Furthermore, ranges differ between ESS surveys. If we were to introduce these categories into our analyses, they would have completely different meanings, and estimates would be difficult to interpret.

To address this issue, we transform income bands into their common-currency mid-points. To give an example, this means that via this transformation, category "€1,800 to under €3,600" is assigned a value of €2,700.[31] Using midpoints has been recognized for some time as an appropriate way to create scores for income categories and has been

---

[29] The wording of this question after 2006 is a bit different, but the meaning remains the same. In 2008 and 2010, "after tax and compulsory deductions" replaces "net."

[30] More precisely, two different cards are shown to respondents, depending on the year of the survey. In the surveys from 2002 to 2006, the card places the respondent's total household income into twelve categories associated with different weekly, monthly or annual ranges. These are the annual ranges associated to each letter category (for country-years before the euro, these were in national currency equivalents). The surveys in 2008 and 2010, on the other hand, use ten categories, which represent the deciles in the country income distribution.

[31] Midpoint value assignments differ among survey waves. For 2002–2006 we used midpoints based on common value categories, while for the 2008 and 2010 surveys, we use midpoints derived from country-specific income deciles.

used extensively in the American politics literature analyzing General Social Survey data (Hout, 2004). A complication arises when defining a midpoint for the open-ended top category (which is undefined because this category has no upper limit). We impute the top-coded income category by assuming that the upper tail of the income distribution follows a Pareto distribution (e.g., Kopczuk et al., 2010). This still leaves us with one remaining problem, namely that the purchasing power of a certain amount of money varies across the countries included in our analysis. Simply put, the meaning of being €10,000 below the mean is different in Germany and in Greece. We address this problem by converting national-currency denominated income into PPP-adjusted 2005 US dollars. The distribution of resulting income distances is quite similar in Western European countries (more than the distribution of untransformed household income). A plot of country-by-country distributions of income distance is available in Figure A.1 in Appendix A.1. There we also provide descriptive information on the population characteristics of this data set.

Our income measure using the GSS follows the same pattern. As mentioned earlier, our transformation of measured income in the ESS follows the predominant approach in the American Politics literature. It should come as no surprise that we rely on a measure of income that is constructed the same way. First income categories (which change over time) are converted into dollar amounts using midpoints. The open-ended top category is imputed assuming that income follows a Pareto distribution. Then, incomes are deflated using the Bureau of Labor Statistics' consumer price index for urban consumers. See the report by Hout (2004) for a more detailed summary. As, again, we are not interested in levels of income, but in the distance from the mean, we finally transform income to be the distance to the national mean in each survey year. Again, Appendix A.1 provides a plot of the distribution of income distances by state.

In contrast to large-scale social surveys like ESS and GSS, household surveys provide information on respondents' and households' income in much greater detail (and with much better quality). Issues such as having to impute midpoint values from categorical responses do not occur in the BHPS. To some extent this is simply a function of survey time spent on measuring it. General social surveys usually only devote a single question to income, while household panels devote whole sections to the measurement of many aspects related to income (and wealth). Furthermore, the fact that household panels provide longitudinal information of the same respondents makes it easier to validate income values in each survey and to correct or impute missing income from past (and future) observations. Thus, household income calculated from the BHPS closely tracks official household income figures (as used by the Department of Work and Pensions) in the United Kingdom (Jenkins, 2010). Household income in the BHPS is derived from detailed household and individual household member questionnaires.[32] A household's gross income is calculated from a number of individual components of each household member such as gross earnings from employment, profits or losses from self-employment, and private and occupational pensions. Also added are social security payments and tax credits. The BHPS itself does not include net household income. Jenkins and colleagues use tax simulation to calculate the amount of taxes and social security contributions to be deducted in order to arrive at net household income figures (Jarvis and Jenkins, 1995; Levy and Jenkins, 2008).[33] We then adjust net household income for inflation and calculate the distance to the mean household income in each year.

Our second household panel data set, the Socio-Economic Panel, provides high-quality income data comparable to the BHPS. Because our use of this data set is limited to an analysis of individuals' income expectations in Chapter 3, which uses only labor income data, we do not need to describe measures of household income here.

1.7 WHERE TO GO FROM HERE

The plan for the rest of the book follows straightforwardly from the previous paragraphs. We have provided a general explanation of the data we use in the book's analyses and a description of the contours of our two main variables of interest: redistribution preferences and income. In this chapter, as in other parts of the book, we make use of figures and maps liberally, and we hope this helps the reader get a feeling for the data before the more systematic analyses.

---

[32] It is interesting to note that compared to our cross-sectional surveys nonresponse to income questions is much lower in the BHPS, which might be the results of trust established with survey respondents (Lynn, 2006: 42).

[33] More precisely, the BHPS net income is derived from the following income components: household gross income is composed of its members' usual gross earnings from employment + earnings from subsidiary employment + profit or loss from self-employment + Social Security benefits and tax credits + private and occupational pensions + income from investments and saving + any private transfers and other income. From this are deducted income tax (for employees and self-employed) + national insurance contributions (for employees and self-employed) + contributions to occupational pension schemes + local taxes.

The substantive chapters in the book are divided into four parts. In Part I, we present our argument about the effects of income expectations on redistribution preferences. Part II is dedicated to the importance of macro-inequality and fear of crime (as its negative externality) to the demand for redistribution. And Part III explores the relationship between population heterogeneity and parochial altruism. Each of these substantive parts of the book consists of two chapters. The first contains the main theoretical argument and an initial analysis of the data. These preliminary analyses are meant to be intuitive and descriptive. The second chapter in each of these parts develops the more systematic empirical tests of the theoretical hypotheses. While some of these analyses are, out of necessity, quantitatively sophisticated, we deemphasize technical details and mathematical formulae in the main text of the book (they are provided in the appendices). In Part IV of the book, we present our argument about the influence of redistribution preferences on vote choice and also explore this relationship empirically. Through the different parts of the book, we attempt to produce explanations that are easy to understand and that focus on the intuitions behind the hypotheses or the techniques. A number of methodological issues are explained in the text, but the main presentation of our different results emphasizes the intuitive use of predicted probabilities or marginal effects (with evident graphical representations).

PART I

MATERIAL SELF-INTEREST: REDISTRIBUTION AND INSURANCE

2

Income, Income Expectations, Redistribution, and Insurance

While the political economy literature has generally been limited to relatively simple material self-interested motivations (an individual's present position in the income distribution determines preferences for redistribution), a number of significant contributions have recently expanded this focus. In this book's next sections, we will explore how negative-externality and other-regarding concerns matter to redistribution preferences. This is a productive endeavor, as we will show, but in this section we take a different tack. Rather than exploring non-pocketbook motivations, our main argument here is that we have been looking at a limited measure of income. We make two related points. Regarding the influence of income, we argue that an individual's expectation of future income is as significant as present income as a determinant of redistribution preferences. Second, we believe that many of the existing approaches in comparative political economy (emphasizing concepts as diverse as risk, insurance, religion, or mobility) are best understood both theoretically and empirically by being integrated into this model of expected life income.

It has been generally noted that the importance of present income as a determinant of redistribution preferences is highly variable, both cross-nationally and temporally. The (still highly relevant) influence of material self-interest as a motivation for redistribution preferences therefore needs to be complemented and improved. In this chapter we argue that material self-interest should not be limited to present income and propose that individuals have preferences that are fundamentally related to their lifetime income. We take the labor economics literature as our inspiration (Mincer,

1958; Ben-Porath, 1967; Mincer, 1974; Heckman et al., 2006) and find that our lifetime income model easily incorporates arguments about social insurance, risk, and mobility (as in Sinn, 1995; Benabou and Ok, 2001; Iversen and Soskice, 2001; Mares, 2003; Moene and Wallerstein, 2003; Rehm, 2009; Alesina and Giuliano, 2011).

2.2 THE ARGUMENT

This chapter attempts to deepen our understanding of one of the most distinct (and influential) approaches to the formation of preferences for redistribution. Most analyses in political economy rely on the idea that the level of redistribution preferred by a given individual is fundamentally a function of relative income or, more specifically, a function of the distance between the individual's own income and the average income of the population covered by the polity in which that person resides. Two different facets of these arguments should be distinguished. One deals with redistribution and the other with insurance, risk, and mobility. Or, as we will argue in more detail in this chapter, one deals with the present, while the other one deals (often implicitly) with the future.

In the following pages, we will explore in more detail these frameworks and elucidate this chapter's claims. In essence, we argue that most material self-interest arguments emphasize present income while not fully exploring the importance of future income. We propose that expectations of future income are as relevant to individuals in forming their redistribution preferences as the levels of income they currently enjoy.

2.2.1 Material Self-Interest: Related and Competing Arguments

Political economy approaches that start from the assumption that an individual's position in the income distribution determines preferences for redistribution are often inspired by the theoretical model proposed by Romer (1975) and developed by Meltzer and Richard (1981). To recapitulate very briefly, the Romer–Meltzer–Richard (RMR) model assumes that the preferences of the median voter determine government policy and that the median voter seeks to maximize current income. If there are no deadweight costs to redistribution, all voters with incomes below the mean maximize their utility by imposing a 100 percent tax rate. Conversely, all voters with incomes above the mean prefer a tax rate of zero.

When there are distortionary costs to taxation, the RMR model implies that, by increasing the distance between the median and the mean incomes, more inequality should be associated with more redistribution. The consensus in the comparative literature on this topic, however, seems to be that there is either no association between market income inequality and redistribution, or, contrary to the prediction of the RMR model, less market inequality is associated with more redistribution (Lindert, 1996; Gouveia and Masia, 1998; Rodrigiuez, 1999: 57–60; Moene and Wallerstein, 2001; Alesina and Glaeser, 2004; Iversen and Soskice, 2009). These findings must be considered with a degree of caution. This is because, until recently, most of this literature relied on macro-comparative empirical analyses (with redistribution as the dependent variable) and did not pay much attention to individual preferences.[1]

It is important to point out that when focusing on the individual demand for redistribution, we (like most of the literature on redistribution preferences) go beyond the standard RMR framework by positing that income should affect preferences for redistribution across the entire income distribution. We expect that an individual in, say, the tenth percentile of the income distribution benefits more from the RMR redistributive scheme (lump-sum payments financed by a linear income tax) than an individual in the thirtieth percentile. As a result, we expect the former individual to have stronger preferences for redistribution than the latter. The converse holds for the upper end of the income distribution as well. At any given tax rate, someone in the ninetieth percentile will lose more income than someone in the seventieth percentile under the RMR scheme. While, arguably, both individuals may like the tax rate to be zero, the intensity of this preference will vary between the two individuals. When looking at individual data, in fact, there is some support for the argument that relative income influences preferences. Using comparative data, a relative income effect is found in, among others, Bean and Papadakis (1998), Finseraas (2009), and Shayo (2009). Using American data, Gilens (2005), McCarty et al. (2008), and Page and Jacobs (2009) (again, among others) find similar effects.

It is nevertheless the case that the importance of income as a determinant of redistribution preferences is highly variable. While it is the case that the rich support redistribution less than the poor almost everywhere, the strength of this relationship is hardly consistent (Dion, 2010; Dion and

---

[1] Even the macro-comparative conclusion is less unambiguous than the consensus in the literature suggests. Milanovic (2000) and Kenworthy and Pontusson (2005) show that rising inequality tends to be consistently associated with more redistribution within countries.

Birchfield, 2010; Beramendi and Rehm, 2016). We propose that one of the reasons for this lack of consistent effects in the literature has to do with a general misconception of the basis of material self-interest. The idea that material self-interest determines redistribution preferences should not be limited to a measure of present income. In the words of Alesina and Giuliano, "(e)conomists traditionally assume that individuals have preferences defined over their lifetime consumption (income) and maximize their utility under a set of constraints. The same principle applies to preferences for redistribution. It follows that maximization of utility from consumption and leisure and some aggregation of individual preferences determines the equilibrium level of taxes and transfers" (2011: 1).

Because of the potential to define material self-interest intertemporally (as lifetime consumption/income), this approach extends the more direct focus on effects of contemporary relative income (as in Romer, 1975; Meltzer and Richard, 1981) and opens the door to arguments about social insurance and risk (as in Sinn, 1995; Iversen and Soskice, 2001; Mares, 2003; Moene and Wallerstein, 2003; Rehm, 2009), and about social mobility and life-cycle profiles (Benabou and Ok, 2001; Haider and Solon, 2006; Alesina and Giuliano, 2011).

Analyses of insurance and mobility are most relevant to the topic of this chapter. Moene and Wallerstein (2001, 2003) articulate the insurance approach most forcefully (cf. also Varian, 1980; Sinn, 1995; Iversen and Soskice, 2001; Mares, 2003). Their model builds on the assumption that demand for insurance rises with income, holding risk exposure constant, and stands the RMR model on its head as far as the predicted association between inequality and redistribution is concerned. As a mean-preserving decline in inequality implies that the income of the median voter is higher, Moene and Wallerstein expect that countries with a more egalitarian distribution of income will have more redistributive governments. More important for the specific argument we present in this section of the book, the model presented in Moene and Wallerstein (2001) is characterized by two parameters: a tax rate that determines the level of aggregate welfare spending and a distributive parameter that determines how welfare benefits are targeted. The main implication in their analysis is that the nature of targeting affects the influence of inequality on redistribution. When the beneficiaries of redistribution are employed, the RMR redistribution effect follows from an increase in inequality. When benefits target the unemployed (who, in Moene and Wallerstein's model have no earnings), the insurance effect dominates. These are very important conclusions, but they are not directly related to the main point of our argument here. While their insights are compatible with our hypotheses, we argue that the insurance logic is relevant to support for redistribution to the extent that individuals anticipate the effects of their future income (and of mobility within the income distribution) and therefore should be integrated into a more general conception of expected income (which includes not only the probability of becoming unemployed).[2]

Other arguments about the importance of insurance have also emphasized the importance of risk in determining redistribution and insurance preferences. In this vein, Rehm (2009, 2016) argues that, while income captures redistribution preferences, occupation characteristics capture risk exposure and insurance motivations. In a highly influential article, Iversen and Soskice (2001) argue that exposure to risk is inversely related to the portability of individual skills. While we agree with Iversen and Soskice that individual expected utility (across a range of possible labor market stages) is the key factor in determining redistribution preferences, we do not emphasize the difference between general and specific skills. Instead, we will consider expected life income to depend on two key factors: education and labor market experience. We therefore want to integrate concerns about insurance and risk into a simpler conception of expected individual life income.

Similarly, religiosity may work as an intermediary between individual insurance considerations and demand for redistribution. Scheve and Stasavage (2006) argue that religion or, rather, active membership in religious organizations provides both tangible and intangible benefits (cf. Pergament, 1997). Inasmuch as the benefits of religion are nonmaterial (e.g., providing solace in times of hardship and therefore decreasing the demand for insurance), we expect its effect to be unrelated to income. However, if religious groups also provide direct material benefits (such as helping out with money in times of unemployment), a religious individual's expectation of his future income stream would be altered. We are agnostic about the influence of religiosity, but the importance of this literature militates for controlling for this potential effect. We return to this topic in the next chapter's analysis.

Some influential contributions within the existing literature hypothesize that individuals with good prospects for upward mobility might be less inclined to support redistribution than their present income would

---

[2] We should also note that our empirical focus in the next chapter is fully on the individual demand for redistribution, unlike Moene and Wallerstein's analysis of aggregate welfare spending.

lead us to expect (e.g., Piketty, 1995; Benabou and Ok, 2001). By the same logic, we argue that individuals who anticipate downward mobility to be more supportive of redistribution than their present income would lead us to expect. Our arguments are perhaps most directly related to those in Alesina and La Ferrara (2005). They explore how individual preferences for redistribution are affected by prospects of future income mobility. Alesina and La Ferrara's measure of expected future profiles are constructed using three types of indicators: individuals' account history of past mobility; individuals' subjective perception of their future standards of living; and objective indexes of mobility for income deciles (based on panel data). While we are inspired by this analysis, we differ in our conceptualization of expected future income.[3] As Alesina and La Ferrara themselves argue, it is the last component in these income profiles that is most novel (2005: 898). Their approach differs from most of the existing empirical literature because of the consideration of the role of a general and objective mobility index as a potential determinant of redistribution. Our argument is similar, inasmuch as it emphasizes an objective but more individual proxy for future positions in the income ladder. However, while their findings emphasize the effects of an individual's likelihood of being in the upper deciles of the income distribution over the next one to five years, we want to explore ways of capturing income prospects over the entire life cycle.

We argue that individuals' anticipated future position in the income distribution is captured by their life-cycle income profile and thus incorporated into their present-day utility calculus via expected income. In this sense, we follow on the steps of the pioneering work of Friedman (1957). And, like Friedman, we rely on a set of explicit theoretical intuitions rather than on a multiperiod maximizing model that can be solved explicitly. Friedman argued that "permanent income" was like a mean of the expected level of income in the future.[4] This intuition very much underpins the labor economics literature on life-cycle profiles that we take as our inspiration (Ben-Porath, 1967; Mincer, 1974; Baker, 1997; Haider and Solon, 2006). Next, we propose a simple way of estimating the value of an individual's expected future income based on the interplay of education and increasing labor market experience.

---

[3] Alesina and La Ferrara also emphasize the effects of beliefs in fairness on redistribution preferences, something that we will not address in detail in this chapter. We focus on nonmaterial considerations (as determinants of redistribution demand additional to expected income) in the next two sections of the book.

[4] Unlike Friedman, however, we do not assume that individuals discount future income and adopt a much shorter time horizon than the remainder of their working lifetimes.

2.2.2 Our Argument

We argue that individuals form their redistribution preferences as a function of two distinct elements: their present income and their expectations about future income. Expectations about future income, we argue, are as influential (possibly more) than present income. Following labor economics models on life-cycle profiles, we suggest a very simple conception of future income. Individuals only look at two factors to form expectations of their future income profile: age (as a proxy for work experience) and education. In essence, we submit (and later test empirically) that individuals have some knowledge about the life-cycle income profile of people with their same level of education. These income profiles are averages that integrate typical labor market experiences (likelihood of experiencing unemployment, of finding a new job if unemployed, of experiencing age-related wage increases or decreases, etc.). With this general idea of how people with their educational level progress through their working lives, they look at their own age and project a likely future income profile. It is both this expectation of future income and the reality of present income that contribute significantly to an individual's demand for redistribution.

Our empirical measure of expected income is based on an extension of the standard human capital earnings function. It expresses the conditional distribution of (log) earnings W given s years of schooling and x years of work experience[5]:

$$W(s,x) = \alpha + f(s) + g(x). \tag{2.1}$$

In typical empirical applications $f(s)$ is a linear function, while $g(x)$ is quadratic yielding the popular "Mincer earnings function," the main idea for which goes back to Mincer (1958, 1974), building on the work of Becker and Chiswick (1966) and Ben-Porath (1967).[6] It describes how income develops over the life cycle for individuals based on the returns to education and growing labor market experience (e.g., via on-the-job training):

$$W(s,x) = \alpha + \beta s + \gamma_1 x + \gamma_2 x^2. \tag{2.2}$$

---

[5] This follows the standard assumption that s and x are additively separable. We focus on the conditional mean of the distribution, $\mu(s,x) = E(W|S = s, X = x)$, but simply write $W(s,x)$ to reduce notational complexity.

[6] The economic literature on the "Mincer model" is enormous. See Psacharopoulos and Patrinos (2004) for a recent review.

Next to an overall intercept, α, returns to education are captured by β, while returns to (increasing) experience are captured by γ_1 and γ_2. The quadratic effect of experience allows for an increasing effect of experience on wages, which usually flattens toward the end of one's working life, representing decreasing returns to investment in human capital. The purely additive effect of schooling and experience in this model specification implies that the effect of work experience on wages is identical across education groups.

To relax this assumption, years of schooling can be replaced by education certificates, as argued by Heckman et al. (2006). Even more important, years of education is a concept of questionable utility in comparative research. It focuses solely on general training and ignores vocational training and higher education. Furthermore, more years of schooling do not necessarily translate into labor market advantages if more able individuals traverse the educational system more quickly, and if differently valued certificates represent similar years spent in educational institutions (Kerckhoff and Dylan, 1999).[7] In other words, focusing on years of schooling ignores the additional employer relevant information signaled by education certificates (Spence, 1974). Thus "(y)ears of education do not provide a particularly good measure of differences in schooling ... If one compares formal schooling it is necessary to go beyond years of schooling and establish some form of equivalence ... " (Freeman and Schettkat, 2000: 8).

Heckman et al. (2006) argue to extend the standard Mincer model of equation (2.2) in two ways. First, one should allow for variable returns to education, instead of specifying a single rate of return. Second, they argue for allowing heterogeneity in returns to experience. Let D be a vector of education certificates with J levels, and let d_j be a 0-1 indicator of the highest completed education certificate. The extended earnings equation

$$W(x, D) = \alpha + \sum_{j=2}^{J} \delta_j d_j + \sum_{j=2}^{J} \gamma_{1j} d_j x + \sum_{j=2}^{J} \gamma_{2j} d_j x^2 \qquad (2.3)$$

now contains education-specific returns to education, δ_j, as well as education-specific returns to experience, γ_{1j} and γ_{2j}.

Figure 2.1 illustrates the income profiles resulting from this extended model, which we adopt for our argument about expected income.

---

[7] For example, the theoretical length of upper secondary education (an education category explained later) varies between two years in Spain, the Netherlands, and the United Kingdom, and more than four years in Austria and Italy (Dunne, 2003: 7).

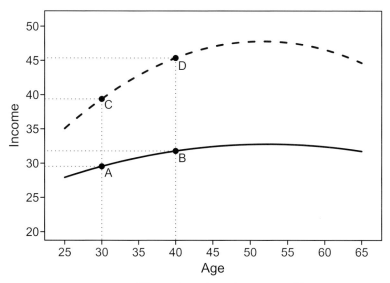

FIGURE 2.1 Illustration of two income profiles

It displays simulated age–income profiles for two individuals with different levels of education. At age thirty these individuals' yearly labor earnings are roughly 10,000 dollars apart (compare points A and C). However, the first individual can expect to earn about 3,000 dollars more when age forty (point B), whereas the second individual's income rises a lot faster. This individual's expected income at age forty is slightly above 45,000 dollars (point D). This also implies that the second individual can expect a higher average lifetime income than the first. More importantly, the difference between them in income averaged over the whole life cycle is greater than the difference in their incomes at age thirty.

It is important to emphasize that our argument is *implicitly* intertemporal. Expected income will be realized in the future. But we introduce these considerations about the future as *explicit* present expectations. In this sense, our approach is not different from the risk and insurance arguments in Rehm (2009, 2016) or Iversen and Soskice (2001). Rehm emphasizes present exposure to occupational unemployment risk and Iversen and Soskice the potential costs of unemployment for those with specific skills (in both cases, individuals demand protection for risks that may be realized in the future). In our argument, we propose that an expectation of future income (in addition to the knowledge of present income) affects the support of redistribution in the present. This approach allows us, like Friedman (1957), to avoid having to solve a multiperiod maximizing model with uncertainties about the level of redistribution in the future. Unlike Moene and Wallerstein (2001) or Iversen and Soskice (2001), however, our argument does not build on individuals' degree of risk aversion. A specific level of risk aversion (against the probability of income loss) is a critical assumption in the articles mentioned: If individuals do not care about risk, they will not demand any insurance. In contrast, our argument does not depend on a specific level of risk aversion because we model individuals as acting on their known future income path (or, rather, their best guess based on a Mincer model), without explicitly modeling the uncertainty around expected income. Our approach implies that expectations of future income have an effect on redistribution even if fully certain and accurate (an individual demands more redistribution today, for example, if she knows she will be poorer in the future).[8]

It is also important to point out that we assume the effects of expected income not to be dependent on present income. As suggested in Chapter 1, we make a distinction between the tax and transfer side of our argument in this chapter (dominated by material interests having to do with present and expected income) and the negative externality and heterogeneity ones to be developed in Parts II and III of this book. The tax and transfer implications of present and expected income are significant to the poor and the rich alike. Empirically, we can confirm this theoretical intuition with an interactive model specification that tests if the effect of income expectations is conditional on present income.[9] This is distinctly different from the arguments dominating the second and third parts of the book. We will show that noneconomic factors (defined as those not directly affecting the income/tax/transfer nexus) affect the poor and the rich differently. As we explain in more detail later, both the negative externalities of inequality and the moral benefits of altruism are more important to the rich.

2.3 CALCULATING EXPECTED INCOME

In the following pages, we apply our theoretical approach and estimate individual expected future income based on the interplay of education and increasing labor market experience. We do this using three different datasets that we will later also employ to estimate the relationship between income expectations and redistribution preferences:

---

[8] As we make clear later, we also assume no discounting of future income.
[9] A Wald test shows no statistically significant difference in the marginal effect of income expectations for the rich and the poor ($p = 0.098$).

the European Social Survey (ESS), the German Socio-Economic Panel, and the British Household Panel Survey.

2.3.1 Expected Income in Western Europe

Our analysis of Western European countries draws on ESS surveys administered in 2002, 2004, 2006, 2008, and 2010.[10] As we have argued earlier, our central variable of interest, expected income, is generated by a statistical model for education–age income profiles. It describes how income develops over the life cycle for individuals with different levels of education. The most commonly used specification for life-earning profiles is the Mincer earnings function (Mincer, 1958, 1974):

$$\log(\text{income})_i = \alpha + \beta_1 s_i + \beta_2 x_i + \beta_3 x_i^2 + \epsilon_i. \tag{2.4}$$

It describes log income as resulting from a linear combination of an individual's education and quadratic years of work experience.[11] The quadratic effect allows for the increasing but flattening effect of experience on wages (representing decreasing returns to experience). In the preceding equation, education is represented by years of schooling, denoted by s_i, and potential work experience is captured by the years following schooling and is denoted by x_i. The purely additive effects of schooling and experience in the Mincer specification suggest that the effect of work experience on wages is similar across education groups. Heckman et al. (2006) extend the Mincer model in two ways. First, they allow for variable returns to education, instead of specifying a single rate of return. Second, they also argue for heterogeneity in returns to experience. Thus, in our model specification, we estimate return-to-education coefficients for different levels of education. We capture (some) heterogeneity in returns by including interactions between each level of education and years of work experience, effectively allowing for differential returns to experience by education groups.[12]

[10] The countries included in our analysis are Austria, Belgium, Switzerland, Germany, Denmark, Spain, Finland, France, United Kingdom, Greece, Ireland, Netherlands, Norway, Portugal, and Sweden. We exclude Italy and Luxembourg because they provide only two waves of data. However, we conducted a robustness test showing that their exclusion does not change our results.

[11] We defer a detailed discussion of variables and their measurement to the next chapter.

[12] Later we use individual-level panel data instead of cross-sections and are thus able to estimate individual-specific returns to experience.

To describe our estimated model more precisely, let y_{ij} be the (log) income of individual i in country j, and s_{ij}, x_{ij} that person's education certificate and work experience, respectively. To ease notation, y_j is a stacked vector of individual incomes of country j. Similarly, stack work experience into x_j. Stacking education certificates yields a vector s_j with four possible values of education certificates: (1) less than upper-secondary, (2) upper-secondary, (3) postsecondary, or (4) tertiary.[13] Because we estimate different rates of return for each education group, we create an education-indicator matrix S_j with one column for each education group that is interacted with work experience. Our estimated income equation is

$$y_j = \boldsymbol{\beta}_{1j}S_j + \boldsymbol{\beta}_{2j}S_jx_j + \boldsymbol{\beta}_{3j}S_jx_j^2 + \boldsymbol{\epsilon}_j. \qquad (2.5)$$

All coefficients are country-specific.[14] Residuals $\boldsymbol{\epsilon}_j$ are white noise within each country. Thus we estimate country-specific life-earning profiles for seventeen West European countries in the ESS spanning the period from 2002 to 2010.[15]

We must point out that the calculation of life-earning profiles proposed earlier depends on the measure of education certificates. The ESS program makes a considerable effort to provide measurements of educational attainment that are cross-nationally harmonized. We use a variable based on the International Standard Classification of Education 1997 (ISCED-97) and developed for the ESS by Silke Schneider. Following UNESCO's recommendations, ISCED-97 attempts to provide data for different countries "on the basis of an internationally accepted standard classification scheme encompassing all types of educational programmes that a country can possibly have" (UNESCO, 1999: 4). Because harmonizing educational measures is a tricky task, however, the ISCED-97 is

---

[13] These categories are mutually exclusive and collectively exhaustive, meaning that no individual belongs to more than one category, and no individual belongs to no category.

[14] Thus we estimate what Gelman and Hill (2007) call completely unpooled models, where estimated country coefficients are not influenced by other countries. We prefer this specification to a multilevel model because our sample size is large enough and, more important, because national labor markets with very different structures might exhibit quite different age–income profiles.

[15] In the absence of detailed work histories for each individual, we proxy experience by age. It is also important to remember that, to minimize complications derived from retirement earnings and household composition, we restrict our analysis to working-age (20–65) male respondents. The household income therefore becomes individual income (whether the household contains just a man or a couple in which the woman is not in paid employment).

a very complex classification.[16] The ESS variable used in this book's analysis is a simplified version of ISCED-97. It consists of five groups. Category (1) "No or basic education" refers to individuals with at most primary education, which refers to the beginning of systematic learning of reading, writing, and mathematics in a nation's starting track of compulsory schooling. Category (2), "lower secondary education," refers to the stage following (1) usually lasting nine years since the beginning of primary education. Its completion usually marks the end of a country's compulsory education. Category (3), "upper secondary," education marks the beginning of higher education (and advanced vocational training) usually concluding in certificates allowing entry into tertiary education. Category (4), titled "postsecondary (but not tertiary)" education represents education programs designed to enhance the knowledge and skills of respondents who have completed category (3). Not all education systems make use of this category. Finally, category (5), "tertiary certificates and beyond," comprises all higher education, including undergraduate and graduate degrees, as well as advanced research degrees.[17] For a detailed functional definition of each category, see UNESCO (1999). Figure 2.2 shows the distribution of education categories by country. All countries have a sizable share of individuals holding tertiary qualifications (e.g., university degrees); the predominant share of individuals holds upper secondary certificates.[18]

---

[16] For a detailed analysis of the ISCED-97 classification and its strengths and weaknesses, see Schneider and Kogan (2008).

[17] To illustrate why a mapping from diverse national education systems to an abstract and simplified, but internationally comparable, classification is needed, consider the case of Germany. Category (1) includes individuals who attended *Kindergarten*/preschool and *Grundschule*. Category (2) comprises of individuals holding the following school-leaving certificates: *Hauptschulabschluss* and *Realschulabschluss*. Category (3) includes individuals who completed vocational training in Germany's dual system, as well as all those holding certificates allowing entry into higher education: *Abitur/allgemeine Hochschulreife*, *fachgebundene Hochschulreife*, or *Fachhochschulreife*. Category (4) includes individuals who conclude dual-system vocational training (as those assigned to category 3) and hold *Abitur* or *Fachhochschulreife*. Category (5) includes all higher education certificates, such as *Diplom*, *Magister*, BA, and MA degrees, as well as doctoral degrees. Also included are individuals with advanced vocational qualifications, such as *Meisterbriefe*, *Berufsakademie* diplomas, or advanced health schools.

[18] Note that the "postsecondary, nontertiary" category is somewhat residual in nature because it is not relevant in all education systems and labor markets. In order to ensure that it does not unduly influence our results, we reestimated our model with individuals falling in this category removed. We still get comparable results.

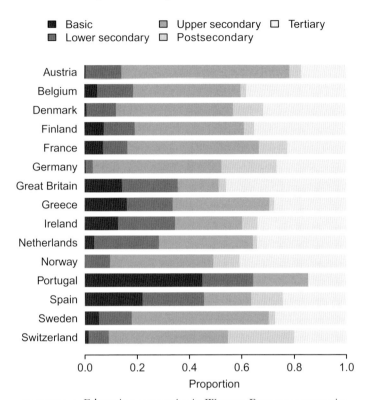

FIGURE 2.2 Education categories in Western European countries

Next, we use these predictions of age–income profiles to calculate average earnings over the remaining working life. Looking forward, what is the average income expected to look like? We simply predict future earnings up to the retirement age of sixty-five. For simplicity, we thus assume away any specific discounting of future income (we weigh income twenty years in the future the same as income 10 years in the future). Denote by $\widehat{y_{ij}(s_i, x_i)}$ income of individual i in country j with level of education s_i and experience x_i predicted from equation (2.5). Let R_i be a scalar indicating years until retirement for each individual. An individual's estimate of annualized expected lifetime income, w_{ij}, is then given by:

$$w_{ij} = R_i^{-1} \sum_{1}^{R_i} \widehat{y_{ij}(s_i, x_i)}. \qquad (2.6)$$

Figures 2.3–2.6 illustrate the resulting age–income profiles by education group in the countries in our sample. The four groups reflect the

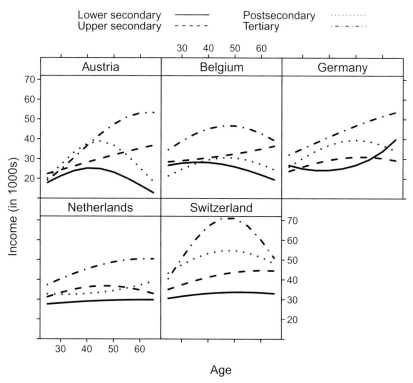

FIGURE 2.3 Age–income profiles by education in continental social market economies

existing macro institutional differences among our countries (and we will come back to the differences later). The figures, however, do show some common patterns. Most earnings curves start out with a steep increase, reflecting both the increasing probability of being employed and the positive effect of work experience. The effect of work experience is not parallel across education groups. Instead, the effect of work experience is steeper for higher educated individuals than for those with primary education. Moreover, most life-earnings profiles show a dip in household earnings after the age of fifty. This dip reflects the increasing probability of unemployment, a reduction in working hours and early retirement.

It is common practice for comparativists to group advanced capitalist political economies into clusters, conceived as coherent and distinct institutional configurations. To cite but three of the best-known examples, Katzenstein (1985) distinguishes among corporatist, liberal, and statist

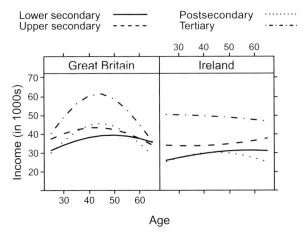

FIGURE 2.4 Age–income profiles by education in liberal market economies

political economies; Esping-Andersen (1990) among social democratic, liberal, and conservative welfare states; and Hall and Soskice (2001) among liberal market economies and coordinated market economies. We are agnostic about these categorizations (and the figures we provide contain a high degree of within-cluster variation), but we use the distinctions, nevertheless, for illustrative purposes. Figure 2.3 shows the age–income profiles by education groups within the continental social market economies. In addition to the general characteristics mentioned earlier, the figure shows some interesting country differences. Increasing levels of education are generally associated with higher wages for all ages. The exception is Belgium (and, partly, the Netherlands), where an upper secondary education is correlated with higher income than a postsecondary one. When looking at tertiary education, Austria, Germany, and Switzerland show the highest age increases in income. But these increases are relatively constant in Austria and Germany, while in Switzerland income experiences a marked decline after individuals reach the age of fifty.

Figure 2.4 contains our two liberal market economies and Figure 2.5 our Mediterranean ones. Perhaps the most remarkable characteristic of Figure 2.4 is the income associated with tertiary education and the compression of incomes in all other levels of education. The range from lower secondary to postsecondary education does not imply as large an increase in income in Great Britain and Ireland as in some other countries in our sample. Regarding tertiary education, income experiences a large age increase in Great Britain until individuals reach the age of fifty

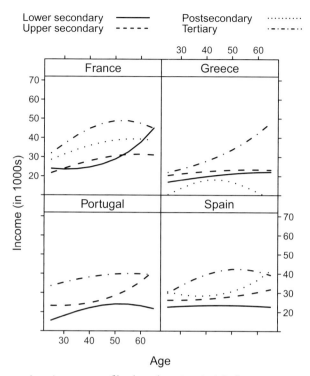

FIGURE 2.5 Age–income profiles by education in Mediterranean economies

and an equally large decrease thereafter. Irish incomes for individuals
with tertiary education starts very high, but decline steadily through the
working life cycle. In the Mediterranean economies, there is again a high
degree of cross-country variation. While having a tertiary education is
associated both with higher income levels and with increases through
the working life cycle in all Mediterranean countries, lower levels of
education are quite distinct. A lower secondary education, for example,
will be associated with quite flat age profiles in Spain and Greece (with
individuals earning pretty much the same when they are thirty as they
earn when they are fifty), but with a dramatic increase in income as an
individual gets older in France (where, by the end of the working life cycle,
incomes are the same whether a person has a lower secondary or a tertiary
education).[19]

---

[19] But we should point out, as we mentioned earlier, that the postsecondary category is
quite empty in some countries.

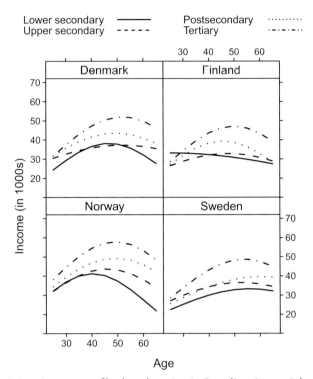

FIGURE 2.6 Age–income profiles by education in Scandinavian social market economies

Figure 2.6, finally, introduces the age–income profiles by education level in the Scandinavian social market economies. In these countries, the income patterns for individuals with lower, upper, and postsecondary education levels look remarkably similar (higher education levels and more work experience is correlated with higher income, until the already familiar dip in earning after the age of fifty). The more significant cross-national differences are visible when we turn our attention to the lower secondary level. While the pattern is the common one in Denmark, at this level of education, income increases steadily with age in Sweden, it declines steadily in Finland, and it experiences an increase and then a dramatic and early decline in Norway.

The overall distribution of expected lifetime income in the countries in our sample is presented in Figure 2.7. Each country's distribution (all rounds of the ESS are aggregated) is summarized by a box plot. Each of the boxes reflects the degree of dispersion (the spread within the box)

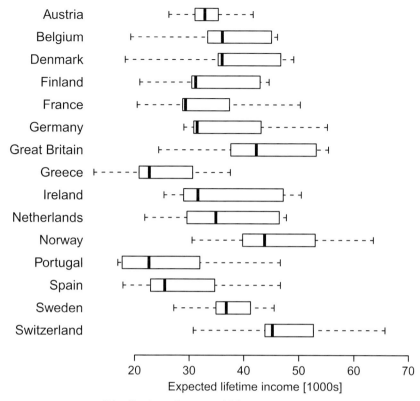

FIGURE 2.7 Distribution of expected lifetime income over countries

and skewness (represented by the position of the median in the box) in the data. The dotted lines reflect the range between minimum and maximum values. Figure 2.7 makes clear the cross-national diversity in our sample. In a country like Austria, the distribution of expected life income is quite compressed, and the median is relatively high. In countries like Belgium or the Netherlands, the median expected lifetime income is similar to that in Austria but the distribution is much more dispersed. The case of Portugal is a good illustration of moderately high levels of dispersion around a very low median of expected lifetime income.

It is perhaps important to point out here that it is not the objective of this book to explain the different patterns in age–income–education profiles (this could be the focus of further research). The important issue for our analysis is how these profiles are translated into expected lifetime income. More meaningful, therefore, for the hypotheses in this chapter, Figure 2.8 reflects the distribution of expected lifetime income for

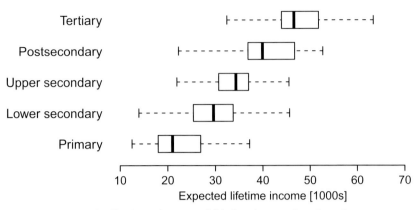

FIGURE 2.8 Distribution of expected lifetime income by education group

different levels of education (for the entire sample). As one would suspect, the figure makes clear how median incomes increase with education. The figure also indicates that dispersion in expected lifetime income is greater when an individual possesses a lower secondary or postsecondary education. Expected lifetime income is more compressed when individuals have either the highest (tertiary) or lowest (primary) levels of education.

2.3.2 Expected Income in Germany and Great Britain

In this section we use more detailed data on individuals' work histories for our expected income calculations. Using panel data, we have access to several observations of an individual's income stream, which allows us to estimate a more flexibly specified lifetime income model. We use household panel data from Germany and the United Kingdom, whose design we discussed in Chapter 1.

Germany

In the analysis using the German Socio-Economic Panel we extend the simplified income process used before to consider full profile heterogeneity (Baker, 1997; Heckman et al., 2006). In other words, we want to allow for the fact that each individual can possess rather idiosyncratic income paths. While education and work experience broadly determine the overall shape of individuals' income profiles, a variety of factors (such as ability and motivation) determine individual outcomes. Two aspects are most relevant here. First, individuals differ in their average levels of income. For example, the starting salaries of two individuals holding the same education certificates might differ simply due to the fact of better negotiation skills or performance at a job talk. Second, returns to experience can be heterogeneous over individuals as well. Some individuals are simply better able to convert work experience into productivity. To flexibly capture this heterogeneity we need to formulate a model that includes individual-specific intercepts as well as individual-specific returns to experience.

Having access to repeated information of individuals' income over time allows us to do exactly that. We model the income of individual i at time t, y_{it} via the following equation[20]:

$$y_{it} = \alpha + \boldsymbol{\beta_1} s_i + \beta_2 x_{it} + \beta_3 x_{it}^2 + [\eta_i + \lambda_i x_{it} + \epsilon_{it}]. \qquad (2.7)$$

Similar to equation (2.4) before, β_1 captures returns to education, while (β_2, β_3) capture quadratic returns to work experience for an *average* individual. The overall intercept is denoted by α. So far this is simply a linear regression model of income on education and quadratic experience.[21] Note that the respective regression coefficients are constant over all individuals (i.e., they do not carry i subscripts).

The value added of having access to repeated observations lies in our ability to model individual specific income patterns. We do so by first including individual-specific constants, denoted by η_i. They capture differences in income between individuals that are not due to their education certificates. Second, we include individual-specific returns to experience, captured by the λ_i term. Thus we allow each individual to deviate from the average education–experience profile. These two extensions move us toward a much more realistic description of individual income expectations. In the previous section, due to data limitations, we assume that two individuals, who are living in the same country, are of the same age, and hold the same education certificate have identical income expectations. In the extended income calculation just described, individuals with the same age and education may have different income expectations due to a number idiosyncratic factors.

---

[20] Income is measured as monthly net labor income. We deflate incomes using the consumer price index with base year 2005. Note that due to German unification there are two CPI series: a preunification series with base year 2005 and a postunification series with base year 2010. We rebase the latter to 2005 to create a common CPI series used in our analyses.

[21] Stochastic errors ϵ_{it} are distributed independent normal with freely estimated variance.

In more technical terms, this constitutes a random coefficient model (Swamy, 1970), where both individual intercepts as well as experience slopes have a distribution over individuals. We specify both terms as arising from a joint normal distribution, i.e., $(\eta, \lambda) \sim N(0, \Sigma)$, where Σ is a variance-covariance matrix that contains variances for both individual-specific effects as well as the covariance between them (see e.g., Gelman and Hill, 2007). The reason to include a covariance between individual intercepts and slopes is that individuals with higher average incomes might have steeper experience–income profiles.

From this model of each individual's income process we can again calculate his or her average life income, which is annualized predicted income from now until retirement age. Let R_i be scalar that denotes for each individual years until retirement and calculate

$$w_i = R_i^{-1} \sum_{r=1}^{R_i} \left[\hat{\alpha} + \hat{\beta}_1 s_i + \hat{\eta}_i + \hat{\beta}_2 (x_{it} + r) + \hat{\beta}_3 (x_{it} + r)^2 + \hat{\lambda}_i (x_{it} + r) \right]$$

(2.8)

to obtain annualized predicted lifetime income taking into account each individual's specific coefficients. In other words, we assume that individuals learn about their performance in the labor market and thus gain knowledge about their idiosyncratic effects (η_i, λ_i). However, individuals face considerable uncertainty when making these predictions, due to (i) their imperfect knowledge of the true income-generating process and (ii) unanticipated shocks occurring in the future. We simulate the fundamental uncertainty a specific individual faces by drawing from a normal distribution with his predicted lifetime income as mean and variance proportional to the variability in his observed stream of earnings:

$$\omega_{it} \sim N \left(E(w_{it}), \psi_i^2 \right).$$

(2.9)

Figure 2.9 shows the resulting age–education profiles for our sample of German individuals. Its construction is slightly more complex than Figures 2.3–2.6. For each individual in our sample we calculate his individual age–income curve. Thus, instead of one population average education–age–income plot as in our previous figures, we now obtain 6,422 age–income curves. Figure 2.9 plots averages for each of our four education groups (the thick black lines). In order to visualize the extent of profile heterogeneity between individuals, we randomly draw 500 individuals and plot their individual age–income profiles (the thin gray lines).

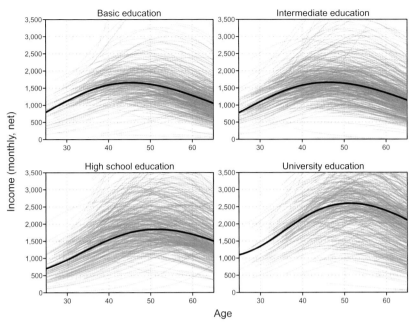

FIGURE 2.9 Heterogeneity in distribution of expected lifetime income by education group in Germany

Even though the estimation of expected lifetime income using the German Socio-Economic Panel is much more detailed and individual specific, the picture that emerges from Figure 2.9 is quite consistent with the one using the much blunter estimation of ESS data in Figure 2.3.

Britain

We repeat the same income expectation calculation with data from the United Kingdom, using the British Household Panel Study. The model for income expectations is the same as described earlier and yields similar patterns of income expectations. The key difference between our German and British data is that the BHPS contains repeated measures of redistribution preferences. We make use of this feature to model more completely the dynamics of expectation formation and preference changes in the next chapter.

3

Income Expectations as Determinants of Redistribution

In this chapter, we test our hypotheses using both cross-sectional and panel-data evidence. While all analyses in our book are restricted to the working-age population, the analyses in this chapter are more restrictive. We limit our sample to males, following the most common choice in the literature on life-cycle income and income mobility. The reason is that there are clear selection concerns about the labor market participation (and fertility choices) of women. Including women in our sample would require a sensible *joint* (selection) model of labor market participation, (household) fertility decisions, and redistribution preferences. Clearly, this is beyond the scope of the current chapter. We thus opt for the more conservative choice and focus on working-age males, where selectivity is less of a concern. The price we pay is that conclusions derived from this chapter are more limited in their generalizability.

3.1 CROSS-SECTIONAL EVIDENCE: EUROPE

We start with a cross-sectional analysis based on the European Social Survey (ESS). We use the expected age–education income profiles calculated from ESS data in the previous chapter and estimate how these profiles influence redistribution preferences. Our use of cross-national data allows us to test the validity of our microlevel argument in varying contexts, characterized by differing political cultures and economic institutions (King et al., 1994: 24). An obvious disadvantage is that the causal status of our findings remains ambiguous. The most obvious criticism is that unobserved individual characteristics (such as ability) might cause both levels of expected income and redistribution preferences.

We tackle this issue later in this chapter, where we rely on panel data collected in two countries (Germany and the UK) to estimate joint models of income expectation formation and preference changes (including individual-specific effects). We find results comparable to the ones with ESS data.

3.1.1 Variable Definitions

EXPECTED INCOME. In the previous chapter, we explained how we generate our central independent variable, expected income, through a statistical model for education–age income profiles. Is expected future income distinct from present income? The theoretical model we have explained earlier and, more important, the implications about redistribution preferences we extract from it, fundamentally depend on future income expectations capturing something that is not highly correlated to present income. It would be tempting for a critical reader to suspect that the relationship between present income (which is also included in the statistical analysis developed later) and future income expectations is in fact very strong. To address this possibility, we present the correlation between expected income and present income for each country in our sample in Table 3.1. The table shows the correlations to be generally low (around 0.2 in some countries, around 0.3 in many others). The only exception is Luxembourg, where the relationship between present income and expected future income is much higher. We address the sensibility of our analysis to this and other country-specific factors in the following sections.

TABLE 3.1 *Correlation between current and expected income*

Country	Corr.	Country	Corr.
Austria	0.240	Italy	0.216
Belgium	0.314	Luxembourg	0.581
Denmark	0.311	Netherlands	0.300
Finland	0.282	Norway	0.269
France	0.363	Portugal	0.317
Germany	0.312	Spain	0.311
Great Britain	0.309	Sweden	0.253
Greece	0.229	Switzerland	0.313
Ireland	0.332		

Note: Correlation between present income and expected lifetime income w_{ij} calculated following equation (2.6).

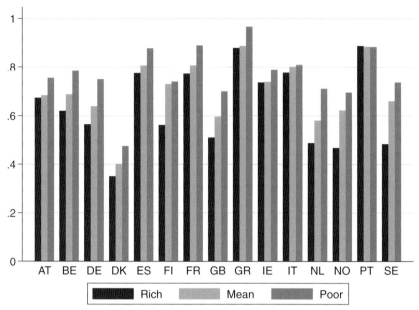

FIGURE 3.1 Support for redistribution (general, among poor, and among rich)

REDISTRIBUTION PREFERENCES. While Table 1.1 on page 24 was informative regarding general support for redistribution in Europe, it did not illustrate the relationship between present income and redistribution preferences. Figure 3.1 shows the level of support for redistribution in each of the countries in the sample (i.e., the percentage of agrees and strong agrees for the question on whether "the government should take measures to reduce differences in income levels"). It also shows the level of support for redistribution among the poor (those individuals with household incomes at most 20,000 PPP-adjusted 2005 US dollars below the country-year mean) and among the rich (those with household incomes at least 40,000 PPP-adjusted 2005 US dollars above the mean).

Figure 3.1 reflects a remarkable amount of cross-national variation. Support for redistribution is generally high in countries like Spain, France, Greece, Ireland, Italy, and Portugal. It is generally low in countries like Denmark, Great Britain, and the Netherlands. The support of redistribution among the rich and the poor mirrors these general trends, but the differences between poor and rich are quite interesting. For example, in Sweden and Norway, where the general support for redistribution is relatively high, the difference between rich and poor is large (around 23 percentage points). In Austria, where the general support for redistribution is again relatively high, the difference between rich and poor is low, only around 7 percentage points (in Portugal the difference is even smaller). There are countries with large differences between the rich and poor that have high general levels of support (like Finland) and that have low levels of support (like the Netherlands).

CONTROL VARIABLES. We include individual-level control variables commonly used in analyses of redistribution preferences.[1] These include age (measured in years) and household size. The model also includes a dummy for being a union member. We expect this variable to be positively associated with support for redistribution. Finally, the model also includes a control for being a foreigner. We introduce this variable to test whether there is a connection between expected future income and identity. A large literature has emerged on the role of racial and ethnic identities on the formation of preferences for redistribution (and we return to this issue in much more detail in Part III).[2]

3.1.2 Statistical Specification

We now turn to a statistical model for how income expectations influence individuals' preferences for redistribution. Our dependent variable is the redistribution preference of individual i living in country j, denoted by R_{ij}^*.[3] We model preferences as a function of income expectations and a number of control variables accounting for individual characteristics:

$$R_{ij}^* = \gamma w_{ij} + \delta x_{ij} + \xi_j + \zeta_{ij}. \tag{3.1}$$

Here γ captures the effect of expected income, w_{ij}. As our respondents are clustered within countries, we include country random effects ξ_j, assumed to be normally distributed with mean zero and freely estimated variance (we also consider a fixed effects specification later). Residuals ζ_{ij} are white noise with variance fixed to $\pi^2/3$, yielding a logit model. Finally, δ is a vector of estimates of control variables (including present income), x_{ij}.

---

[1] Previous analyses of individual preferences using similar controls include Corneo and Grüner (2002), Blekesaune and Quadagno (2003), Cusack et al. (2006), Iversen and Soskice (2001), Rehm (2009), and Stegmueller et al. (2012).

[2] A more detailed description of the data and its population characteristics is available in Chapter 1 and Appendix A.1.

[3] Using a logit formulation, R_{ij}^* is a latent variable determining observed survey responses, such that a respondent "agrees" or "strongly agrees" that "the government should take measures to reduce differences in income levels" if $R_{ij}^* \geq 0$. He does not support redistribution ("disagrees," etc.) when $R_{ij}^* < 0$. Our results do not change substantively if we employ an ordered logit specification.

ESTIMATION. Our statistical analysis consists of two stages. In the first stage, explained in the previous chapter, we calculated annualized expected lifetime income following equations (2.5) and (2.6) estimated using least squares. The second stage consists of our analysis of redistribution preferences as given in equation (3.1). We estimate this equation via maximum likelihood using fifteen-point adaptive Gaussian quadrature to integrate over the random effects distribution. Because first-stage expected lifetime income, w_{it}, is based on estimates, we need to account for its uncertainty (the standard error of the prediction) in order to avoid well-known error-in-variables attenuation (Chesher, 1991; Greene, 2002: 84). We incorporate this first-stage uncertainty into our preference equation estimates via nonparametric bootstrapping (Cameron and Trivedi, 2005: 357). To be precise, we take 500 bootstrap samples and for each sample we estimate first-stage expected lifetime income (from equations 2.5 and 2.6), which we then insert into equation (3.1). This strategy yields estimates corrected for errors-in-variable bias and conservative standard errors.

In order to check the robustness of our results against specific statistical choices, we estimate three more model specifications. First, we simply omit all control variables including only present and expected income as right-hand-side variables. In the next specification, we replace country random effects by fixed effects, i.e., we include a set of country dummies. Finally, we jettison our bootstrapping procedure and employ simple heteroscedasticity-consistent standard errors.

3.1.3 Results

Table 3.2 presents estimates of our redistribution preference equation using these different specifications. Our interest is focused on the effects of the two measures of income on redistribution preferences. Are redistribution preferences mainly a function of how individuals do currently, or – as we argue in this book – do considerations of expected income play a role as well? A first look at the results in Table 3.2 suggests that both measures of income play a significant role. Looking at the respective magnitudes of each of these effects, however, we find that considerations of present and future income matter very differently. Our results in fact suggest that a one-dollar change in expected lifetime income has a much larger impact on redistribution preferences than a one-dollar change in actual current income.

TABLE 3.2 *Expected income and redistribution preferences*

	(1)	(2)	(3)	(4)
Expected income	−0.272	−0.260	−0.258	−0.273
	(0.021)	(0.021)	(0.021)	(0.017)
Current income	−0.095	−0.097	−0.097	−0.096
	(0.006)	(0.006)	(0.006)	(0.006)
Household members		−0.010	−0.010	−0.010
		(0.010)	(0.010)	(0.010)
Union member		0.429	0.433	0.434
		(0.028)	(0.028)	(0.030)
Age		0.008	0.008	0.007
		(0.001)	(0.001)	(0.001)
Foreigner		0.145	0.144	0.146
		(0.046)	(0.046)	(0.046)
Time dummies	Yes	Yes	Yes	Yes
Country effects	Random	Random	Fixed	Fixed
Standard errors	Bootstrap	Bootstrap	Bootstrap	Robust

Note: N = 29,766. Bootstrapped standard errors based on 500 replicates.

Looking at estimates for individual control variables, our results show some to be relevant determinants of redistribution preferences. Consistent with previous findings in the literature, factors such as age, being a union member, and being a foreigner increase the probability of agreeing that the government should reduce income differences.

Going back to the income effects that are the main focus of this book, Table 3.2 is unequivocal in showing the statistical significance of both measures of income but it is germane to ask what the substantive effects of income expectations on preferences are. Figure 3.2 reveals the magnitude of expected income effects in a more substantive way and compares them with the effects of current income. We calculate predicted probabilities of demand for redistribution before and after a standard deviation change in current and expected income. The figure displays the differences in predicted probabilities and their associated 95 percent confidence intervals. A positive standard deviation shock to current labor income reduces an individual's probability of redistribution support by almost 6 percentage points. On the other hand, a positive standard deviation change in expected income reduces support for redistribution by almost 11 percentage points. For both estimated effects we find narrow confidence intervals that are clearly bound away from zero.

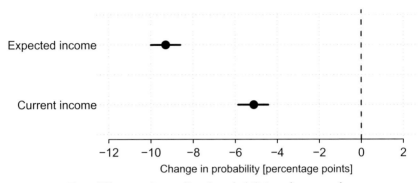

FIGURE 3.2 First differences in predicted probabilities of support for redistribution

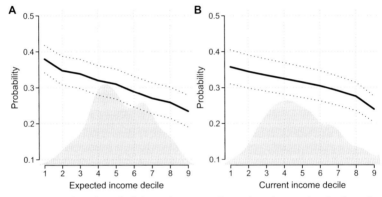

FIGURE 3.3 Predicted probability of support for redistribution by deciles of expected (A) and current (B) income, Europe

We illustrate our results in one final way in Figure 3.3. It shows predicted probabilities of redistribution support over deciles of the distribution of expected (A) and current income (B). In other words, for each decile we calculate the predicted probability of supporting redistribution holding all other individual characteristics constant. Figure 3.3 plots these predicted probabilities and their associated 95 percent confidence intervals. The shaded areas in the background are the distributions of both variables.[4] Moving up the deciles of the distribution of expected income, and holding all other relevant individual-level factors constant, support

---

4 The displayed distribution is calculated via kernel density estimation evaluated over a 200-point grid.

for redistribution decreases considerably. Confirming our central argument, we find that expected income is just as relevant as (if not more than) present-day income in shaping citizens' preferences.

3.1.4 Robustness Tests

Table 3.3 presents a set of robustness tests designed to address alternative explanations of redistribution demand (as well as possible criticisms of our approach).

Previous research indicates that average support for redistribution tends to fall when the existing levels of redistribution are high. The idea that there is some threshold at which the disincentive effects of redistribution become more severe (see for example Tanzi and Schuhknecht, 2000) provides a possible explanation for this relationship. Arguably, people who live in countries with large redistributive welfare states are more concerned about, and more aware of, the disincentive effects of redistribution. It also seems likely that some respondents take actual levels of redistribution into account when expressing their preferences, i.e., that they are expressing agreement or disagreement with the proposition that the government should do *more* (or *less*) to reduce income differences. It is finally common to react to the data in Figure 1.3 on page 25 by pointing out that the general levels of support for redistribution in Spain, Portugal, and Greece (countries with well-known problems of tax compliance) are much higher than in Sweden or Denmark. Perhaps, it is argued, those paying low taxes are more likely to agree that redistribution is, in principle, desirable.

We address these concerns in two ways. In specification (1) we control for the effect of existing levels of social policy generosity. Spending data are total public social spending (in cash and in kind), per head, in constant 2006 prices and PPP US dollars from the OECD's SOCX database. The main social policy areas covered are old age, survivors, incapacity-related benefits, health, family, active labor market programs, unemployment, and housing. Second, in specification (2), we restrict our sample to strictly wage-earners, excluding all individuals whose income contains nonwage elements (e.g., self-employment, income from investments). The reason for this is that we know that even in Southern Europe (where tax compliance is limited) cheating is more difficult among wage-earners (and easier for the self-employed). This yields a reduced sample of 25,124 cases. But neither specification changes our substantive results.

TABLE 3.3 *Robustness of expected and current income estimates under various model specifications*

		Expected income		Current income	
		Est.	s.e.	Est.	s.e.
(1)	Redistribution	−0.262	0.021	−0.097	0.006
(2)	Wage-earners	−0.268	0.040	−0.094	0.008
(3)	Religion	−0.261	0.021	−0.096	0.006
(4)	Social class	−0.132	0.023	−0.082	0.006
(5)	Skill specificity	−0.202	0.024	−0.093	0.006
(6)	Occupational risk	−0.175	0.028	−0.090	0.006
(7)	Altruism	−0.277	0.022	−0.095	0.006
(8)	Ideology	−0.310	0.022	−0.095	0.006
(9)	Country × time FE	−0.258	0.024	−0.096	0.006
(10)	Country jackknife	−0.276	0.038	−0.096	0.011

Note: Bootstrapped standard errors, based on 500 replicates.

As discussed earlier, religion might provide direct material benefits, such as help from fellow church members in times of unemployment (Scheve and Stasavage, 2006; Stegmueller et al., 2012). If the material benefits of religiosity enter income expectation considerations in an additively separable fashion (in other words, if an individual's expectation has two additive components, Mincer expected income, and income from one's church in the event of unemployment), its effect will be captured by the residual term in our income expectation equation. However, to explicitly allow for that not being the case, and to account for any direct preference effects of religion (those not captured by income expectations), specification (3) includes an indicator variable of regular church attendance. We find that our core results are indeed unchanged.

Specification (4) tests whether our main results are robust to controlling for the effects of social class. While income and class are clearly strongly related, we argue that within the broad class categories usually used in political–sociological research, both income expectations and actual income can vary considerably (Brynin, 2010). Thus we expect to find an effect of income expectations even when including class. We rely on the six-category version of the Erikson–Goldthorpe social class scheme (Erikson and Goldthorpe, 1992).[5] Our estimates show a reduced,

---

[5] The six classes are: service class I (higher-level controllers and administrators), service class II (lower-level controllers and administrators), routine nonmanual employees, skilled workers, unskilled workers, and the self-employed.

Cross-Sectional Evidence: Europe

but still highly relevant, effect of expected income. This suggests that income is a mechanism linking class and preferences, but that income also shapes preferences beyond social class.

As we mentioned in the previous chapter, an influential literature in comparative political economy has argued that redistribution preferences are affected by the demand for insurance against an uncertain future (Moene and Wallerstein, 2001; Iversen and Soskice, 2009; Rehm, 2009). To address this, we introduced explicit measures of risk into the analysis. An important component of the demand for insurance and redistribution has to do with the risk of becoming unemployed. Iversen and Soskice (2001) argue that individuals who have made risky investments in specific skills will demand insurance against the possible future loss of income from those investments. Thus, we introduce measures of skill specificity and unemployment risk based on occupational job categories. Skill specificity is calculated following Cusack et al. (2006), while the occupational unemployment rate follows Rehm (2009).[6] Results are presented in specifications (5) and (6) and show a similar picture to the one we find when including social class.

A most significant approach to noneconomic motivations for redistribution preferences has focused on other-regarding concerns (for reviews, see Fehr and Schmidt, 2006b; DellaVigna, 2009).[7] To address this issue directly, we introduce a control for other-regarding preferences. Due to the sparsity of data on altruism, we rely on a proxy measure. The ESS surveys ask respondents to listen to a description of different kinds of persons and to declare whether these persons are (or are not) like them. One of the descriptions is as follows: "She/he thinks it is important that every person in the world should be treated equally. She/he believes everyone should have equal opportunities in life." Respondents can then decide whether this person is "Very much like me," "Like me," "Somewhat like me," "A little like me," "Not like me," or "Not like me at all." We create an indicator variable equal to one for respondents who indicate full agreement with this statement of equality (by responding 'Very much like me'). Our results in specification (7) show that including other-regarding preferences does not alter our basic findings.

Our main analysis excludes a measure of ideology or left–right self-placement because we believe that explaining economic preferences helps

---

[6] We are indebted to Philipp Rehm for providing us with both data sets.
[7] We return to this issue in more detail in Part III.

us understand a key constituent of ideology and therefore it should not be an "explanatory" variable in our model. Nonetheless, it has been argued that ideological positions are an independent source of redistribution preferences (see Margalit, 2013), and we can show that the expected income–redistribution preferences link is robust to the inclusion of this variable. In specification (8), we account for respondents' ideology through an indicator equal to 1 if a respondent self-classifies as left of center on a standard left–right scale. Again, we find our results confirmed.

In specification (9) we change our model to specify country-specific constants as fixed instead of random effects. Besides the fact that we now do not need to make a distributional assumption about country-specific effects, this has two important implications. First, the model allows for a correlation between individual-level characteristics and country-specific effects. Second, it accounts for the effect of time-invariant macrolevel confounders (such as Left party dominance or the progressivity of the tax and transfer system) on preferences. Of course, this leaves open the possibility of omitted time-varying macro-variables. We therefore also add country-specific time trends (both linear and quadratic).[8] Again, we find our core insight confirmed.

Finally, in a more technical robustness test, we study the sensitivity of our results against the extreme values of a single country. It is well known that results from pooled analyses might be driven by a few influential units (Van der Meer et al., 2010). We use jackknifing (Wu, 1986), which successively deletes one country at a time, re-estimates the model, and then produces standard errors adjusted for the (possible) additional variation between models (this is different from the bootstrap we used earlier, where we resampled individuals). While this specification shows increased uncertainty in our estimates, we still find our core results confirmed.

3.2 PANEL EVIDENCE I: GERMANY

We now turn to an analysis exploiting some of the advantages of panel data. As described in the last chapter, using the German Socio-Economic Panel, we have repeated observations of individuals' earnings allowing us to calculate individual-specific income paths. Before detailing how we

---

[8] In this chapter (and unlike the following ones) we focus exclusively on a micro-level relationship. We thus prefer the "saturated" fixed effects specification to estimating a large number of robustness tests, including country-level controls.

use these in our statistical model, we describe variable definitions specific to the German case.

3.2.1 Variable Definitions

INCOME AND EDUCATION. As mentioned in the last chapter, income is measured via monthly net labor income. We deflate incomes using the consumer price index for unified Germany.[9] Our conceptualization of education is again categorical, in order to capture distinct returns to different certificates. We use four broad categories that delimit the major education certificates in the German labor market (Braun and Müller, 1997): (1) elementary education (including those without any education certificate), (2) intermediate education, (3) high school degrees, and (4) university degrees.[10]

PREFERENCES. Similar to the analysis of British household data to be developed later, our measure of redistribution is based on respondents' statements regarding governments' intervention on the economy via active job creation.[11] More specifically, the SOEP question we rely on asks respondents "Who should be responsible for the following areas: job creation schemes." Respondents are invited to respond using five labeled categories: "only the state, mostly the state, state and private forces, mostly private forces, only private forces." In contrast to income, our measure of preferences is purely cross-sectional (it is only available in 2002).[12]

CONTROLS. As further controls for heterogeneity between individuals we include a respondent's household size, indicator variables for union membership, and being a foreigner. To account for possibly distinct preferences of individuals that grew up in the former German Democratic

---

[9] Due to German unification there are two CPI series: a preunification series with base year 2005 and a post-unification series with base year 2010. We rebase the latter to 2005 to create a common CPI series used in our analyses.

[10] These are based on the CASMIN scheme, and, in the German context, correspond to (1): "Hauptschulabschluss" with and without vocational training; (2): "Mittlere Reife" with and without vocational training; (3): "Fachhochschulreife/Abitur" with and without vocational training; (4): "Hochschulabschluss" and "Fachhochschulabschluss."

[11] As mentioned earlier, we follow previous work using government job creation questions as an appropriate proxy for redistribution demand. See Ansell (2014), who uses BHPS data, and Ashok et al. (2015), who use ANES data asking respondents whether the government in Washington should see to it that every person has a job and a good standard of living.

[12] The analysis of British household data in the next section does not have this limitation.

Republic (Alesina and Fuchs-Schündeln, 2007; Svallfors, 2010), we include an indicator variable for living in the Eastern part of Germany in 1989. As a (rough) proxy for wealth we include an indicator variable for house ownership (which is a stronger indicator of wealth as compared to the UK or US, where ownership rates are much higher).

3.2.2 Statistical Specification

We model individuals' preferences for redistribution, R_i^*, as function of expected income and a set of controls using the following model:[13]

$$R_i^* = \gamma w_i + \delta x_i + \zeta_i + v_j. \tag{3.2}$$

Here γ captures the effect of expected income, δ is a vector of estimates of control variables x. Residuals ζ_i are white noise with variance fixed to 1, yielding an ordered probit model. To capture regional differences, we include a vector of federal state fixed effects, v_j.

We estimate this equation via standard maximum likelihood. Once again the uncertainty of our first-stage expected lifetime income estimates, w_i, needs to be incorporated into these second-stage preference estimates (Brownstone and Valletta, 2001). As was the case in our cross-sectional analysis, we incorporate this estimated variance via bootstrapping. To be precise, we take 100 bootstrap samples and for each sample we estimate first-stage expected lifetime income (from equations 2.7 and 2.8), which we then insert into equation (3.2). This yields more conservative standard errors accounting for errors-in-variables and prediction uncertainty. All standard errors in tables and plots that follow are obtained via this bootstrapping procedure.

3.2.3 Results

Table 3.4 shows estimates, standard errors, and 95 percent confidence intervals for both our income equation and preference equations. The value added of this analysis is the more detailed model for individual

---

[13] We use an ordered probit specification, where an individual's preferred level of redistribution, R_i^*, is a latent continuous variable, related to observed categorical survey responses, $y^{(r)}$, by a threshold specification, $y_{it}^{(r)} = c$ if $R_i^* \in (\mu_{c-1}, \mu_c]$, with a monotonically ordered threshold vector μ. To reduce the number of thresholds to be estimated, we combine the first two and last two categories of our observed variable (creating a contrast between responsibility ascribed to the state, private forces, or a neither-nor response).

TABLE 3.4 *Income dynamics and redistribution preferences in Germany*

	Est.	s.e.	95% CI	
(A) Income dynamics equation[a]				
Intermediate	0.030	0.017	−0.005	0.064
High school	0.109	0.031	0.048	0.170
Degree	0.502	0.033	0.438	0.566
Experience	0.081	0.002	0.077	0.085
Experience^2	−0.016	0.000	−0.017	−0.015
Indiv. effect variance	0.412	0.029	0.355	0.470
Experience variance	0.011	0.001	0.009	0.013
(B) Preference equation[b]				
Expected income	−0.143	0.029	−0.200	−0.086
Current income	−0.084	0.036	−0.154	−0.015
Controls				
Household size	0.025	0.011	0.004	0.047
Union member	0.137	0.037	0.064	0.210
Age	−0.003	0.002	−0.007	0.000
Foreigner	0.232	0.055	0.124	0.340
East	0.074	0.103	−0.128	0.276
House owner	−0.106	0.034	−0.173	−0.040

Note: Bootstrapped maximum likelihood estimates, and standard errors, with 95% confidence intervals. Results based on 100 bootstrap replicates. Normal-based confidence intervals. Experience squared scaled by 10. Covariance between random individual constants and experience effects is −0.657(0.023).
[a]Based on panel waves A to S, 1984–2002.
[b]Based on panel wave S, 2002.

income dynamics. Panel (A) of Table 3.4 shows the clear payoff of education and experience in the German labor market. Individuals holding more advanced educational certificates earn higher wages, an effect that is most pronounced among those holding university degrees. Keeping education constant, we also find the expected returns to accumulated human capital. Increasing experience is associated with rising earnings. The experience-earnings profile is quadratic, signifying that returns to human capital are lower toward the end of one's working life. The estimates presented here were used to calculate the predicted education by experience income curves plotted in Figure 2.9 on page 57. That plot hinted at considerable individual variation in individual income paths. Our estimates for the variances of individual-specific effects in panel (A) confirm this. We find considerable variation in both levels of earnings as well as the slope of experience. Thus, our analysis using SOEP panel data more adequately takes into account individual heterogeneity in income expectations. If and how this changes the estimated relationship between income expectations and preferences is what we turn to next.

Panel (B) of Table 3.4 shows estimates of our preference equation taking into account individual heterogeneity in expected income as well as individuals' current income. Starting with individual background variables, we largely find the expected effects. As in our European analysis, being a union member increases (latent) redistribution support. In contrast, house ownership, our proxy for respondents' wealth, decreases redistribution support. Both individuals from the Eastern part of Germany and the non-native born are more likely to support redistributive policy; however, the confidence interval for the former is too wide to support statistically reliable conclusions. Turning to our two central variables of interest, we find clear support for our hypotheses in this analysis as well. An individual's expected income matters significantly for his (because we only have males in our sample) redistribution preferences. In order to appreciate the substantive magnitude of this effect, we calculate average marginal effects of both current and expected income on the probability of supporting redistribution. By support we mean that a respondent thinks that "only the state" or "mostly the state" should be responsible for job creation. The marginal effect of current income on preferences is -0.032 with a standard error of $.016$, while the marginal effect of expected income is -0.048 with standard error $.014$. This shows, first, that the pure Meltzer–Richards model should be extended. Expected income matters at least as much as current income for individuals' preference formation. The higher one's future expected income, the less likely one is to support redistributive government policy. This effect is not just statistically significant but also highly substantively relevant. Moving a respondent from, say, the median of the distribution expected income up to the ninetieth percentile decreases his probability of supporting redistribution by almost four percentage points.[14] Thus, we conclude that even when taking into account the considerable heterogeneity in individuals' future income streams, we find clear evidence that expected income matters for current redistribution preferences.

---

[14] More precisely, it reduces the probability of supporting redistribution by 3.9 percentage points with a standard error of 1.0. Standard errors for all quantities reported in this paragraph are also based on 100 bootstrap replicates.

TABLE 3.5 *Robustness checks; expected and current income estimates under alternative specifications*

		Expected income		Current income	
		Est.	s.e.	Est.	s.e.
(1)	Divorce, unemployment	−0.143	0.029	−0.091	0.037
(2)	Occupational unempl.	−0.129	0.029	−0.062	0.034
(3)	Skill specificity	−0.120	0.029	−0.068	0.035
(4)	Religion	−0.138	0.030	−0.084	0.039
(5)	Social class	−0.099	0.028	−0.016	0.032
(6)	Industry effects	−0.134	0.030	−0.078	0.037
(7)	Ideology	−0.143	0.029	−0.084	0.036

Note: Based on 100 bootstrap replications. Sample sizes are: specification (1) 5,276, (2) 5,344, (3) 5,228, (4) 4,888, (5) 5,351, (6) 5,116, and (7) 5,198.

3.2.4 Robustness Tests

How robust are our SOEP-based results to changes in model specification? Table 3.5 presents a number of robustness tests.

INCOME SHOCKS. Our first concern is to explicitly include income shocks, such as becoming unemployed or getting divorced. We argued earlier that the income-relevant effects of this shock are already captured in our model. However, there might be other channels linking, say, the experience of unemployment to preferences. In our first robustness test we allow for this possibility. We include indicators for unemployment and divorce. Our results show that their inclusion changes little in our conclusion about the link between income expectations and preferences.

OCCUPATIONAL UNEMPLOYMENT RISK. One might argue that our analysis mostly captures specific preferences for insurance against occupational risks (rather than the general effect of income expectations that we argue encapsulates insurance demand). Being employed in an occupation with a higher risk of unemployment, we should expect individuals to respond positively to statements promising government job creation schemes. To account for this criticism, robustness specification (2) includes occupational unemployment rates (Rehm, 2005; Cusack et al., 2006). Our results show that accounting for unemployment risk does indeed reduce our estimated effects. But we still find our core result confirmed.

SKILL SPECIFICITY. Related to the previous argument, individuals with specific skills are expected to hold more favorable views on government intervention in the labor market (e.g., Iversen and Soskice, 2001). We thus include a measure of skill specificity calculated following Cusack et al. (2006) on the two-digit ISCO level. Estimates in specification (3) show that, while somewhat reduced in size expected, income still matters.

SOCIAL CLASS AND RELIGION. We include robustness tests for both religion and social class. Previous research has stressed the role of religion on determining redistribution preferences (Scheve and Stasavage, 2006; Stegmueller et al., 2012; Stegmueller, 2013b). We include a categorical measure of religion (contrasting Seculars with Catholics and Protestants). However, we expect the role of religion to be orthogonal to the heterogeneity-preferences nexus. This is borne out in specification (4), where we find that the effect of expected income is still highly relevant. The inclusion of social class is somewhat more problematic. Clearly, social class and expected income are closely related, to such an extent that some scholars consider long-term income expectation purely a result of social class. The debate about the role and meaning of social class is not our concern here. What we want to stress is the argument that even *within* social classes, individuals will vary in their expected income streams (remember, our income models explicitly accounts for heterogeneity in income streams due to both observed and unobserved individual characteristics). Thus, we expect that even when including social class, we will obtain a detectable (if reduced) effect of expected income. In specification (5) we include the six-class version of the Erikson–Goldthorpe class scheme. Our results provide quite clear evidence for the relevance of considering expected income when explaining redistribution preferences. While the inclusion of social class renders the estimate of current income small and statistically indistinguishable from zero, expected income still matters.

INDUSTRY EFFECTS. In specification (6) we include industry fixed effects in order to capture unobserved systematic differences (such as unemployment risk, export dependence, promotion schedules, etc.) between industrial sectors in the German labor market. We use one-digit industry codes, contrasting nine major industrial sectors. Our results show that accounting for industry effects does not substantively alter our conclusions.

IDEOLOGY. Finally, we include a measure of ideology. As was the case in the cross-sectional analysis, we argue that explaining economic preferences helps us understand a key constituent of ideology and therefore it should not be an "explanatory" variable in our model. Because there are arguments about ideological positions as an independent source of redistribution preferences (Margalit, 2013), in specification (7), we account for respondents' ideology through an indicator equal to 1 if a respondent strongly self-identifies with a Left party.[15] Again, we find our core results to be substantively robust.

3.3 PANEL EVIDENCE II: UNITED KINGDOM

We now provide additional evidence based on a dynamic analysis of individual panel data based on the British Household Panel Survey from 1991 to 2007. While of course more limited in scope than our comparative analysis, here we have available repeated observations on both earnings and preferences. This allows us to build an explicit dynamic model for changing income expectations and how they influence preferences for redistribution. We use the British Household Panel Survey (BHPS), described in Chapter 1. As in our previous analysis, we limit our sample to working-age males. We create a balanced panel using individuals who provide responses to all seven waves. This yields information on 1,023 respondents observed between 1991 and 2007.[16]

3.3.1 Variable Definitions

PREFERENCES. Our dependent variable is support for active social policy, more specifically stated support for the government's active role in implementing a "full-employment policy" (Ansell, 2014), as described in Chapter 1. There we illustrated aggregate over-time changes in preferences of our panel (see Figure 1.5 on page 28). However, such aggregate preference patterns can hide considerable individual-level dynamics. In Figure 3.4 we calculate, for each individual, how often he changes his preferences over the span of our seven-wave panel. Our definition of change is moving between our three-category measure of redistribution support

---

[15] SOEP contains a two-stage party identification questions. The first one asks respondents for the party (or parties) they identify with. We define Left parties as the Social Democrats and Party of Democratic Socialism. The second questions probes the strength of party identification. We define strong identification to be present when respondents respond that their support for their party is either "Strong" or "Fairly Strong."

[16] Note that we conducted a robustness test using an unbalanced panel of a larger size and found similar results.

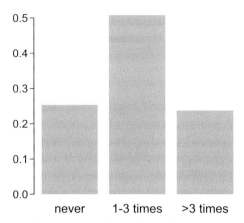

FIGURE 3.4 Number of observed within-individual preference changes, UK 1991–2007

(contrasting agree with indifference and disagree categories). Thus the changes described are not just minor adjustments in response strength (as in adding "strongly" when already agreeing) but quite clear shifts in position vis-a-vis redistributive policy. Looking at Figure 3.4, we find that more than half of our respondents change their preferences at least once, while one-quarter never changes. In contrast, roughly one-quarter of our sample changes preferences more than three times over the span of our seven-wave panel. The fact that there is considerable *within*-individual change in preferences is what we will exploit in the statistical model that follows.

INCOME, EDUCATION, AND WORK EXPERIENCE. We capture income using a respondent's annual labor income, deflated using the UK consumer price index with base year 2005. An indicator variable captures if he gets income from other sources (i.e., it is 1 if income from all sources minus labor income is nonzero). For a detailed discussion of income measures in the BHPS, see Jenkins (2010). We measure experience as potential work experience, which is a person's potential time in the labor market after leaving school (calculated as current age minus school-leaving age). Education is measured by standard UK school-leaving certificates.

CONTROLS. In order to capture effects of wealth, we employ an indicator variable equal to 1 if our respondent is a house owner. Respondents are also asked to estimate the value of their house. We take this estimate and deflate it (cf. Ansell, 2014). Finally, we include indicator variables for being nonwhite, member of a union, divorced, or unemployed.[17]

3.3.2 Statistical Specification

INCOME DYNAMICS. As explained in more detail in the previous chapter, our income model is the profile heterogeneity model (Baker, 1997), an extension of the classic Mincer equation approach. It models income as function of returns to education and experience, which are heterogeneous over individuals due to unobserved individual factors, such as ability or motivation.

PREFERENCE DYNAMICS. In this analysis of BHPS data, we model individual preferences as a dynamic process as well. Denote an individual's preferred level of redistribution at time t by R_{it}^*.[18] We employ a dynamic panel specification, where preferences R_{it}^* are a function of past preferences and expected and current income, while controlling for observed and unobserved individual heterogeneity.

$$R_{it}^* = \phi z_{it-1} + \gamma \omega_{it} + \delta_1' x_{it} + \xi_i + \zeta_{it}, \quad t = 2, \ldots, T \qquad (3.3)$$

here γ represents the net effect of expected income ω_{it} on preferences. Preference persistence is captured by ϕ, whereas δ captures effects of controls in x_{it}, which includes a measure of household size, a union membership indicator, age, a nonwhite indicator, a house ownership indicator, and house value. Individual-specific effects are captured by ξ_i, which is specified as emerging from a normal distribution with freely estimated variance.[19] Finally, stochastic errors ζ_{it} are independent over individuals and time, and we fix their variance to 1 to identify the ordered probit structure.[20] Following Heckman (1981a, b), we model initial conditions R_{i1}^* as a function of individual-specific effects (ξ_i scaled by θ), individual

---

[17] Again, a more detailed description of the data and its population characteristics is available in Chapter 1 and Appendix A.1.

[18] As before, R_{it}^* is a latent continuous variable, related to observed categorical survey responses by a threshold specification $y_{it}^{(r)} = c$ if $R_{it}^* \in (\mu_{c-1}, \mu_c]$, with a monotonically ordered threshold vector $\boldsymbol{\mu}$. We set $\mu_1 = 0$ for identifications as a constant is included in x_{it}, which follows.

[19] Stegmueller (2013a) shows this model to be robust under a more flexible semiparametric specification.

[20] We assume that $\mathrm{Cov}(\epsilon_{it}, x_{it}) = 0$ and $\mathrm{Cov}(\epsilon_{is}, \epsilon_{it}) = 0 \forall s \neq t$. Furthermore, we employ the usual random effects assumptions, namely that $\mathrm{Cov}(\xi_i, \epsilon_{it}) = 0$ and $\mathrm{Cov}(\xi_i, x_{it}) = 0$.

controls at the beginning of the panel, and parents' educational background (collected in w_i), in order to capture possible socialization effects
(for more details on this dynamic specification see Stegmueller, 2013a).

$$R_{i1}^* = \delta_0' w_i + \theta \xi_i + \zeta_{i1} \qquad (3.4)$$

We estimate the model in a Bayesian framework using MCMC sampling. Details on priors are given in Appendix A.2. We jointly estimate
the income and preference equations and our approach propagates all
uncertainty through the model. Thus, we include both fundamental uncertainty as well as estimation uncertainty, e.g., we account for the errors
in variables problem caused by the fact that ω_{it} in equation (3.3) is an
estimated quantity.

3.3.3 Results

Table 3.6 shows estimates from our unified income and preference dynamics model. Panel (A) shows income dynamics estimates. As expected, we
find that individuals with higher levels of education, especially those holding degrees, have higher average levels of income. Returns to experience
are positive but decrease toward the end of one's working life. However,
behind these average patterns lies considerable individual variation. Most
of this is due to unobserved individual differences, such as ability or motivation, as indicated by the large estimated variance of individual specific
effects. A purely cross-sectional analysis of preferences does not take these
into account.

To assess how expected income shapes preferences, panel (B) of
Table 3.6 shows our preference dynamics estimates. An individual's
income expectations shapes his preferences. We find that higher expected
income reduces one's support for redistribution considerably, even when
accounting for current income levels and sources of wealth. As expected
from the basic Meltzer–Richards model, we find a negative effect of
current income as well. Before we examine the role of expected and
current income in more detail, we discuss our control variables and the
remaining features of the dynamic panel model.

Our control variables point in the expected directions. Union members are more likely to support redistribution. We also find that asset
ownership matters: individuals with high value homes are more opposed
to redistributive activity. On the other hand, the effects of the size of
one's household and being nonwhite are not precisely estimated. As

TABLE 3.6 *Estimates of unified income and preference dynamics model for Great Britain, 1991–2007*

	Est.	s.e.	95% Interval	
(A) Income dynamics equation				
Intercept	0.790	0.056	0.680	0.899
Education: O-levels	0.536	0.076	0.389	0.689
Education: A-levels	0.728	0.084	0.562	0.890
Education: Degree	1.148	0.094	0.971	1.339
Returns to experience	0.059	0.004	0.053	0.067
Returns to experience^2	−0.030	0.006	−0.042	−0.018
Individual effects variance	0.843	0.089	0.677	1.022
Experience variance	0.003	0.000	0.002	0.003
(B) Preference dynamics equation				
Expected income	−0.099	0.022	−0.146	−0.058
Current income	−0.065	0.017	−0.099	−0.032
Other income	−0.092	0.046	−0.179	0.001
Household size	0.027	0.046	−0.065	0.116
House owner	−0.035	0.054	−0.136	0.073
House value	−0.287	0.058	−0.398	−0.173
Union member	0.167	0.055	0.059	0.274
Nonwhite	0.328	0.193	−0.041	0.711
Preference persistence	0.259	0.032	0.199	0.322
Individual effect variance	0.956	0.066	0.829	1.086
Deviance		20,340		

Note: Estimate refers to posterior mean, s.e. to posterior standard deviation. 95 percent interval is highest posterior density region. Based on 5000 MCMC samples. $N = 7,161$. Initial condition effect is 1.226 ± 0.123. Initial condition equation estimates δ_0 and thresholds μ not shown. Covariance between individual effects variance and returns to experience variance is $−0.031 \pm 0.004$.

discussed earlier, our model (in contrast to cross-sectional analyses) accounts for both preference persistence and unobserved individual differences. The estimates in panel (B) of Table 3.6 show that these factors cannot be ignored. The parameter capturing dependence of one's current preferences on past ones is clearly nonzero. Similarly, we find a high degree of unobserved individual variability, which indicates that unobserved individual characteristics play a large role in shaping individual preferences.

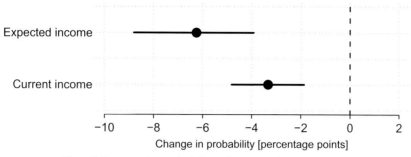

FIGURE 3.5 First differences in probability of support for redistribution resulting from a standard deviation change in income

What is the substantive effect of income expectations on preferences? Figure 3.5 helps us visualize the magnitude of expected income effects. We calculate predicted probabilities of demand for redistribution before and after a standard deviation change in current and expected income. Figure 3.5 displays differences in predicted probabilities with associated 95 percent confidence intervals. Simulating a positive standard deviation shock to current labor income only (think of a one-time bonus payment), reduces one's probability of redistribution support by more than three percentage points. A positive standard deviation change in expected income (think of increasing returns to experience) reduces support for redistribution by more than six percentage points. For both estimated effects we find wide confidence intervals, due to the fact that we include estimation and substantive uncertainty in our calculations. However, both intervals are clearly bound away from zero, indicating that the effects of current and, especially, expected income are significant both in the substantive and statistical sense.

We can further illustrate the importance of income expectations by constructing levels of redistribution support over the distribution of expected and current income. Figure 3.6 shows predicted probabilities of redistribution support over deciles of the expected and current income distribution (calculated as in previous sections). We find considerable heterogeneity around the average level of redistribution support. Moving up deciles in the distribution of expected income, and holding all other relevant individual-level factors constant, one is less and less likely to encounter individuals supporting active government. The same holds for the distribution of current income, but we find that the suppressing effect on preferences is far less pronounced when compared to the role of expected income.

TABLE 3.7 *Robustness checks; expected and current income estimates in the United Kingdom under alternative specifications; posterior means and standard deviations*

		Expected income		Current income	
		Est	s.e.	Est	s.e.
(1)	Unemployment, divorce	−0.097	0.022	−0.063	0.017
(2)	Social class	−0.085	0.024	−0.046	0.018
(3)	Religion	−0.103	0.022	−0.066	0.017
(4)	Region effects	−0.099	0.022	−0.064	0.017
(5)	Industry effects	−0.099	0.023	−0.062	0.018
(6)	Skill specificity	−0.128	0.027	−0.068	0.018
(7)	Occupational unempl.	−0.124	0.027	−0.069	0.018
(8)	Ideology	−0.095	0.022	−0.067	0.017
(9)	Unbalanced panel	−0.109	0.018	−0.038	0.012

Note: Sample size is 982 in specifications (7) and (8), 2,051 in (12), and 1,023 in remaining ones. Estimate refers to mean of posterior distribution, s.e. to its standard deviation.

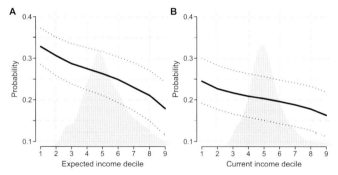

FIGURE 3.6 Predicted probability of support for redistribution by deciles of expected (A) and current (B) income

3.3.4 Robustness Checks

We conduct again a number of robustness checks. Our income dynamics equation is based only on income streams observed by the respondent, without explicitly including adverse life events such as becoming unemployed or getting divorced. We prefer this specification because the monetary effects of such shocks will be captured by changes in income. In specification (1), where we add unemployment and divorce to the income dynamics equation, we find no difference in the results. One might argue that the "real" drivers of preferences are one's class position. We disagree with this view because even within classes there exists considerable variation in expected income. Consequently, specification (2) which includes social class does not change our core results. Recent research shows that an individual's religious beliefs shapes redistribution preferences (Scheve and Stasavage, 2006; Stegmueller et al., 2012). Again, we consider this orthogonal to our income model; a view that is confirmed by specification (3). To capture the specificities of local labor markets and employment sectors, specifications (4) and (5) include region and industry dummies. We find our substantive results unchanged. A more interesting robustness test is carried out in specifications (6) and (7). As mentioned in previous sections, recent research stresses the relevance of specific skills and associated labor market risks (e.g., Iversen and Soskice, 2001; Rehm, 2009). Including a measure of skill specificity as well as unemployment risk and re-estimating our models does not change our core results, but rather leads to slightly increased effects of expected income. Including a respondent's ideology in (8) similarly leaves our central findings in place. Finally, specification (9) uses an unbalanced panel of now 2,051 respondents, with virtually unchanged results.

PART II

BEYOND INCOME: EXTERNALITIES OF
INEQUALITY

4

Externalities and Redistribution

While we have focused on the importance of individual expected income in the previous section and shown its relevance to the demand for redistribution, we move away in this section from exclusive economic considerations and complement our argument with concerns about the negative externalities associated with higher levels of macroinequality. The relationship between macrolevels of income inequality and redistribution preferences is a hotly contested topic in the literature on the comparative political economy of industrialized democracies. In this section of the book we want to make three related points. First, in agreement with most of the existing literature, we argue that material self-interest is an important determinant of redistribution preferences. We confirm the results in the previous section and show that income (measured both as present and as expected) explains a significant part of an individual's support for redistribution. Second, and more important, we also show that, once material self-interest motivations are accounted for, there is still a great degree of variation in redistribution preferences. We argue that this variation has to do with the preferences of the presently rich (and not those of the poor) and that they can be explained by taking into account one of the externalities of inequality, namely the relationship between macroinequality and crime. Third, using data from the European Social Survey (ESS) and the British Household Panel Survey, we present a set of empirical tests that support our hypotheses (and provide limited evidence in favor of alternative explanations).

The arguments in this section challenge some influential approaches to the politics of inequality, particularly those contending that second-dimension issues (both cultural and social) outweigh economic ones.

We will elaborate on our differences from these approaches in the pages that follow.

4.1 THE ARGUMENT

This chapter's theoretical argument makes three distinct points about the formation of preferences for redistribution. The first one relates to the idea that the level of redistribution preferred by a given individual is fundamentally a function of her economic self-interest. The second point distinguishes between current tax and transfer considerations and externality-related motivations and maintains these motivations are long term and low stakes. As such, they matter most to the rich. We will argue that, if we accept that the influence of economic self-interest is sufficiently captured by the microeffect of relative income (and future income expectations), macrolevels of inequality matter to the presently rich – and mostly to the rich – because of negative externality reasons. Our third point proposes that the macroeffect of inequality can be explained by different micro-level factors and contends that the most important of these is crime as a very visible negative externality of inequality.

4.1.1 Material Self-Interest

As we have argued in the previous chapters, most analyses in political economy rely on the idea that the level of redistribution preferred by a given individual is fundamentally a function of that person's relative income. More specifically, it is a function of the distance between someone's own income and the average income of the population covered by the polity in which one resides. In the rest of the book, we adopt the framework developed in the first section and continue to assume that the economic motivations for redistribution preferences should not be limited to a measure of present income. In the analysis in this section, we assess the two different facets of material self-interest arguments emphasized in Part I: the first one dealing with redistribution (and captured by present income) and the other with insurance, risk, and mobility (and captured by expected future income). Our analysis confirms that expectations of future income are as relevant to individuals in forming their redistribution preferences as the levels of income they currently enjoy.

4.1.2 Externality-Related Motivations

The possibility that noneconomic motivations may influence redistribution preferences has received increasing amounts of attention in the recent political economy literature. In this chapter we define noneconomic motivations simply as not related to income, tax, and transfer considerations. As we will document later, support for redistribution is widespread in Western Europe and extends into income groups whose support for redistribution could not possibly be motivated by income maximization alone. We will also show that while support for redistribution by the poor is quite constant, support by the rich is shaped by different macrolevels of inequality. In the section that follows, we will explain in more detail the reasons why crime is a significant externality of inequality but we start now by clarifying the relationship between current tax/transfer considerations and concerns for the negative externalities associated with inequality.

As in the Meltzer–Richard model, our argument implies that a rise in inequality that increases the distance between an individual's income and the mean will change distribution preferences. More important, our argument also implies that the current pocketbook consequences of inequality are fully contained in the individual income distance shifts produced by this inequality rise. Insurance motivations are captured by the effects of expected future income. In other words, the tax and transfer consequences of inequality are picked up by individual (present and expected) income changes.

Macrolevels of inequality, however, can indirectly affect the individual utility function implicit in the previous paragraph. Following Alesina and Giuliano (2011), we can think about this utility function as one in which individuals care not only about present and expected future income but also about some macromeasure of income distribution.[1] If inequality produces economic externalities, we would expect individual preferences to be affected. Of consequence to our argument, this model allows for even the rich to be negatively affected by macroinequality and, therefore, for them to support redistribution for purely self-interested reasons.

---

[1] As suggested by Alesina and Giuliano (2011), different individuals may be affected by different kinds of inequality. For simplicity, in this section of the book we focus on the Gini coefficient, which is the most commonly used measure of inequality in the political economy literature.

We are not the first authors to recognize the externalities of inequality as a specific case of a more general model of support for redistribution with macroinequality concerns as well as individual tax and transfer considerations. The literature in economics and political economy has identified a number of other externalities. If we assume the poor to be less educated, a less-effective democracy has been considered a negative externality of inequality by authors like Milton Friedman (1982). There is also some research connecting inequality and environmental degradation (Boyce, 1994). And see Beramendi (2012) for an analysis of the externalities of regional inequality.

But perhaps the clearest example is the literature on externalities of education, which connects average levels of education with aggregate levels of productivity (see, for example, Nelson and Phelps, 1966; Romer, 1990; Perotti, 1996). This framework proposes that, with imperfect credit markets, more inequality means more people below an income level that would allow them to acquire education. The rich, in this case, would support redistribution because of the benefits of a higher education average. But, to our knowledge, we are the first to emphasize crime as the key explanatory factor behind the affluent's support for redistribution.

Why, however, should we focus on crime as the most relevant negative externality of inequality to the demand for redistribution? There are several reasons. First, the intuition connecting inequality to crime is *a priori* more generally accepted than the link between inequality and democracy or productivity. We mentioned in the initial chapter of this book some evidence on the consequences of inequality for "survival crime" (based on semi-structured interviews with policy-makers, focus groups with frontline welfare practitioners, and repeated qualitative longitudinal interviews with a diverse sample of 480 welfare recipients in the UK). We also referred to newspaper stories illustrating the concerns of the affluent with regard to the security consequences of increases in inequality. Second, and perhaps more important, the connection between inequality and crime has a long and distinguished lineage in economics (starting with Becker, 1968), sociology (see, for example, Runciman, 1966) and political science (Wilensky, 1975). Finally, we also attempt to address this issue empirically. In the analysis to be presented in the next chapter, we show that our measure of fear of crime "explains" a large part of the inequality effect among the rich. We also perform a placebo test that demonstrates it is not the case that the inclusion of any variable measuring political perceptions or beliefs could render the effect of inequality insignificant.

The preceding paragraphs suggest that both tax/transfer and externality considerations matter to redistribution preferences. To integrate the arguments about these two distinct dimensions, however, we will argue that a hierarchy of preferences exists. We propose that poor people (regardless of their expected future income) value redistribution for its immediate tax and transfer consequences. The redistributive preferences of the rich, on the other hand, are less significantly affected by current tax and transfer considerations. For the rich, the negative externalities of inequality can become more relevant.

We conceive of the solution to the negative externalities of inequality as both time-horizon and stakes related. The possibility that the poor have shorter-term motivations than the rich has been explored in the economics and sociology literature before. In economics, the poor have been argued to be more constrained in their investment decisions than the rich (explaining the lower likelihood by the poor to invest in long-term objectives like increasing human capital or saving for retirement).[2] Complementarily, sociological research has illustrated that lower social class (itself closely related to low income) leads to shorter time horizons (see, for example, O'Rand and Ellis, 1974). It is also reasonable to argue that the relative importance of receiving benefits is greater for the poor than the relative importance of paying taxes is for the rich. This difference can be illustrated as follows. From 2001 to 2005, the relative size of benefits (including public pensions) for households in the bottom decile of the distribution represented 71.7 percent of household disposable income in Western European countries.[3] For households in the top decile of the distribution, on the other hand, market income was reduced by just 27.7 percent after subtracting taxes.[4] We expect that, as the stakes of redistribution decline, longer-term considerations related to inequality and crime will increase. We therefore argue in this section of the book that longer time horizons and lower stakes (in relation to current tax and transfer considerations) mean that the negative externalities of inequality will be more important to the rich.

It is important to emphasize here that the underlying logic for our argument about the externalities of inequality concerns a distinction

---

[2] See, for example, Lawrance (1991) or Dynan et al. (2004).

[3] Even in Greece, where this component is the lowest, it amounted to a 44 percent of disposable income. Authors' calculations based on EUROMOD tax simulation data from Paulus et al., 2009, Appendix A, Table 2.

[4] Authors' calculations based on EUROMOD tax simulation data from Paulus et al., 2009, Appendix A, Table 3.

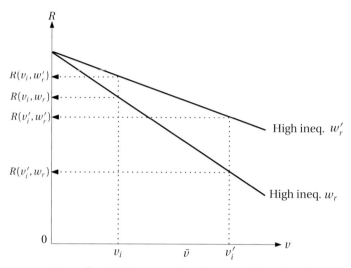

FIGURE 4.1 Inequality (w), income (v), and support for redistribution (R)

between the presently rich and the poor. An ongoing theme throughout the second and third parts of this book is that noneconomic factors (defined as those not directly affecting the income/tax/transfer nexus) affect the poor and the rich differently. While in the previous chapters we argued (and presented evidence to support) that the effects of expected income were not dependent on present income, we propose in this part of the book that the influence of negative externalities is linked to it (more important to the affluent, less relevant to the poor).

The implications of this chapter's argument are summarized in Figure 4.1. We expect the negative externalities of inequality to be associated with less support for redistribution. Because we argue that for the poor externality concerns are trumped by material tax-transfer incentives, redistribution preferences converge regardless of the level of inequality as income declines. Thus, the redistribution preferences of an individual with low income v_i in a low-inequality region w_r, denoted $R(v_i, w_r)$, and in a high-inequality region $R(v_i, w'_r)$ do not differ by much. In contrast, we expect more inequality to promote concerns for its negative externalities only for the rich, so that redistribution preferences of a rich individual in a low-income region $R(v'_i, w_r)$ differ starkly from those in high-inequality regions $R(v'_i, w'_r)$.

4.1.3 Macroinequality and Fear of Crime

We will show later that the association between macroinequality and redistribution preferences summarized in Figure 4.1 is supported by the empirical evidence and is extraordinarily robust. We argue that the effect of macroinequality is channeled by a number of different microfactors. The most important of this, as mentioned earlier, is crime, as a most visible negative externality of inequality.[5]

The canonical model for the political economy of crime and inequality was originally developed by Becker (1968) and first explored empirically by Ehrlich (1973). The basic argument is simple (see a nice explanation in Bourguignon, 1999). Assume that society is divided into three classes (the poor, the middle, and the rich) with increasing levels of wealth. Assume further that crime pays a benefit, that there is a probability that crime will result in sanction/punishment and that the proportion of "honest" individuals (people who would not consider crime as an option regardless of its economic benefits) is independent of the level of income (and distributed uniformly across classes). It follows from this straightforward framework that rich people for whom the benefit of crime is small in proportion to their initial wealth will never find crime attractive. It also follows that there will always be a proportion of people among the poor who will engage in crime, and that the benefits from crime are proportional to the wealth of the population. The crime rate implied by this simple model would be positively correlated to the extent of poverty and inequality and negatively correlated to the probability of being caught, the cost of the sanction/punishment, and the proportion of "honest" individuals.

Following this framework, the intuition that crime is related to inequality is easy to understand. With more inequality, the potential gain for the poor from engaging in crime is higher and the opportunity cost is lower. Some early empirical analyses supported this intuition (Ehrlich, 1973; Freeman, 1983) and, more recently, Fajnzlber et al. (2002) use panel data for more than thirty-seven industrialized and nonindustrialized countries from the early 1970s until the mid-1990s to explore the relationship between inequality and violent crime. They find crime rates and inequality

---

[5] In the analysis to be developed later, we focus on the relationship between macroinequality and fear of crime. A number of political economy models emphasize the connection between inequality and altruism instead (i.e., models in which, in addition to self-interest, individuals exhibit concern for the impact of inequality on others). See Dimick et al. (2016) for an analysis.

to be positively correlated within countries and, particularly, between countries.[6] But the evidence is not unambiguous.

While earlier we have described the relationship between inequality and objective levels of crime, it is fear of crime by the affluent that matters most to our argument. We do understand that, as shown by a well-established sociology literature, fear of crime does not exactly reflect the objective possibility of victimization. As early as 1980, DuBow et al. showed that crime rates reflect victimization of the poor (more than the rich) and that fear levels for particular age–sex groups are inversely related to their victimization (elderly women having the lowest victimization rates but the highest fear of crime, young men having the opposite combination).[7] While we do model explicitly the determinants of fear of crime in the empirical analysis we develop later (and show that macroinequality is a significant one), we are not interested in them *per se*. Our argument simply requires rich individuals to perceive regional crime rates and to believe that there is a connection between macroinequality and crime (following the intuitive logic of the Becker model summarized earlier). This connection makes sense even if the affluent have concerns for crime that are disproportionately high given their objective probability of victimization.

We should note that there is an implicit temporal side to this economic approach to crime because it involves the probability of being caught (in the future) for a crime being committed or not (in the present). Arguably, "the core message of the economic model of criminal behavior is that it can be discouraged by raising its expected 'price' " (Lee and McCrary, 2005: 1). This, in turn, makes the importance of the price of crime crucially depend on how much potential offenders discount their future welfare.[8] The individuals who are most likely to consider committing crime, i.e., the poor, are generally thought to have very high discount rates (Wilson and Herrnstein, 1985; Katz et al., 2003). Because the likelihood of committing crime is not the focus of our analysis (the determinants of concern for crime are, and particularly the role of inequality) we do not address the

---

[6] See also Mehlum et al. (2005) for cross-country evidence.

[7] On the other hand, the effect of victimization on fear of crime may not be a direct one exactly reflecting the objective possibility of being a victim. The indirect victimization model in sociology proposes that fear of crime "is more widespread than victimization because those not directly victimized are indirectly victimized when they hear of such experiences from others, resulting in elevated fear levels" (Covington and Taylor, 1991: 232).

[8] For an explicit temporal model, see, for example, Davis (1988).

price of criminal behavior. But the high discount of future welfare by the poor (who are more likely to consider committing crime in this economic framework), is indeed the basis of our theoretical argument. We adopt the concern for future welfare from this political economy approach to crime but, as suggested earlier, change the focus to the likelihood that an individual considers himself/herself to be a potential crime victim.

To anticipate some of our empirical choices later, two additional observations are needed about our argument that macroinequality reflects individual concerns about crime as a negative externality. The first one is about the level of macroinequality. Our theoretical argument proposes that the importance of inequality emerges from its relationship to crime as a negative externality. As we argued in Chapter 1, this implies that the relevant level of inequality should be one at which a visible connection to crime could be made by individuals. We therefore move away from national data and use regional levels of inequality in the analysis later. We argue that, unlike more aggregate levels, regional inequality is visible and that it is plausible to assume that it would be related to fear of crime by rich individuals. While it would be interesting to use even more disaggregated units, the availability of the data at our disposal limits what we can do, and, perhaps more important, it is unclear smaller is necessarily better for an empirical test of our hypotheses.

Our argument also implies that rich individuals who are concerned about crime (because they live in unequal areas) are more likely to support redistribution. We assume the affluent's concern for crime to be causally connected to macroinequality, and higher redistribution to be perceived as one of the solutions to the problem. It is clear that other solutions are possible. Most importantly, the affluent may demand protection as a solution to crime (rather than redistribution as a solution to its cause). Recall that objective crime rates in Becker's model are negatively correlated to the probability of being caught and the cost of the sanction/punishment.

As argued by Alesina and Giuliano (2011), the implicit assumption in the kind of argument made in this chapter is that it should cost less for the rich to redistribute than to increase spending on security (i.e., policing, incarceration, etc.). This is not an unreasonable assumption. The topic of incarceration in the United States, because it is the focus of a large literature, is a good illustration. The cost of incarceration is high. In his widely cited 1996 paper, Freeman calculated that crime control activities cost 2 percent of GDP. Also, incarceration costs often crowd out spending on social policy (for a state comparison within the United States, see Ellwood and Guetzkow, 2009). And, while in the short run incarceration reduces unemployment (and the costs of unemployment benefits or active labor market policy), in the long run the costs increase substantially as ex-inmates find themselves in need of public assistance and are often confined to casual or illegitimate employment (e.g., Western, 2006). More explicitly, Donohue and Siegleman (1998) find that diverting resources from incarceration and directing the savings to successful social policy (like preschool interventions) would reduce crime without increasing spending in the United States.

While we recognize this as an important issue, we do not consider demands for protection to be incompatible with preferences for redistribution. A number of issues make the comparative costs and benefits of these policies difficult to quantify. They include the implications of these policies in terms of investment in human capital, the encouragement of individual behaviors with positive externalities, the discouragement of behaviors with negative externalities, the spillover from one domain to another (such as education and health investments that affect human capital and work effort), the benefits of avoided crime (e.g., early childhood interventions that produce the primary intended impact, better cognitive development, but also later gains in schooling and employment that reduce criminal behavior), the effects of parental incarceration on children's prospects, etc.[9] For many rich individuals, uncertainty influences the assessment of the costs and effectiveness of redistribution and security as solutions to crime.[10] Considering this uncertainty, demands for protection should not be incompatible with preferences for redistribution. In Western Europe, where the empirical analysis that follows focuses on, we argue that the rich think of redistribution and protection as complementary policies to mitigate regional crime.[11]

4.2 PRELIMINARY ANALYSIS

We have argued earlier that rich individuals who are more concerned about crime because they live in more unequal areas will be more likely to

---

[9] For a review of these assessment issues, see Vining and Weimer (2010).

[10] Moreover, if the poor as potential offenders value their future significantly less than their present welfare, as argued in this chapter, the effectiveness of deterrence and punishment is put in question (see Lee and McCrary, 2005).

[11] It is also reasonable to expect the level of privately financed security available in Western Europe to be lower than, for example, in the United States (where gated communities, private protection, and residential segregation are more common). We will return to the American case in the next chapters.

TABLE 4.1 *Overview of ESS countries and years included in the analysis*

Country	ESS years
Austria	2002, 2004, 2006
Belgium	2002, 2004, 2006, 2008
Denmark	2002, 2004, 2006
Finland	2006, 2008
France	2002, 2004, 2006, 2008
Germany	2002, 2004, 2006, 2008
Ireland	2002, 2004
Netherlands	2002, 2004, 2006, 2008
Norway	2002, 2004, 2006, 2008
Portugal	2002, 2004, 2006, 2008
Spain	2002, 2004, 2006, 2008
Sweden	2002, 2004, 2006, 2008
Switzerland	2002, 2004, 2006, 2008
United Kingdom	2002, 2004, 2006, 2008

support redistribution. In this section of the chapter we provide a series of intuitive and illustrative figures that illuminate the relationships of interest for our arguments about income, inequality, fear of crime, and redistribution preferences.

As we mentioned in Chapter 1, we will use two different sources of data in this chapter and the next. First we use data from the ESS, which includes consistent regional-level identifiers allowing us to match individual and regional information while working with adequate sample sizes. Our sample covers 129 regions in 14 countries: Austria, Belgium, Germany, Denmark, Spain, Finland, France, Great Britain, Ireland, Netherlands, Norway, Portugal, Sweden, and Switzerland, surveyed between 2002 and early 2009. For a detailed list of countries and years included in the analysis, see Table 4.1, but the reader should keep in mind that the data in this part of the book does not include ESS waves after 2009 and that some countries/waves are excluded because of lack of time-consistent regional identifiers.[12]

We then use data from the British Household Panel Survey (BHPS) from 1991 to 2007. We analyze the original ("Essex") sample of the BHPS and create an unbalanced panel using individuals who provide

---

[12] We treat missing data using multiple imputation (King et al., 2001), more details are provided when explaining the analysis in Chapter 5.

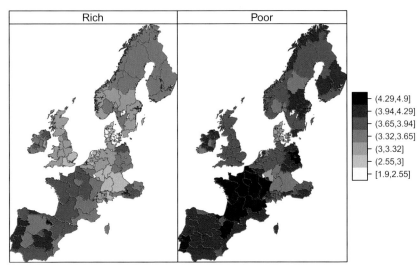

FIGURE 4.2 Average regional redistribution preferences among rich and poor, ESS (2002–2008)

responses to at least three waves.[13] As mentioned before, in order to obtain a more homogeneous sample, we limit our sample to working-age individuals (ages 20 to 65), including both employed and unemployed persons (yielding information on 3,173 respondents observed between 1991 and 2007). We summarized the ESS and BHPS measures of relative income and redistribution preferences in Chapter 1, and readers should return to the description in those pages to get an intuitive sense of the data. Figure 4.2, however, represents a more concrete first illustration of the two things our argument is about: the existence of regional variation in support for redistribution among the rich and the poor in Western Europe. Figure 4.2 captures the average level of support (i.e., the mean of the five-point scale) for redistribution in each of the regions in the ESS sample.[14] First among the rich (those with household incomes 30,000 PPP-adjusted 2005 US dollars above the mean, the ninetieth percentile in the sample's income distribution) and then among the poor (with household incomes 25,000 PPP-adjusted 2005 US dollars below the country-year mean, the tenth percentile).

[13] Redistribution items are available in waves A, C, E, G, J, N, and Q.
[14] Note that here and in the following these are unadjusted regional means (without any spatial smoothing or poststratification) intended to illustrate relative patterns.

Figure 4.2 strongly suggest the existence of a general relative-income effect. By looking at the two panels side by side, we can see that the support for redistribution of the poor is almost always higher than that of the rich (there are some exceptions, but these are limited to very few regions where support for redistribution is generally very high for both groups). While the poor's average regional support for redistribution is close to 4 in the 5-point scale (the "Agree" choice), the average for the rich is closer to 3 (the "Neither agree nor Disagree" choice). Figure 4.2 also shows a remarkable amount of regional variation. The lowest support for redistribution among the rich (2.2 on the 5-point scale, close to the "Disagree" choice) can be found in a Danish region (Vestsjællands Amt), while the highest support among the rich (4.6) is in a Spanish one (La Rioja). For the poor, the highest support for redistribution (4.5) is in France (Champagne-Ardenne, Picardie and Bourgogne) while the lowest support (2.6) is again to be found in Vestsjællands Amt.

More important for the arguments in this section of the book, the degree of regional variation within countries in Figure 4.2 is remarkable. Looking at the redistribution preferences of the rich, this variation can be illustrated by comparing two regions in the United Kingdom. In the South East of England, the rich exhibit a low support for redistribution (2.8) while in Northern Ireland they are much more supportive (3.8, a whole point higher). The preferences of the poor can also be used as an illustration. In Denmark, the poor in Storstrøms Amt are much more supportive of redistribution (3.7) than in Vestsjællands Amt (2.6).

The existence of regional variation in support for redistribution among the rich and the poor is also explored in Figure 4.3, but this time the data come from our BHPS analysis. Like Figure 4.2, Figure 4.3 reflects the existence of a general relative-income effect. The poor in the UK are almost always more supportive of redistribution than the rich (there are some exceptions, but these are limited to very few regions with low numbers of respondents within the poor or the rich).[15] While the poor's average regional response to the redistribution survey question[16] is 3.4 in the 5-point scale (close to 4, the "Agree" choice), the average for the rich is 2.7 (closer to 2, the "Disagree" choice).

---

[15] They are Eastern Scotland, the East Yorkshire and Northern Lincolnshire region, and the Northumberland and Tyne and Wear region. The white regions in Figure 4.3 do not have any respondents within our categories of rich or poor (they are North Eastern Scotland, the Highlands and Islands region, and the Cornwall and Isles of Scilly region).

[16] Recall that the BHPS question captures support for the statement that "it is the government's responsibility to provide a job for everyone who wants one."

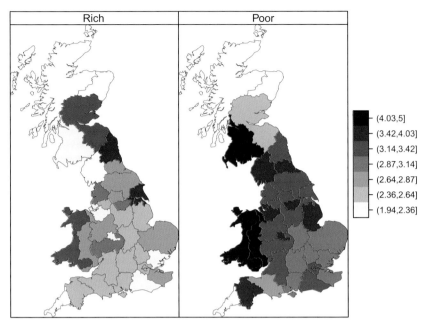

FIGURE 4.3 Redistribution preferences among rich and poor, BHPS (1991–2007)

Regarding regional variation, the lowest support for redistribution among the rich (1.9 on the 5-point scale, lower than the "Disagree" choice) can be found in Cumbria, while the highest support (3.3) is in the West Wales and The Valleys region. For the poor, the highest support for redistribution (4.6) is again to be found in the West Wales and The Valleys region, while the lowest support (2.5) is in Eastern Scotland.

Both Figures 4.2 and 4.3 reflect important regional differences between the rich and the poor. Figure 4.2 suggested that support for redistribution was generally high in regions in Spain, France, Ireland, and Portugal and low in regions in Denmark, Germany, Great Britain, Belgium, and the Netherlands. In Figure 4.3, general support for redistribution is high in regions in Wales, but low in some regions of the south of England.

The support of redistribution among the rich and the poor mirrors these general trends, but the differences between poor and rich are interesting. For example, in some regions in France, Sweden, and Norway, where the general support for redistribution is relatively high, the difference between rich and poor is large (around 1, of the 5-point scale). In Britain, this is also the case in, for example, South Western Scotland. In some regions in Spain and Portugal, where the general support for

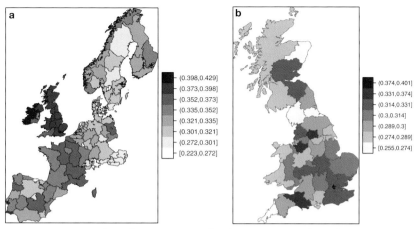

FIGURE 4.4 Gini index of income inequality by region. Panel (a) shows Western Europe (ESS 2002–2008), panel (b) the United Kingdom (BHPS 1991–2007)

redistribution is again relatively high, the difference between rich and poor is low (below 0.5). There are regions with low general levels of support for redistribution that have small differences between the rich and poor in Denmark (Viborg Amt and Frederiksborg Amt), Austria (Salzburg), or (in Figure 4.3) Essex. And there are regions with similarly low general levels of support that have big differences between the rich and poor in the Netherlands (Friesland, Noord-Holland, and Zeeland) or Germany (Berlin and Hamburg).

4.2.1 Regional Variation in Inequality and Fear of Crime

The more systematic analysis to be developed in the next chapter will help explain the redistribution patterns shown in Figures 4.2 and 4.3, but an initial illustration of our main explanatory variables can be offered in this section. Panel (a) of Figure 4.4 captures regional inequality in our Western European ESS sample, while panel (b) does the same for our BHPS data. In both maps we present regional Gini indexes calculated from the individual-level surveys.[17] While most of the variation in our ESS analysis is cross-sectional, the BHPS offers us a more extensive time period to explore. Figure 4.5 reflects the change in regional Gini in Britain from the 1990s to the 2000s.

---

[17] The detailed explanation of these calculations is provided in the next chapter.

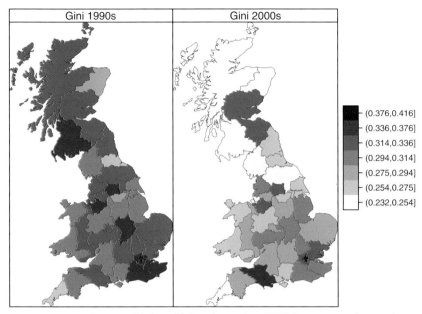

FIGURE 4.5 Average Gini coefficient by region (BHPS, 1990s, and 2000s)

The figures again show a remarkable amount of regional variation. In Western Europe (from 2002 to 2008), regional inequality was highest in Ireland (particularly in the Midwest, Midlands, West, South-West, and Border), some regions in the UK (Scotland, Northern Ireland, and London), and Portugal (Lisboa and Algarve). The most equal regions were distributed among a higher number of countries: Spain (Cantabria), Denmark (Roskilde Amt and Viborg Amt), Austria (Vorarlberg, Salzburg, Kärnten, and Niederösterreich), Switzerland (Ostschweiz and Ticino), and the Netherlands (Zeeland). In Great Britain from 1991 to 2007, the most unequal regions were East Anglia, Cheshire, West Yorkshire, the Dorset and Somerset region, and the Leicestershire, Rutland, and Northamptonshire region. The more equal regions were the Cornwall and Isles of Scilly region, the Tees Valley and Durham region, North Eastern Scotland, Cumbria and the East Yorkshire and Northern Lincolnshire region.

Temporal change in regional inequality levels is reflected in Figure 4.5. The figure makes clear that there is a general decrease in regional inequality in Britain from the 1990s to the 2000s. In fact, this is the case in all regions in our sample except Lincolnshire and the Dorset and Somerset region. The biggest decreases in inequality take place in South

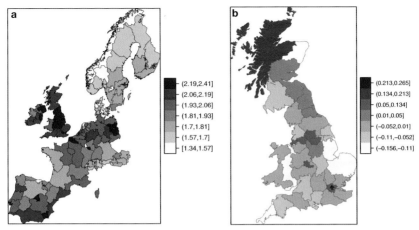

FIGURE 4.6 Fear of crime by region. Panel (a) shows Western Europe, panel (b) shows United Kingdom

Western Scotland, Merseyside, the Highlands and Islands region, and North Yorkshire.

We have argued earlier that the reason why rich individuals who live in unequal regions support redistribution is because they are more concerned about crime. We can now turn to some preliminary figures illustrating this point. As was the case in our analysis of inequality, the left panel of Figure 4.6 captures fear of crime (measured as the regional average) in our Western European ESS sample, while panel (b) does the same for our BHPS data. As we explain in more detail in the next chapter, when analyzing ESS data, we measure individuals' crime concerns via a survey item that has become "the de facto standard for measuring fear of crime" (Warr, 2000: 457). It prompts a respondent if he or she is afraid of walking alone in the dark with four category responses ranging from "very safe" to "very unsafe." When exploring BHPS data, we use a broader measure capturing individuals' fear of crime. We argue that a number of survey items capturing the extent to which individuals perceive threatening actions in their neighborhood can be summarized by an underlying (or latent) *fear of crime* variable.[18]

Panel (a) of Figure 4.6 shows that in Western Europe (from 2002 to 2008), fear of crime was most significant in the UK (particularly in the North West, West Midlands, Yorkshire and The Humber, and Northern

---

[18] See a more detailed explanation in the next chapter.

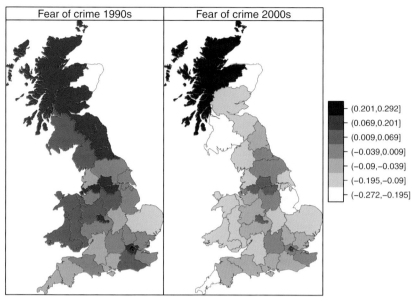

FIGURE 4.7 Regional changes in fear of crime (BHPS, 1990s, and 2000s)

Ireland), Spain (Murcia and Madrid), and also in one French region (Nord-Pas-de-Calais). The regions with the lowest concern from crime were in Denmark (Bornholms Amt, Ringkøbing Amt, and Viborg Amt) and Norway (Nord-Norge, Hedmark og Oppland, Vestlandet, and Trøndelag). Panel (b) shows that in Great Britain from 1991 to 2007, the areas with the highest level of fear of crime (measured as our latent variable) were the Cornwall and Isles of Sicily region, East Anglia, Lincolnshire, and East Wales. The highest levels of fear of crimes were in Inner London, the Highlands and Islands region, and the West Midlands.

Temporal change in regional levels of fear of crime are captured in Figure 4.7. Just as was the case when looking at inequality, the figure suggests that there is a general decrease in fear of crime in Britain from the 1990s to the 2000s. In fact, this is the case in all regions in our sample except one (the Highlands and Islands region). The biggest decreases in fear of crime take place in South Western Scotland, Eastern Scotland, and the Cornwall and Isles of Scilly region.

Most significantly for our argument, the figures in this section show a general correlation between inequality and fear of crime. Using ESS data, the lowest levels of inequality and fear of crime can be found in regions of Denmark and Switzerland (and also in Cantabria, Spain). The highest levels of both variables are in some regions in the UK (like London, the North West, or the East Midlands), in Ireland's Mid-East, and in Portugal (Lisboa). We explore these patterns in a more systematic way in the next chapter.

5

Analysis of Externalities

To explore the theoretical claims explained earlier, we focus on the effects of income distance at the individual level, the macrolevel of inequality, and their interaction (while controlling for expected future income and a number of other factors). Present and expected future income are meant to capture the effects of individual material preferences and macroinequality those of noneconomic (meaning unrelated to immediate income, tax, and transfer) considerations. The first expectation is that income distance will be a significant determinant of redistribution preferences. We also expect, however, that increasing levels of regional inequality will make the rich more likely to support redistribution. We then will show that the very robust effects of inequality are in fact the product of fear of crime among the affluent.

We begin by analyzing data from the European Social Survey (ESS), described in Chapter 1. To obtain usable regional sample sizes, we select countries who participated in at least two rounds and provide consistent regional identifiers over time (see Table 4.1). As mentioned in the previous chapter, we limit our analyses to surveys collected between September 2002 and January 2009, which was still a time of relative economic calm.[1]

---

[1] We also examined if eliminating surveys after 2007 changes our results and found no change in substantive findings.

5.1.1 Variable Definitions

THE MEASURES OF INCOME. We have argued that individuals form their redistribution preferences as a function of two distinct economic elements: their present income and their expectations about future income. Present income is measured as the distance between the income of respondents and the mean income in their country (at the time of the survey). As we explained in more detail in Chapter 1, the ESS captures income by asking respondents to place their total net household income into a number of income bands (12 in 2002–06, 10 in 2008) giving yearly, monthly, or weekly figures. To create a measure that closely represents our theoretical concept, income distance, we transform income bands into their midpoints, convert the top-coded income category by assuming that the upper tail of the income distribution follows a Pareto distribution, convert euros or national currencies into PPP-adjusted 2005 US dollars, and, for each respondent, we calculate the distance between household income and the mean income for the country-year survey.[2]

Following labor economics models on life-cycle profiles, in the previous section of this book we proposed a very simple conception of future income that depended on age (as a proxy for work experience) and education. These income profiles are averages that integrate typical labor market experiences (likelihood of experiencing unemployment, of finding a new job if unemployed, of experiencing age-related wage increases or decreases, etc.).[3] We introduce expectations of future income as an explanatory variable in our analysis.

FEAR OF CRIME. We measure individuals' crime concerns via a survey item that has become "the de facto standard for measuring fear of crime" (Warr, 2000: 457). It prompts a respondent if he or she is afraid of walking alone in the dark with four category responses ranging from "very safe" to "very unsafe." As we discussed earlier, this captures crime concerns as externality of inequality, instead of actual crime.[4]

INEQUALITY. To measure inequality, we follow the majority of the literature and use the Gini index (Cowell, 2000). Because we need regional

---

[2] A more detailed description of the data and its population characteristics is available in Chapter 1 and Appendix A.1.

[3] In previous chapters, we explained how we generate our measure expected income in a first-stage statistical model following equations (2.5) and (2.6).

[4] We also use a measure of actual crime victimization as a predictor of fear of crime (see details later). This variable is based on asking respondents if they or a member of their household have been a victim of burglary or assault within the last five years.

inequality measures, we calculate the Gini index for each region from our full sample of individual-level survey respondents (pooling survey waves), while adjusting for small-sample bias following the correction proposed by Deltas (2003). In the statistical analysis developed later we also account for its estimation uncertainty.[5]

INDIVIDUAL- AND REGIONAL-LEVEL CONTROLS. We control for a range of standard individual characteristics, namely a respondent's gender, age in years, years of schooling, indicator variables for currently being unemployed, or not in the labor force, and the size of one's household. As controls for existing regional differences we include the harmonized regional unemployment rate, gross-domestic product, the percentage of foreigners (see, e.g., Alesina and Glaeser, 2004; Finseraas, 2008a), and a summary measure of a region's high-tech specialization.[6]

5.1.2 Statistical Models

In the first stage of our analysis we study the link between regional levels of inequality, relative income, and redistribution preferences R_i^*. Our model specification is

$$R_i^* = \alpha \, (v_i - \bar{v}) + \beta w_j + \gamma w_j (v_i - \bar{v}) + \delta' x_{ij} + \epsilon_{iR}. \qquad (5.1)$$

Here α captures the effect of relative income, the difference between an individual's income v_i, and country-year average income $\bar{v}$. The remaining (noneconomic) effect of macroinequality w_j is captured by β. Because we argue that inequality effects are more relevant among the rich than among the poor, our model includes an interaction between inequality and individual income with associated effect coefficient γ. Finally, we include a wide range of individual and regional level controls x_{ij} (including, in some models, expected future income) whose effects are represented by δ.

Redistribution preferences R_i^* are a latent construct obtained from observed categorical survey responses R (with K_r categories) via a set of thresholds (e.g., McKelvey and Zavoina, 1975; Greene and Hensher,

---

[5] To address the errors-in-variables problem, we use household (inclusion probability) weights and a jackknife-based estimator (Karagiannis and Kovacevic, 2000). See later section for more details.

[6] We used a factor model to generate a summary measure for regional high-tech specialization. We collected Eurostat data on regional information on the share of a region's total workforce employed in science and technology sectors, the share of the economically active population that hold higher degrees, a head count of personnel employed in R&D, and regional total R&D expenditure.

2010) such that $R = r$ if $\tau_{r-1} < R^* < \tau_r$ $(r = 1, \ldots, K_r)$.[7] Thresholds τ are strictly monotonically ordered and the variance of the stochastic disturbances is fixed at $\epsilon_{iR} \sim N(0,1)$ yielding an ordered probit specification.[8]

In the second stage of our analysis we jointly model fear of crime and preferences for redistribution. Our fear of crime variable C is also ordered categorical, and we use the same ordered probit specification as earlier, i.e., $C = c$ if $\tau_{c-1} < C^* < \tau_c$ $(c = 1, \ldots, K_c)$ with strictly ordered thresholds and errors $\epsilon_{iC} \sim N(0,1)$ for identification. Errors from the redistribution and crime equations are correlated and thus specified as distributed bivariate normal (Greene, 2002: 711f.):

$$\epsilon_{1i}, \epsilon_{1i} \sim BVN(0, 0, 1, 1, \rho),$$

where ρ captures the residual correlation between both equations.

A direct test for our argument that fear of crime is an important externality shaping redistribution preferences is to estimate its effect in our redistribution equation. We thus arrive at the following simultaneous (recursive) system of equations (Greene and Hensher, 2010: ch.10)[9]:

$$C_i^* = \alpha_1(v_i - \bar{v}) + \beta_1 w_j + \delta_1' x_{1ij} + \epsilon_{iC} \tag{5.2}$$
$$R_i^* = \lambda_1 C_i + \lambda_2 C_i(v_i - \bar{v}) + \alpha_2(v_i - \bar{v}) + \beta_2 w_j + \gamma w_j(v_i - \bar{v})$$
$$+ \delta_2' x_{2ij} + \epsilon_{iR}. \tag{5.3}$$

Thus this model can be seen as a straightforward extension of the more familiar bivariate probit model to ordered data (Butler and Chatterjee,

---

[7] This model thus imposes what is known as the single-crossing property, which follows directly from the theoretical assumption of single-peaked preferences: as one moves along the values of x, the predicted probability $Pr(y = r)$ changes only once (Boes and Winkelmann, 2006; Greene and Hensher, 2010). As Greene and Hensher (2010) argue at length, models that do not enforce this restriction (such as multinomial or generalized ordered logit modes) are not appropriate for strictly ordered preference data. An argument that is sometimes made (especially in the sociology literature) is that one should conduct a Brant test, which compares an ordered specification with an "unordered" one. However, because an unordered specification is clearly an inappropriate *behavioral* model for the data used here, we do not pursue this further. For further arguments against these kind of test see Greene and Hensher (2010).

[8] An ordered probit model needs two identifying restrictions. Besides setting the scale by fixing the error variance, we fix the location by not including a constant term (but estimate all thresholds).

[9] The system is recursive because C_i is allowed to influence R_i but not vice versa. The model employs the standard assumption that $E(\epsilon_{iC}|x_{1ij}, x_{2ij}) = E(\epsilon_{iR}|x_{1ij}, x_{2ij}) = 0$.

1997).[10] In order not to rely on function form alone for identification, x_{1ij} should contain at least one covariate excluded from the redistribution equation. The literature on determinants of fear of crime includes a number of "standard" variables related to the probability of victimization, such as social class, education, age, and gender. However these variables are all relevant controls in our redistribution equation as well. Thus we use actual victimization, that is if the respondent reports that he, or a member of his household, has been a victim of crime, which is plausibly excluded from the redistribution equation.

We estimate these two equations jointly by maximum likelihood (Butler and Chatterjee, 1997). In this setup, individuals within the same region and country will share unobserved characteristics, rendering the standard assumption of independent errors implausible (e.g., Moulton, 1990; Pepper, 2002). Thus, to account for arbitrary within region and country error correlations, we estimate standard errors using a nonparametric bootstrap resampling regions and countries (e.g., Wooldridge, 2003).[11]

In this second stage, our main interest lies on λ_1 and λ_2, which capture the effect of fear of crime (and its interaction with income) on redistribution preferences net of all other covariate effects. Our model still includes the main effect of income distance α_2 as well as the remaining effect of inequality β_2 and its interaction with income distance, captured by γ. Estimates of individual and regional level controls x_{ij} are given by δ. Ideally, if fear of crime plays a significant role in explaining redistribution preferences, we expect to see at least (i) a significant effect of inequality on fear of crime: $\beta_1 \neq 0$, (ii) a significant effect of fear on preferences: $\lambda_1 \neq 0$, and (iii) a reduction of the (remaining) effect of inequality on the rich γ vis-à-vis equation (5.1).

MULTIPLE IMPUTATION AND MEASUREMENT ERROR. We use multiple imputation to address missing values. More importantly, decomposing Gini into regional values involves calculating the distance of individual household income from a regional income mean. These

---

[10] See Yatchew and Griliches (1985) for a discussion of the disadvantages of two-step estimation. Freedman and Sekhon (2010) caution against convergence to local maxima, which we check by (i) running our model several times from dispersed initial values, and (ii) bootstrapping individual observations. In each case we get essentially the same results.

[11] An alternative, less computationally demanding, strategy is to employ cluster-robust variance estimation. This does not substantively change our results.

TABLE 5.1 *Income inequality and redistribution preferences in Western Europe*

Eq.: Redistribution	(1)		(2)	
	Est.	s.e.	Est.	s.e.
Income distance	−0.054	0.003	−0.056	0.003
Inequality (Gini)	1.508	0.771	1.297	0.635
Income distance × Gini	0.217	0.104	0.237	0.102
Income expectations			−0.173	0.032
Covariates				
Individual & regional[a]	Included		Included	

Note: Maximum likelihood estimates, standard errors, and 95 percent confidence intervals of equation (5.1). Bootstrapped, multiple overimputation standard errors based on 500 samples from 129 regions and 14 countries. $N = 75,112$.
[a]Individual level controls are age, female, education, labor force status, houschold size. Regional level controls are percentage of foreigners, unemployment rate, gross-domestic product, and high-tech specialization. Estimates for τs and controls not shown.

means can carry considerable uncertainty when calculated from survey data. Thus, Gini values are measured with error, a fact that is often ignored and leads to classical errors-in-variables bias in results. In our analyses we correct for measurement error following the methodology outlined by Blackwell et al. (2017), who propose to treat measurement error in the framework of missing data. Details are provided in Appendix A.3.

5.1.3 Results: Inequality

Table 5.1 shows parameter estimates and standard errors for our basic model estimating the effects of relative income, regional inequality, and their interaction. Because of the interaction, the interpretation of our variables of interest is not straightforward. We develop a stricter test of our argument later by calculating the specific effects of being rich or poor conditional on different levels of macroinequality. Suffice it to say at this stage that these three variables are statistically significant. As expected, we find that income distance has a negative effect on redistribution preferences: the further above someone is from the mean income, the more she opposes income redistribution. We also find that increasing levels of income inequality go hand in hand with higher preferences for redistribution, and that this relationship increases with an individual's income distance.

As mentioned earlier, specification (2) contains our measure of expected future income. The results in Table 5.1 simply confirm those in Chapter 3: a one-dollar change in expected lifetime income has a large and significant impact on redistribution preferences. Although not the focus of this chapter's analysis, the results in Table 5.1 also show some of the individual control variables to be significant determinants of redistribution preferences in a manner compatible with the existing literature. Older individuals and women are more in favor of redistribution, while those with higher education oppose it. Potential recipients of transfer payments – the currently unemployed – support income redistribution. Among our regional level controls we find higher average support for redistribution in high unemployment regions, whereas regions specializing in high-tech display lower average levels of support.

To gain a more intuitive understanding of the role of inequality, we use specification (1) to calculate average predicted probabilities for supporting redistribution among rich and poor individuals living in high- or low-inequality regions, respectively.[12] In Figure 5.1, the only factors that change in the comparison of predicted probabilities, therefore, are income distance to the mean (in the x-axis) and the two levels of macroinequality (in the solid and dashed lines). High inequality refers to Gini values at the ninetieth percentile of the regional distribution, while low inequality refers to the tenth. The results provide a clear picture of the correspondence between our theoretical argument (in Figure 4.1) and our empirical findings.

The results in Table 5.2 take the predicted probabilities in Figure 5.1 and compare the likelihood of supporting redistribution for the rich and the poor (defined as the ninetieth and tenth percentiles of the income distribution). Like before, high inequality refers to Gini values at the ninetieth percentile of the regional distribution, while low inequality refers to the tenth. The results in Table 5.2 again provide strong confirmation of our

---

[12] "Simple" predicted probabilities are calculated by setting the variables in question to the chosen values (e.g., rich or poor in high- or low-inequality regions) while holding all other variables at one observed value (e.g., the mean values). Average predicted probabilities, however, are calculated by setting the variables in question to the chosen values while holding all other variables at all their observed values. The final estimates are the average of these predictions. We do the same later when calculating average marginal effects. See Hanmer and Kalkan (2013) for a recent discussion of the advantages of these estimates in a political science context.

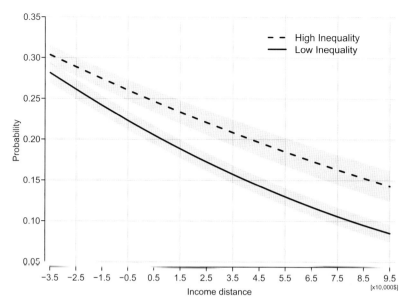

FIGURE 5.1 Predicted probability of support for redistribution in Western Europe as function of income distance in inequality

initial expectations. Among the poor the probability of strongly supporting redistribution only changes from 25.7 to 28.6 percent when moving from low- to high-inequality regions. In contrast, the effect of inequality is more pronounced among the rich: explicit support for redistribution rises from 15.7 percent in low-inequality regions to 20.8 percent in high-inequality areas. In other words, the difference in predicted support for redistribution due to increased inequality is almost twice as large among the rich.[13]

To put this conclusion to a stricter test we calculate average marginal effects of income inequality for rich and poor individuals, shown in Table 5.3 together with their respective standard errors and 95 percent confidence bounds. The results further support our argument. The marginal effect of inequality among rich individuals is large and

---

[13] It is worth reminding the reader that the current evidence is based on a cross-sectional analysis comparing different levels of inequality in different regions. Thus all references to changes are strictly counterfactual (and model-based): They refer to the hypothetical operation of moving one region's level of inequality to that experienced by another, while holding all else equal. In the next section we will study the impact of inequality in an explicitly longitudinal setting.

TABLE 5.2 *Probability of support for redistribution among the rich and the poor in low- and high-inequality regions*

		Gini	
		Low	High
Income	Poor	25.7	28.6
	Rich	15.7	20.8

Note: Calculated from equation (5.1). Average predicted probabilities. Region-country bootstrapped, multiple overimputation standard errors. All probabilities are significantly different from zero.

TABLE 5.3 *Marginal effect of inequality for the rich and poor; average marginal effects for predicted strong support of redistribution*

	Marginal effect of Gini			
	Est.	s.e.	95% CI	
Poor	0.323	0.188	−0.053	0.700
Rich	0.575	0.257	0.066	1.084

Note: Calculated from equation (5.1). Region-country bootstrapped, multiple overimputation standard errors.

statistically different from zero. In contrast, we find a considerably smaller marginal effect among the poor.[14]

It is important to point out that the estimates in Tables 5.1–5.3 represent a significant amount of support for the relationship hypothesized in Figure 4.1. As we expected, redistribution preferences converge for the poor regardless of the level of inequality. We also find the redistribution preferences of the rich to diverge as macroinequality becomes larger. Some influential alternative hypotheses are contradicted by our evidence.

An important literature posits that, in high-inequality contexts, the poor are diverted from the pursuit of their material self-interest. This effect would imply that, in contradiction to Figure 4.1, redistribution preferences would diverge for the poor and converge for the affluent. Perhaps

[14] Note that the results in Rueda and Stegmueller (2016) are even more pronounced, showing this difference for the poor to be statistically insignificant. This is caused by a less restrictive estimation strategy in this book, which does not include class and skill specificity as controls in the main analysis.

the most well-known example of these arguments is its application to the high-inequality example of the United States and the contention that second-dimension issues (particularly cultural and social ones) outweigh economics for the American working class.[15] More comparatively, Shayo's (2009) important contribution to the political economy of identity formation follows a similar logic.[16] If these arguments were to hold in our data, we would expect the poor in unequal countries to be distracted from their material self-interested redistribution preferences, to the extent that these second-dimension concerns are correlated with inequality. The results presented here suggest that the poor are not distracted from the pursuit of their present material self-interest in regions with higher levels of macroinequality, whether because of second-dimension concerns or prospects of upward mobility.

In another theoretical alternative, Lupu and Pontusson (2011) propose that macrolevels of equality are related to empathy. They argue that, because of social affinity, individuals will be inclined to have more similar redistribution preferences to those who are closer to them in terms of income distance. While Lupu and Pontusson emphasize skew (rather than Ginis) and the position of the middle class, their argument implies that social affinity would make the rich have higher levels of support for redistribution as inequality decreases (the opposite of the predictions in Figure 4.1). A similar relationship would be expected by the approach that relates beliefs in a just world to redistribution preferences. To the extent that macrolevels of inequality are related to these beliefs (for example that inequality rewards the hard-working and punishes the lazy), we would observe lower levels of support for redistribution from the rich in countries with higher inequality and a higher normative tolerance for it (Alesina and Glaeser, 2004; Benabou and Tirole, 2006). Our evidence fails to support these arguments.

As we mentioned earlier, an influential literature in comparative political economy has argued that, if inequality means that the rich are more likely to become poor, current generosity may not reflect noneconomic concerns but the demand for insurance against an uncertain future (Moene and Wallerstein, 2001; Iversen and Soskice, 2009; Rehm,

---

[15] See Frank (2004), the critique in Bartels (2006), and the comparative analyses by De La O and Rodden (2008) and Huber and Stanig (2011).

[16] This logic has also been applied to arguments about population heterogeneity (ethnic or racial diversity distracting the poor from their material self-interest). We return to them in the next section of the book.

2009).[17] To address this, we need to refer back to our expected future income results in Table 5.1. We argued in Part 1 of the book that the insurance logic is relevant to support for redistribution to the extent that individuals anticipate the effects of their future income (and of mobility within the income distribution) and therefore should be integrated into a more general conception of expected income. Controlling for these factors directly through our measure of expected future income, therefore, indicates that our negative externality results are robust to the effects of insurance/risk/mobility.[18]

5.1.4 Results: Fear of Crime

In the previous sections, we went on to argue that one of the mechanisms linking inequality and redistribution preferences is fear of crime. Table 5.4 presents estimates from our simultaneous ordered probit model linking inequality to fear of crime, which then is expected to shape preferences for redistribution. In our fear of crime equation, we include a number of factors identified in the literature (e.g., Hale, 1996), but we do not report them here for reasons of space. Suffice it to say that we find, not surprisingly, that having previously been a victim of crime increases a person's fear of crime and that other variables affect fear of crime in the expected directions. More importantly, the results in Table 5.4 show that, in agreement with our argument, in regions with higher levels of inequality, respondents – whether rich or poor – are more afraid of crime.

Turning to the redistribution equation in Table 5.4, we find clear evidence that fear of crime matters for redistribution preferences. Individuals who are more afraid of crime show higher levels of support for redistribution, a relationship that is slightly stronger among those with higher incomes. A test for independence of fear of crime and redistribution equations is rejected ($F = 12.7$ at 2df.). We also find that the direct effect of inequality becomes statistically insignificant once we explicitly estimate the effect of fear of crime.

---

[17] A similar expectation emerges from the "prospect of upward mobility" (POUM) hypothesis. Benabou and Ok (2001) argue that the poor do not support high levels of redistribution because of the hope that they, or their offspring, may make it up the income ladder. To the extent that mobility is correlated with macrolevel inequality (something that is in any case not clear), we would expect a different relationship between income and preferences from that depicted in Figure 4.1.

[18] We also introduced an explicit measure of risk into the robustness analysis later.

TABLE 5.4 *Fear of crime, relative income, inequality, and redistribution preferences*

Eq.: Fear	(1)		(2)	
	Est.	s.e.	Est.	s.e.
Crime victim	0.271	0.022	0.268	0.022
Income distance	−0.019	0.003	−0.019	0.003
Inequality (Gini)	4.884	0.770	4.882	0.832
Eq.: Redistribution				
Income distance	−0.071	0.005	−0.069	−0.006
Inequality (Gini)	0.720	0.770	0.237	0.666
Income distance × Gini	0.179	0.089	0.207	0.101
Fear of crime	0.235	0.075	0.312	0.075
Income distance × Fear	0.011	0.003	0.009	0.003
Expected income			−0.169	0.031
Error correlation	−0.169	0.066	−0.238	0.067
Test	12.73 $p = 0.00$		21.78, $p = 0.00$	

Note: System of equations (5.2) and (5.3). Maximum likelihood estimates, region-country bootstrapped, multiple overimputation standard errors, and 95 percent confidence intervals. N = 75,112. Test against model without fear equation, $F = 157.2, p = 0.000$. Distribution of tests is based on Barnard and Rubin (1999). Estimates for τs and controls not shown. See Appendix A.3.1 for complete table of estimates.

Again, a stricter test of our hypotheses can be obtained by calculating average marginal effects. We expect to find (i) a significant (both in the statistical and substantive sense) marginal effect of fear of crime on redistribution preferences, and (ii) that the size of the remaining effect of macroinequality (operating through other channels) is reduced. Table 5.5 shows average marginal effects of fear of crime and inequality among the rich. As already indicated by our coefficient estimates, the marginal effect of fear of crime is strong and clearly different from zero. More importantly, we find the remaining marginal effect of inequality to be greatly limited. In fact, it is reduced to such an extent that its confidence interval includes zero. This result does, of course, not negate the existence of other relevant channels linking inequality and preferences, but it at least signifies that externalities go a long way in explaining the effect of inequality on redistribution preferences.

TABLE 5.5 *Effects of fear of crime and inequality among the rich; average marginal effects for predicted strong support of redistribution*

| | Marginal effect among rich | | | |
	Est.	s.e.	95% CI	
Fear of crime	0.094	0.033	0.030	0.159
Inequality	0.346	0.278	−0.203	0.896

Note: Calculated from eqs. (5.2) and (5.3). Region-country bootstrapped, multiple overimputation standard errors.

5.1.5 A Placebo Test

Before describing a number of robustness tests we subject our analysis to in the following section, we perform a placebo test. One may argue that the inclusion of any variable measuring political perceptions or beliefs could render the macroeffect of inequality insignificant. If so, the fact that our measure of fear of crime "explains" a large part of the inequality effect among the rich would be far less noteworthy. To check for this possibility we replace our theoretically important variable, fear of crime, with a "catchall" variable: an individual's ideology (measured on a standard left–right scale). We do indeed find that ideology affects preferences. The marginal effect of ideology is substantial, estimated as −0.076 with a standard error of 0.004. However, unlike in our models involving crime fears, the effect of inequality among the poor remains highly significant and not reduced in magnitude at all. It is still estimated as 0.583 with a standard error of 0.225, indicating that this alternative political variable does not contribute to explaining the effect of inequality.

5.1.6 Robustness Checks

While the previous section is quite convincing at providing support for our hypotheses, there are alternative arguments in the existing literature with implications about the relationship between income and redistribution preferences that are connected to the ones proposed in this section of the book. These alternative explanations rest on very different causal claims that we can test directly. The tests are reported in Table 5.6, focusing on our variables of interest, the marginal effects of Gini and fear of crime for the rich.

TABLE 5.6 *Overview of robustness checks; average marginal effects among the rich from basic model and model including fear of crime; estimates whose 95 percent confidence interval includes zero are marked with †*

| | | Basic model | | Model with endogenous fear | | | |
| | | Gini | | Fear | | Gini | |
Robustness tests		Est.	s.e.	Est.	s.e.	Est.	s.e.
(1)	Social spending	0.732	0.293	0.084	0.033	0.529	0.299†
(2a)	Regional social spending	0.554	0.244	0.095	0.034	0.325	0.252†
(2b)	Federalism	0.626	0.274	0.102	0.032	0.390	0.281†
(3a)	Population density	0.616	0.266	0.090	0.035	0.426	0.270†
(3b)	Urban area	0.569	0.250	0.093	0.035	0.344	0.259†
(3c)	Urban region	0.565	0.244	0.098	0.035	0.329	0.252†
(4)	Religion	0.504	0.230	0.100	0.033	0.264	0.241
(5a)	Ideology (redist. eq.)	0.592	0.235	0.097	0.029	0.355	0.239†
(5b)	Ideology (both eq.)	0.592	0.235	0.098	0.029	0.352	0.240†
(6)	Altruism	0.580	0.250	0.062	0.031	0.419	0.261†
(7)	Skill specificity	0.575	0.255	0.093	0.034	0.348	0.262†
(8)	Social class	0.583	0.257	0.101	0.034	0.337	0.263†
(9)	Wage earner sample	0.593	0.258	0.111	0.038	0.322	0.268†

Note: Robust, multiple imputation standard errors clustered by 129 regions and penalized for 5 imputations.

EXISTING LEVELS OF REDISTRIBUTION. Previous research indicates that average support for redistribution tends to fall when the existing levels of redistribution are high. As we mentioned in previous chapters, the idea that there is some threshold at which the disincentive effects of redistribution become more severe (see, for example, Tanzi and Schuhknecht, 2000) provides a possible explanation for this relationship. It also seems likely that some respondents take actual levels of redistribution into account when expressing their preferences, i.e., that they are expressing agreement or disagreement with the proposition that the government should do more to reduce income differences. In an alternative, but related, explanation, high levels of redistribution are argued to be connected with encompassing welfare and labor market institutions that provide the poor and the rich with more information about redistributive issues (see Kumlin and Svallfors, 2007). This would imply more extreme redistribution preferences by poor and rich in high welfare state countries.

To test these alternatives, we include existing levels of social spending in our estimation.[19] The results in model (1) in Table 5.6 show that while the inclusion of preexisting redistribution marginally increases the direct effect of inequality in the model with endogenous fear (the 95 percent confidence interval still includes zero), it leaves our core result – the role of fear of crime – virtually unchanged.

NATIONAL VERSUS REGIONAL REDISTRIBUTION. We consider the measure of redistribution preferences in the chapter's analysis to (mostly) capture national redistribution. It is possible that in federal countries (where regional government have more of a role in providing redistribution), respondents integrate a combination of national and regional policy into their assessment of redistribution. We address this issue in two ways. First, we create a measure of regional social spending. The regional measure weights national expenditure by the regional share of the recipient population (because region-specific spending data are only available for a very limited number of countries in our sample).[20] Second, we use a measure of federalism by creating an indicator variable that equals one if, within a country, regions are an autonomous source of government spending (based on Eurostat's Government revenue and expenditure database). Specifications (2a) and (2b) in Table 5.6 show that our main conclusions are robust to these considerations.

POPULATION DENSITY/URBANIZATION. Although our analyses emphasize the regional level, one may argue that we ignore political geography, i.e., the distinct preferences of individuals living in high-density, urban areas (see, for example, Cho et al., 2006). As argued by Rodden (2010: 322), it is clear that individuals sort themselves into neighborhoods with similar demographic, occupational, income, and ultimately political preferences.[21] We address this concern in two

---

[19] Spending data are total public social spending (in cash and in kind), per head, in constant 2000 prices and PPP US dollars from OECD's SOCX database. The main social policy areas covered are: Old age, Survivors, Incapacity-related benefits, Health, Family, Active labor market programs, Unemployment, and Housing.

[20] We calculate the regional share of the recipient population from our available survey data as the population share of unemployed, the disabled, and those in retirement.

[21] Note that sorting also entails the possibility of "sorting out," namely that individuals evade the negative externalities of rising inequality by moving. We address this issue in more detail in our analyses using panel data later.

ways. First, we simply include an individual-level survey variable, which indicates if the respondent lives in an urban area. Second, we construct variables measuring the degree of urbanization of a region (this is simply the regional mean of our individual level variable) and population density (data from Eurostat). Table 5.6, specifications (3a), (3b), and (3c) show that both individual and contextual measures do not change our core results.[22]

RELIGION. Previous research has stressed the role of religion for redistribution preferences (Scheve and Stasavage, 2006; Stegmueller et al., 2012; Stegmueller, 2013b). Including religion (indicator variables for Catholic and Protestant, as well as a measure of church attendance) in model (4), we find a somewhat reduced effect of inequality among the rich, but it is still significant (its confidence interval excludes zero). Similar to our previous checks, results in Table 5.6 confirm that including fear of crime substantially reduces the remaining effects of inequality.

IDEOLOGY. As in other parts of this book, our main analyses exclude a measure of ideology or left–right self-placement. We have argued that explaining economic preferences helps us understand a key constituent of ideology and therefore it should not be an "explanatory" variable in our model. As we also have mentioned in previous chapters, other authors have proposed that ideological positions are an independent source of redistribution preferences, and we can show that the inequality–fear link is robust to the inclusion of this variable. In Table 5.6, specification (5), we account for respondents' ideology in two ways. First, we simply include ideology in our redistribution equation and find the results unchanged. Second, we allow for the fact that conservative respondents might be more likely to indicate fear of crime, by including ideology in our fear of crime equation. Again, we find our results confirmed.

ALTRUISM. As we will explain in more detail in Part III, a most significant approach to noneconomic motivations for redistribution preferences has focused on other-regarding concerns (for reviews, see Fehr and Schmidt, 2006b; DellaVigna, 2009). Other-regarding concerns are particularly relevant to our arguments because of the possibility that the rich could be more willing to support redistribution in highly unequal societies because they can afford to be more compassionate. This would be the opposite of the relationship between empathy and

---

[22] While controlling for population density marginally increases the direct effect of inequality in the model with endogenous fear (but note that the 95 percent confidence interval still includes zero), the effect of fear of crime remains virtually unchanged.

inequality proposed by Lupu and Pontusson (2011) and analyzed in more detail in the discussion of our main results. To address this issue directly, we introduce a control for other-regarding preferences. Due to the sparsity of data on altruism, we rely on a proxy measure provided in the ESS (see the details in Section 3.1.4). Our results in specification (6) show that including other regarding preferences does not alter our basic findings.

SKILL SPECIFICITY. Returning to the arguments (summarized earlier) that understand redistribution as insurance against an uncertain future (Moene and Wallerstein, 2001; Iversen and Soskice, 2009; Rehm, 2009), we introduce an explicit measure of risk into the analysis. An important component of the demand for insurance and redistribution has to do with the risk of becoming unemployed. We operationalize risk as specific skills. Iversen and Soskice (2001) argue that individuals who have made risky investments in specific skills will demand insurance against the possible future loss of income from those investments. In specification (7) we use the original measure of skill specificity of Iversen and Soskice (2001). Skill specificity is calculated following Cusack et al. (2006).[23] We find our core results unchanged.

SOCIAL CLASS. There is a well-established literature in sociology connecting class with redistribution. Class (partly as a factor influencing insurance and risk and partly as a source of socialization profiles) needs to be accounted for in our empirical analysis. In model (8) we include a control for class. We once again use the six-category version of the Erikson–Goldthorpe social class scheme (Erikson and Goldthorpe, 1992).[24] The variation of income within class categories is high enough to allow us to assess whether our main results regarding relative income, inequality, and fear of crime are robust to controlling for the effects of class. Table 5.6 makes clear that controlling for class does not affect our main substantive conclusions.

LABOR INCOME. Owing to the usual constraints of large-scale comparative survey projects, the income measure in the ESS is based on a single item with discrete categories. In the following specifications we test the robustness of our results to changes in the sample composition of

---

[23] We are indebted to Philip Rehm for providing us with skill specificity measures on the ISCO 1d level.

[24] The six classes are service class I (higher-level controllers and administrators), service class II (lower-level controllers and administrators), routine nonmanual employees, skilled workers, unskilled workers, and the self-employed.

income earners.[25] In specification (9) we only include respondents who currently obtain labor income. Again, our core results are quite robust.

ADDITIONAL TESTS. We carry out a number of more technical tests in Appendix A.3. They address some issues related to our measurements of income and inequality, the nature of our ESS sample, and the inclusion of fixed effects into the model. Our estimates show that our core conclusions remain valid under these alternatives.

5.2 PANEL EVIDENCE: UNITED KINGDOM

As discussed in Chapter 1, the availability of repeated observations of individual preferences allows us to construct stricter statistical tests. In a purely cross-sectional analysis we are unable to account for unobservable individual confounders, such as ability or motivation. Inasmuch as these are correlated with redistribution preferences, not accounting for them will likely overstate the importance of observed individual-level variables such as income. In the following pages, we describe a model where individual-specific unobservables are taken into account and where changes in redistribution preferences are a function of changing individual incomes and regional levels of inequality. We then extend our model to include individuals' crime fears, as a microlevel externality of inequality.

A further advantage of this analysis is that we can make some headway in tackling a major endogeneity issue that possibly affects the previous analysis: sorting. If one assumes that individuals move freely (and easily) in response to changes in their environment, one can envision a situation in which they completely sort themselves into regions based on their preferences. For our analysis, this raises the possibility that our respondents react to an increase in the local externalities associated with rising inequality by moving to a different region. While a complete model of the joint determination of preferences and the decision to move (or stay) is beyond the scope of the analysis here, we tackle this issue by making use of the longitudinal nature of our data. For each individual we know if he or she moved from one period to the next, and we can thus restrict our analysis to those respondents who did not move out of a given region over the course of our panel. It is noteworthy that only 16 percent of our sample is classified as movers, thus 84 percent (2,672 individuals) has stayed within a given region and was exposed to

---

[25] For the same reasons as those explained in the previous section of the book.

changing levels of regional inequality. It is this subset of individuals that we analyze in the following pages (but we also analyze our full sample in a robustness test).

5.2.1 Variable Definitions

REGIONAL INEQUALITY. In order to obtain a regional measure of inequality in the United Kingdom, we calculate the Gini index from BHPS data for 37 NUTS2 regions (based on annual net incomes for all households).[26] In order to maximize the sample size on which we base our Gini calculation (and because our data on redistribution preferences are not in yearly intervals) we use a three-year window of household incomes for each Gini by region and year. Standard errors of our measure of inequality are obtained via jackknifing (Karagiannis and Kovacevic, 2000). The models we estimate later will take into account that our inequality measure is based on estimates with limited precision.

FEAR OF CRIME. The BHPS offers us the opportunity to use a broader measure capturing individuals' fear of crime. We measure it via the extent to which they perceive threatening behavior in their neighborhood, ranging from disorderly conduct to vandalism and assault. The survey contains a number of items that capture such neighborhood issues. The first two are subjective assessments about one feeling safe and worrying about crime.[27] The following eight items capture (subjective) perceptions of neighborhood decay: the extent of graffiti in one's area, drunks on the street, teens hanging around, vandalism and property damage, incidence of racial insults, homes and cars being broken into, and violent attacks on persons.[28] Using multiple measures produces a more reliable estimate of

---

[26] In other words, we exploit the maximum available sample size when calculating regional Gini. In our statistical models the number of households is lower (due to selection criteria and missing data). Net household income is obtained via a tax simulation model. See Jenkins (2010) for more details.

[27] The exact item wordings are: "How safe do you feel walking alone in this area after dark?" with response options "Very safe, Fairly safe, A bit unsafe, Very unsafe, Never go out after dark;" and "Do you ever worry about the possibility that you, or anyone else who lives with you, might be the victim of crime?" with response options "No" and "Yes."

[28] The exact item wording is "Please look at this card and tell me how common or uncommon each of the following things is in your area:" "Homes broken into," "Cars broken into or stolen," "People attacked on the streets," "Vandalism and deliberate damage to property," "Drunks or tramps on the streets," "Teenagers hanging around in streets," "Graffiti on walls or buildings," "Insults or attacks to do with someone's race

individuals' fear of crime (e.g., Ansolabehere et al., 2008). Furthermore, they are available at several points in time (in three waves), a central element in our panel analysis later, where we investigate the role of changes of crime fears on changing preferences.[29]

Because we are not interested in each single issue, we argue that these can be summarized by an underlying (or latent) *fear of crime* variable. To do so, we estimate a mixed factor model (Quinn, 2004; Skrondal and Rabe-Hesketh, 2004), where we model an individual's response $y_{ijt}^{(c)}$ to item j ($j = 1, \ldots, 10$) in panel wave t ($t = 1, \ldots, 3$) as a function of fear of crime θ_{it}:

$$y_{ijt}^{(c)} = \mu_j + \lambda_j \theta_{it} + \psi_{jt} \tag{5.4}$$

Here, θ_{it} is an individual's crime fear at time t, μ_j and λ_j are item intercepts and loadings, respectively. Because each item is only an imperfect proxy for fear of crime, parts of the variation in individuals' responses are unrelated to crime fears. This residual variance is captured by ψ_{jt}. To set the scale of the neighborhood factor, the loading of the first item is fixed to 1.0.[30] Our results in Table 5.7 show that each item is significantly related to our crime variable θ: all loadings are of substantial magnitude and different from zero. Figures 4.6 and 4.7 show the distribution of individuals' crime fears by region.

5.2.2 Statistical Models

We start with a model of redistribution preferences of individual i in region j at time t, R_{ijt}^*.[31] We regress it on an individual's income distance from the national mean, denoted by $\tilde{v}_{it}$, regional income inequality, w_{jt}, and a number of individual and regional control variables, x_{ijt} using the following specification:

$$R_{ijt}^* = \alpha \tilde{v}_{it} + \beta w_{jt} + \gamma w_{jt} \tilde{v}_{it} + \delta' x_{ijt} + \xi_i + \zeta_j + \epsilon_{ijt}. \tag{5.5}$$

---

or colour." Response options were "Very common, Fairly common, Not very common, Not at all common."

[29] Items were asked in waves G, L, and Q.

[30] The Bayesian specification of the model is completed by assigning priors to all parameters. We use a "noninformative" Inverse Gamma prior for the variance of θ_i with shape and scale set to 0.001. We use normal priors for intercepts and loadings with prior mean zero and variance of 10; inverse gamma priors with shape = 1 and scale = 2 for residuals.

[31] As before, R_{ijt}^* is a latent variable generated by a threshold crossing mechanism $R_{ijt} = k$ if $\tau_{k-1} < R_{ijt}^* \tau_k$ (Albert and Chib, 1993).

TABLE 5.7 *Mixed measurement model for perception of neighborhood problems as function of latent crime fears; estimates and standard errors*

	Intercepts		Loadings	
	Est.	s.e.	Est.	s.e.
Feel unsafe	2.142	0.012	1.000[a]	
Crime worry	0.147[b]	0.007	1.084	0.070
Graffiti	1.903	0.009	1.629	0.071
Drunks	1.606	0.008	1.533	0.066
Teens	2.616	0.010	1.822	0.080
Vandalism	2.015	0.009	1.956	0.083
Racial insults	1.433	0.007	1.194	0.052
Homes broken into	2.105	0.009	1.634	0.070
Cars broken into	2.175	0.009	1.888	0.080
Attacks	1.517	0.007	1.386	0.059

Note: Based on 5,000 MCMC samples. Estimates are posterior means, standard errors refer to posterior standard deviations. Residual variances not shown.
[a]Fixed parameter
[b]Probit threshold

Here, the coefficients α and β capture the role of income distance and inequality, respectively, while the conditional (on income) effect of inequality is captured by γ. Coefficients for observed control variables are represented by δ. As in the previous section analyzing ESS data, in our alternative main model we include expected future income as one of our explanatory variables. Effects of unobserved individual-specific and time-constant characteristics (say, ability) are captured by ξ. Region-specific effects are captured by ζ_j.[32]

FEAR OF CRIME. To capture the effect of externalities of inequality on redistribution preferences, we extend our previous model and include fear of crime of individual i at time t, θ_{it}:

$$R_{ijt}^* = \alpha \tilde{v}_{it} + \beta w_{jt} + \gamma w_{jt} \tilde{v}_{it} + \delta' x_{ijt} + \lambda_1 \theta_{it} + \lambda_2 \theta_{it} \tilde{v}_{it} + \xi_i + \zeta_j + \epsilon_{ijt}.$$

$$(5.6)$$

All existing parameters of the model are unchanged. As before, we take into account regional and individual-specific effects. What is new are coefficients λ, which capture the effect of (changing) fear of crime. The

---

[32] Residuals ϵ_{ijt} are white noise. Random effects are distributed mean zero with estimated variance $\xi \sim N(0, \sigma_\xi^2)$. We assume that $\text{Cov}(\epsilon, \xi) = 0$.

main effect of fear of crime on preferences is captured by λ_1, which we expect to be positive. Coefficient λ_2 denotes the differential effect of fear for the rich. We expect λ_2 to be positive as well signifying that fear of crime matters more to the rich.

Thus a straightforward test of the relevance of fear of crime as a negative externality influencing redistribution preferences is if $\lambda(\lambda_1, \lambda_2) > 0$. More substantively, if externalities matter to preferences, we expect that their inclusion will reduce the size of the remaining income–inequality interaction (represented by γ). We estimate these models using Markov Chain Monte Carlo simulation.[33] We take uncertainty in our Gini estimates into account by estimating the model on repeated data sets, which represents the variation in Gini due to measurement error, and combining the final estimates. See Quinn and Martin (2002: 410) for a similar strategy.

5.2.3 Results

Our resulting estimates are displayed in Table 5.8. Before turning to our variables of interest we note that estimates of most other covariates are in the expected direction. As in the previous section and the previous chapters, specification (2) shows that our measure of expected future income has a large, negative and significant impact on redistribution preferences. Regarding the individual and regional controls, we can submit that women support redistribution more than men, as do union members and minorities. Education has a negative effect: individuals holding higher degrees are much less likely to opt for more government intervention in the economy. Interestingly, being unemployed has no statistically clear effect of preferences (which is all the more remarkable given the nature of our dependent variable).[34] In regions with higher levels of unemployment, support for redistribution is higher. In contrast, in regions with a higher share of foreign-born population individuals support redistribution less.

---

[33] We use "uninformative" priors to obtain results similar to maximum-likelihood based techniques. Priors for parameters are mean zero with variance 100. Priors for variances of random effects are inverse gamma with shape and scale 0.001. Thus our analysis does not use any "subjective" prior information, and results can be interpreted like classical estimates one would obtain in a maximum-likelihood based analysis.

[34] Note that this result is in line with the one reported in Stegmueller (2013a). Further note that, in contrast to most previous research, we explicitly account for individual unobservables.

TABLE 5.8 *Inequality, income distance, and redistribution prefer-ences in the United Kingdom, 1991–2007*

	(1)		(2)	
	Est.	s.e.	Est.	s.e.
Income distance	−0.110	0.020	−0.095	0.021
Inequality	0.958	0.171	0.982	0.169
Inequality × Income	0.226	0.059	0.167	0.060
Income expectations			−0.016	0.004
Controls				
Individual & regional[a]	Included		Included	
Random effects [variance]				
Individual	2.486	0.041	2.457	0.041
Region	0.061	0.014	0.060	0.013

Note: Estimates are posterior means, s.e. refers to posterior standard deviation. Multiple overimputation estimates taking into account measurement error in Gini estimates. Based on 10,000 MCMC samples. [a]Controls are age, gender, union membership, nonwhite indicator, unemployed, household size, education certificate, regional unemployment rate, regional GDP, and regional share of foreigners.

Turning to estimates of the effect of income and inequality, we find that both income and inequality matter for people's preferences. Individuals with incomes above the average prefer less redistribution. An increase in inequality is associated with an increase in support for redistribution (all else equal). We find a positive and significant interaction, indicating that an increase in inequality produces a larger preference change for richer individuals. As interpreting raw interaction coefficients can be mis-leading, especially in limited dependent variable models, a more intuitive picture is provided in Figure 5.2. It plots average predicted probabilities of support for redistribution at different levels of income in both high- and low-inequality regions (defined as regions in the tenth and ninetieth percentiles of the Gini distribution). Even though this analysis is stricter than our previous one (accounting for unobserved individual characteris-tics), Figure 5.2 shows a pattern remarkably similar to Figure 5.1. First, as expected, we find that as an individual's income increases with respect to the mean, the probability of supporting redistributive action by the state declines considerably. Second, we find that a change in regional income inequality (all else equal) affects the preferences of the poor very little. However, the picture for the rich is quite different: their support for redistribution is higher if they live in a region with higher levels of

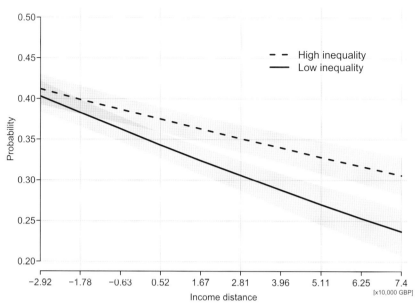

FIGURE 5.2 Predicted probability of support for redistribution as function of income distance and inequality; United Kingdom, 1991–2007

inequality. Consider someone with an income of 50,000 UK pounds above the mean. Her probability of supporting redistribution is 27 percent if she lives in a region with low inequality. All else equal, this figure rises to 33 percent if she lives in a highly unequal region.

We explore more specific quantities of interest in Table 5.9. We calculate first differences in average predicted probabilities of support for redistribution (that is, either "agree" or "strongly agree") contrasting regions with high and low inequality. As before, we define regions of low inequality as those at the tenth percentile of the Gini distribution, and as high-inequality regions those at the ninetieth percentile, and we define rich and poor respondents as those at the tenth and ninetieth percentile of the United Kingdom's income distribution (averaged over all years). Table 5.9 shows that, in contrast to our finding using ESS data, inequality matters for both the rich and the poor. However, in keeping with our central argument we find that an increase from low to high inequality (as defined earlier) matters much more to the rich: the increase in redistribution preferences among the poor is 1.9 percentage points, while for the rich it is twice as large at 3.8 percentage points.

TABLE 5.9 *Effect of inequality among rich and poor in the United Kingdom, 1991–2007*

| | First difference in predicted probability | | | |
	Est.	s.e.	95% CI	
Poor	1.85	0.57	0.76	2.89
Rich	3.81	0.56	2.75	4.84

Note: First differences in predicted probabilities of redistribution support in low-versus high-inequality regions. Calculated from 10,000 MCMC samples.

We now consider individual-level manifestations of externalities of inequality, that is, a model including individuals' (changing) crime fears. Our resulting parameter estimates, displayed in Table 5.10, show that fear of crime significantly affects preferences: The higher the fear, the higher the tendency to agree to more government intervention. We also find that the effect of fear tends to be larger for the rich. The confidence interval of these effects is bound away from zero, indicating that this finding is highly statistically reliable. Does fear of crime explain (part of) the conditional effect of inequality among the rich? It does. While its impact is far less dramatic compared to our results in the previous section, we still find the estimate of the income × inequality interaction reduced. In terms of the probability of redistribution support, the effect of inequality is reduced by 15 percent from 3.8 to 3.2 percentage points when accounting for fear of crime.

5.2.4 Robustness Checks

Table 5.11 presents results from several robustness checks. It displays first differences of average predicted probabilities of redistribution support among the rich (defined, once more, as those in the ninetieth percentile of the United Kingdom's income distribution, averaged over all years).

MOVERS. Because of our concerns about sorting, a robustness test specific to this analysis is the inclusion of "movers." As discussed earlier, we excluded from our analysis the 14 percent of individuals who moved at least once during the length of our panel. When comparing individuals who moved to "stayers," we find that the former have somewhat lower preferences for redistribution. The difference is small but statistically significant. Thus we expect our main findings to be weakened when includ-

TABLE 5.10 *Inequality, income, fear of crime, and redistribution preferences in the United Kingdom, 1991–2007*

	Est.	s.e.	95% CI	
Fear of crime	0.126	0.019	0.088	0.163
Fear of crime × income	0.038	0.011	0.016	0.060
Income distance	−0.075	0.021	−0.116	−0.032
Inequality	0.950	0.171	0.617	1.286
Income distance × Inequality	0.106	0.062	−0.017	0.228
Controls	Included			
Random effects [variance]				
Individual	2.445	0.042	2.364	2.531
Region	0.059	0.013	0.037	0.087

Note: N = 15,318. Estimates are posterior means, s.e. refers to posterior standard deviation. Multiple overimputation estimates taking into account measurement error in Gini estimates. Based on 10,000 MCMC samples.

TABLE 5.11 *Overview of robustness checks; first differences in probabilities for several specifications*

	Simple model		Model including fear			
	Gini		Fear		Gini	
Robustness tests	Est.	s.e.	Est.	s.e.	Est.	s.e.
(1) Movers	3.48	0.54	1.76	0.27	3.05	0.51
(2) Population density	3.52	0.56	1.87	0.28	3.24	0.59
(3) Regional social spending	3.27	0.58	1.85	0.30	2.57	0.70
(4) Social class	3.58	0.55	1.83	0.29	3.18	0.56
(5) Religion	3.60	0.58	1.89	0.29	3.28	0.57
(6) Skill specificity	2.79	0.62	1.99	0.29	2.56	0.62
(7) Ideology	3.02	0.55	1.75	0.27	2.70	0.57

Note: Calculated from 1,000 MCMC samples. Sample sizes are: 3,173 in specification (1), 2,609 in specification (6), 2,672 in remaining ones.

ing movers in our analysis. Our results in specification (1) in Table 5.11 show that our core finding still obtains under this specification, albeit, as expected, in somewhat weaker form.

POPULATION DENSITY. As an alternative way to account for possible sorting of individuals into neighborhoods (based on income, occupation, and preferences, e.g., Rodden, 2010: 322) we include a region's population density (data from Eurostat) in specification (2).[35] Our results still show the effects of inequality and fear of crime.

EXISTING SPENDING LEVELS. We argue in our analysis that redistribution policy is set at the national level and thus constitutes the focal point of individuals' redistribution preference formation. However, inasmuch as regions have autonomy in steering social spending, respondents might consider both national and regional redistribution policy and outcomes when deciding on their preferred amount of redistribution. To consider this possibility we include a measure of regional social spending at the level of the nine UK government office regions in specification (3). Table 5.11 shows that our results are robust to these effects.

SOCIAL CLASS AND RELIGION. We also add measures for religion and social class in specifications (4) and (5). Religion is a five-category variable representing Protestantism, Catholicism, other Christian denominations, other denominations, and "none." Social class is measured the same way as in our analysis earlier. Our core results is not substantively effected by these model changes.

SKILL SPECIFICITY. To address labor market risk arguments as in the previous analyses in this chapter, we include a measure of skill specificity calculated following Cusack et al. (2006) at the two-digit ISCO level. Specification (6) shows that controlling for individuals holding more or less specific skills explains part of their redistribution preferences. Nonetheless, our core finding is confirmed: the effect of inequality is larger among the rich and is (partly) explained by their fear of crime.

IDEOLOGY. In this data set we do not have a direct measure of ideology. Instead we use a respondents' stated party identification as a proxy for his or her ideological leanings. We create a four category variable that captures those who identify with Labor, the Conservatives, the Liberal Democrats, or another party (including "none"). Specification (7) shows that our core results are robust to the inclusion of this variable.

---

[35] In contrast to the analysis in the previous section we lack information on whether individuals live in an urban or rural area.

PART III

BEYOND INCOME: POPULATION HETEROGENEITY

6

Heterogeneity and Redistribution

This chapter examines a set of assumptions underlying most arguments about the importance of economic circumstances to political outcomes. We make three related points. First, we argue for an integration of material self-interest and other-regarding concerns. As was the case in previous parts of the book, in terms of the influence of relative income, we adopt a slightly modified version of the model proposed by Romer (1975) and Meltzer and Richard (1981). We also complement our understanding of economic material self-interest with an explicit assessment of the role of expected future income. Second, we argue for the importance of something that, for now, we will term "altruism." We will explain that we consider other-regarding preferences an important motivation for individuals. Moral benefits are derived from the support of redistribution, but, we will further argue, these moral benefits are inextricably dependent on the identity of the poor. Altruism is most relevant when the recipients of benefits are similar to those financing them. Third, we argue that the material benefits of redistribution dominate the preferences of the poor. The rich, on the other hand, can afford to be altruistic. Combining the preceding second and third points, we will show that group homogeneity magnifies (or limits) the importance of altruism for the rich. We finally show that the effects of this "parochial altruism" on the demand for redistribution are distinct from those emerging from the negative externalities of inequality.

In making this distinction about the influence of altruism and group homogeneity on the poor and the rich, the arguments in this chapter challenge some influential approaches to the politics of inequality. We will elaborate on this in the pages that follow, but we will make two general points here. The first relates to the role of altruism in the political economy literature while the second addresses population heterogeneity in Europe and the United States.

The political economy literature has generally been limited to relatively simple material self-interested motivations: an individual's position in the income distribution determines her preferences for redistribution. Most political economy arguments (one could, in fact, say most comparative politics arguments) start from this initial assumption and address other factors in more complex causal chains (the role of parties, labor market institutions, the nature of government, federalism, international factors, etc.). An increasing amount of convincing evidence indicates, however, that other-regarding concerns are an important motivation for individuals. As argued by Alesina and Giuliano, political economy models "can accommodate altruism, i.e., a situation in which one agent cares also about the utility of somebody else. But altruism is not an unpredictable 'social noise' to be randomly sprinkled over individuals" (2011: 94). Altruistic concerns need to be systematized into predictable political economy hypotheses. This section of the book represents an effort in that direction.

The future of the welfare state has come under increasing pressure from immigration and ethnic heterogeneity. A comprehensive welfare state, the argument goes, was possible in Western European countries because of homogenous societies. More ethnically heterogeneous societies are expected to display lower levels of support for redistribution (see, for example, Alesina and Glaeser, 2004; Freeman, 2009). Migration has produced an "Americanization"[1] of European welfare politics by making the poor less likely to support redistribution (even though they economically benefit from it) because of noneconomic concerns (cultural, values, etc.) related to population heterogeneity. The analysis presented in the following pages will challenge these arguments. The significant differences in support for redistribution in Western Europe and the United States have little to do with the poor (who consistently support redistribution regardless of population heterogeneity) and a lot to do with the altruism of the rich.

---

[1] This term has been used by Freeman (2009: 61), who argued that migration "has reduced the political clout of those social strata that have traditionally been the chief source of support for welfare state development, and it has contributed to the erosion of the political consensus on which the welfare state rests. It has led to the Americanization of European welfare politics."

6.1 THE ARGUMENT

This chapter's theoretical framework attempts to integrate three distinct approaches to the formation of preferences for redistribution. As in previous parts of the book, the first one relies on the idea that the level of redistribution preferred by a given individual is fundamentally a function of her material self-interest. The second approach maintains that other-regarding concerns matter. Altruistic individuals derive utility not only from their own material gains but also from those of other people. The third approach emphasizes identity and in-group solidarity, arguing that ethnic, national, or religious fractionalization reduces overall support for redistribution.

This chapter will consolidate insights from these three approaches into one argument and focus on the relationship between in-group identity and altruism. In the following pages, we will explore in more detail these general frameworks and elucidate this chapter's claims. In essence, we argue for the importance of nonmaterial factors but propose that (1) they matter most to those in less material need and (2) they are conditional on the identity of the poor. Relative income, we will argue, sets the material baseline from which the influence of altruism and identity emerges.

6.1.1 Material Self-Interest

Little needs to be written at this stage about our general approach to material self-interest. As in previous sections of the book, the material baseline for our argument proposes that a significant determinant of redistribution preferences is the difference between an individual's income and the mean in her country. The lower below the mean the income is, the more an individual gains from redistribution and the stronger we expect her support for it to be. The higher above the mean, the more an individual loses from redistribution and the weaker we expect her support to be. Also as before, we argue that expectations about future income can be as influential in determining the demand for redistribution as present income. In this section of the book, we continue to treat expected future income as a good proxy for concerns for insurance, mobility, and risk.

6.1.2 Altruism

The possibility that other-regarding concerns influence redistribution preferences has received increasing amounts of attention in the recent political economy literature (see, e.g., Shayo, 2009; Lupu and Pontusson, 2011;

Cavaillé and Trump, 2015). There is neural evidence that individuals have a dislike for unequal distributions, independent from social image or potential reciprocity motivations. Tricomi et al. (2010) use functional magnetic resonance imaging to test directly for the presence of inequality-averse social preferences in the human brain. In laboratory experiments, individuals have been shown to have concerns for the welfare of others (see, for example, Fehr and Gächter, 2000; Charness and Rabin, 2002). A number of alternative models have been presented to analyze different kinds of other-regarding concerns (for reviews, see Fehr and Schmidt, 2006a; DellaVigna, 2009). As we have shown in the previous sections of this book, support for redistribution is widespread in Western Europe. We will document later that this support extends into high-income groups whose support for redistribution could not possibly be motivated by short-term income maximization not only in Europe but, more important, also in the United States. Altruism constitutes one plausible reason why affluent individuals might support redistribution even though its effect is to reduce their disposable income and their share of total income.

The dimension of altruism that is most relevant to this chapter's argument pertains to the willingness of individuals to make sacrifices in order to realize welfare gains for those in society who are worse off. The kind of altruism we are interested in, therefore, is not characterized by unconditional kindness (which would imply that an individual's utility increases as the material gains received by any other individual increase). It is a conditional form of altruism that has often been defined as *positive inequity aversion*.[2] Fehr and Schmidt argue that an "individual is inequity averse if, in addition to his material self-interest, his utility increases if the allocation of material payoffs [in his society] becomes more equitable" (2006a: 620).[3]

6.1.3 Identity and In-Group Altruism

We also build on a significant recent literature exploring the role of identity on the formation of preferences for redistribution. There are material self-interest reasons why identity could matter to redistribution

---

[2] For a related analysis focusing on trade policy preferences that looks at both positive and negative inequity aversion, see Lü et al. (2010).

[3] Some of these inequity aversion arguments can be traced back to the pioneering contribution by Adams (1965) on inequity in social exchanges. The main intuition in this social psychology work is that an individual's social behavior is affected by feelings about the justice in her relationship to others.

preferences. Group homogeneity could promote information sharing, the identification of free riders, and communication.[4] In this chapter, however, we emphasize the connection between altruism and group homogeneity. Much of the literature on altruism emphasizes that other-regarding considerations are bounded by racial, ethnic, or religious cleavages or, in other words, take the form of "in-group solidarity" or "parochial altruism."[5] Habyarimana et al. aptly summarize this line of argument by recognizing that individuals may attach positive utility to the welfare of fellow ethnic group members but no utility (or negative utility) to the welfare of non-group members (2007: 710).

There is a clear relationship between this identity approach and the altruism arguments analyzed in the previous section. While positive inequity aversion implies that an individual's utility will increases as the poor benefit from more redistribution, identity arguments emphasize that this may be dependent on who the poor are. Perceiving the poor as different, these arguments suggest, detracts from altruism. A significant literature (see, for example, Easterly and Levine, 1997) find that ethnically fragmented countries provide fewer public services. And there can be little doubt that racism has served as an obstacle to redistributive politics in the American case (Luttmer, 2001; Alesina and Glaeser, 2004; Gilens, 2009).

While the arguments about self-interest presented in the previous section require that support for redistribution will decrease with income, conceptions of altruism and identity mean there are "moral" benefits attached to the promotion of equality within in-group members. The implications of these arguments are reflected in panel (a) of Figure 6.1. The lines represent the relationship expected in models proposing that altruism promotes redistribution (for example, Alesina and Glaeser, 2004). In the figure, all individuals (poor and rich alike), obtain moral benefits from supporting redistribution when group homogeneity is high, which means that altruism pushes preferences for redistribution upward. More concretely, the redistribution preferences of an individual with low income v_i in a low-homogeneity region h_r, denoted $R(v_i, h_r)$ are much lower than the redistribution preferences of an individual with the same level of income in a high-homogeneity region h'_r, denoted $R(v_i, h'_r)$. The same increase in redistribution preferences in regions with high homogeneity is expected of an individual with high income v'_i in Figure 6.1.

---

[4] For an analysis of the mechanisms underlying these effects, see Habyarimana et al. (2007).
[5] For an analysis of parochial altruism, see Bernhard et al. (2006).

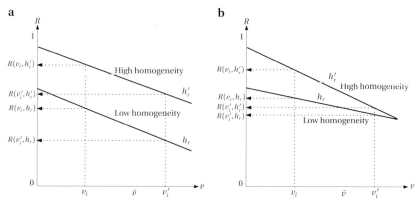

FIGURE 6.1 Population homogeneity (h), income (v) and support for redistribution (R)

Alternatively, some of the existing literature posits that ethnic, religious, or national cleavages matter more to the preferences of the poor than to the preferences of the affluent or, in other words, that "identity politics" diverts the poor from the pursuit of material self-interest. This effect is shown in panel (b) of Figure 6.1 with, again, a lower line for the scenario with less group homogeneity (h_r). A well-known example of these arguments is its application to the United States and the contention that second-dimension issues (particularly cultural and social ones) outweigh economic ones for the American working class.[6] More comparatively, the important contribution to the political economy of identity formation in Shayo (2009) follows a similar logic.[7] In these arguments, altruism does not matter. But, to the extent that these second-dimension concerns are correlated with population heterogeneity, they would lead us to expect that the poor in heterogenous regions have weaker redistribution preferences (not because of lack of altruism, but because they are distracted from their material self-interest). Redistribution preferences would then converge as income grows (as suggested by Figure 6.1). In this framework, the redistribution preferences of an individual with low income v_i in a low-homogeneity region h_r, again denoted $R(v_i, h_r)$, are lower than the redis-

---

[6] See Frank (2004) and the critique in Bartels (2006).

[7] Although not dealing directly with ethnicity, Shayo's theoretical model emphasizes two identity dimensions: economic class and nationality. As a result of status differences, the poor are more likely than the rich to identify with the nation rather than their class. Because they take group interests into account, moreover, the poor who identify with the nation are less supportive of redistribution than the poor who identify with their class.

tribution preferences of an individual with the same level of income in a high homogeneity region h'_r, denoted $R(v_i, h'_r)$. Because second-dimension issues outweigh economic ones for the poor (and these cultural and social issues are affected by population heterogeneity), their preferences diverge when homogeneity is low. In this arguments the rich, however, are not as affected by second-dimension issues. The redistribution preferences of an individual with high income v'_i in a low-heterogeneity region $R(v'_i, h_r)$ and in a high-heterogeneity region $R(v'_i, h'_r)$ do not differ by much in Figure 6.1.

6.1.4 Altruism: Short Time-Horizon and High Stakes for the Poor

The preceding sections suggest that both material self-interest and altruism should matter to redistribution preferences. To integrate the arguments about these two distinct dimensions, however, we will argue that a hierarchy of preferences exists. As we did in Part II of this book, we propose that poor people value redistribution for its material consequences. Once again, the redistributive preferences of the rich, on the other hand, are less significantly affected by their immediate material self-interest. For the rich, altruism can become more relevant.

As was the case in our analysis of the negative externalities of inequality, we conceive the relevance of altruism to be affected by both time horizons and stakes. As before, we argue that the poor have shorter-term motivations than the rich and that the relative importance of receiving benefits is greater for the poor than the relative importance of paying taxes is for the rich. And again we expect that, as the stakes of redistribution decline, less immediate and lower stakes considerations related to the moral benefits of altruism will matter more. The relationship between altruism and population heterogeneity will therefore be more important to the rich.[8]

An alternative but similar approach to altruism is possible. Our expectations are compatible with an argument proposing that the moral benefits of altruism are a luxury good that will be more likely to be consumed when the need for other basic goods has been satisfied. The

---

[8] Once again we emphasize here that the underlying logic for our argument about altruism and identity concerns a distinction between the *presently* rich and the poor. As in our analysis of inequality, we argue that (while the effects of expected income are not dependent on present income) noneconomic factors (defined as those not directly affecting the income/tax/transfer nexus) affect the poor and the rich differently.

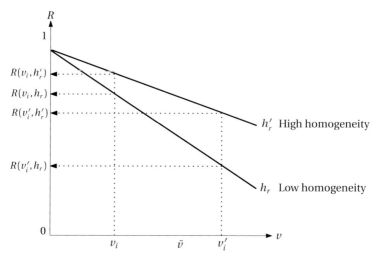

FIGURE 6.2 Population homogeneity (h), income (v) and support for redistribution (R) in our argument

idea that altruistic concerns will be trumped by material ones for the poor is consistent with previous political economy work on material and nonmaterial incentives. Levitt and List construct a model in which individuals maximize their material gains but, when wealth-maximizing action has a moral cost, they deviate from that action to one with a lower moral cost (2007: 157). More importantly, they also argue that, as the stakes of the game rise, wealth concerns will increase in importance relative to moral concerns. For us higher stakes (i.e., the poor's need for the benefits of redistribution) increase the importance of relative income as a determinant of redistribution preferences. Lower stakes for the rich (there are material costs to increasing redistribution, but for the rich they do not involve dramatic consequences comparable to those for the poor) mean that altruistic concerns will be more important.

The implications of this chapter's argument are summarized in Figure 6.2. We expect population heterogeneity to be associated with less support for redistribution. Because we argue that for the poor altruism is trumped by material incentives, redistribution preferences converge regardless of group homogeneity as income declines. We expect group homogeneity to promote altruism only for the rich. In Figure 6.2, the redistribution preferences of an individual with low income v_i (regardless of her expected future income) in a low-homogeneity region h_r, denoted $R(v_i, h_r)$, and in a high-homogeneity region $R(v_i, h'_r)$ do not differ by much. In contrast, we expect more homogeneity to promote altruistic concerns only for the rich (again regardless of their expected future income), so that redistribution preferences of a rich individual in a low-homogeneity region $R(v'_i, h_r)$ differ starkly from those in high-homogeneity regions $R(v'_i, h'_r)$.

In the analysis to be developed in the next chapter, we follow an approach that is quite similar to the one we undertook when exploring the negative externalities of inequality. We test our theoretical alternatives by considering the effects of income distance at the individual level and of population heterogeneity on the macro level. Income distance is meant to capture the effects of present material self-interested preferences and the macro-measure of heterogeneity the influence of in-group altruism. The first expectation is that income distance will be a significant determinant of redistribution preferences. We also expect, however, that decreasing levels of heterogeneity will make the rich (much more than the poor) more supportive of redistribution.

Exploring the importance of altruism and group heterogeneity by looking at the interaction of income distance (at the individual level) and heterogeneity (at the macrolevel) is a direct test of this chapter's hypotheses. It is, however, an approach that is dependent on a particular conception of altruism. There are two ways of thinking about altruism or other-regarding preferences in the political economy literature. The first analyzes altruism as an individual characteristic (a personality trait[9] or "taste for giving"[10]). The second one understands other-regarding concerns to be affected by a "situational" logic. Previously in this chapter, we have referred to one of the most common expressions of this approach: "in group solidarity" or "parochial altruism." While we accept that the role of altruism as an individual characteristic in determining redistribution preferences may be an important one, we emphasize a situational approach in this section of the book. We agree that, for many economic outcomes, personality measures may be as predictive as cognitive ones (see, for example, Almlund et al., 2011) but find this compatible with our main argument. It is certainly possible that there are some individuals that

---

[9] In this research altruism has often taken the form of a self-reported measure (the Self-Report Altruism, SRA, Scale) aggregating different items capturing an individual's engagement in altruistic behaviors (pushing a stranger's car out of the snow, giving money to a charity, etc.). See, for example, the research on altruistic personality by Rushton et al. (1981).

[10] See, for example, Andreoni (1989, 1990).

have more altruistic personalities than others. But this would not affect the general implications of our argument unless these personality types were highly correlated with individual income and ethnic or racial macro-heterogeneity (and we have no reason, theoretical or empirical, to believe this is the case).

We will make a final observation about the theoretical claims. As mentioned in previous chapters, an influential literature in comparative political economy has argued that redistribution preferences are affected by the demand for insurance against an uncertain future (Iversen and Soskice, 2001; Moene and Wallerstein, 2001; Rehm, 2009). A related set of arguments connects ethnic identity to risk. The basic intuition in this approach is that some identity groups may be linked with particular profiles regarding risk, mobility, etc. (as in Piketty, 1995 or Benabou and Ok, 2001). Consequently, in segmented labor markets where the poor are different from the rich, the rich may feel less vulnerable to risk. To the extent that it is possible, we will try to address these concerns empirically later (by introducing an explicit measure of risk into the analysis). However, as argued by Alt and Iversen (2017) in a recent contribution, arguments about altruism and social "distance" and arguments about insurance in segmented labor markets have very similar empirical implications (even if based on very different microfoundations).[11] The analysis to be developed in the following pages will not be able to fully resolve this issue.

6.2 PRELIMINARY ANALYSIS

We have argued above that rich individuals in heterogeneous societies will be less likely to have other-regarding motivations and therefore will tend to support redistribution less than rich individuals in homogeneous societies. In this section, we provide an introduction to what we mean by "heterogeneity" as well as a series of intuitive and illustrative figures that illuminate the relationships of interest for our arguments about income, population homogeneity and redistribution preferences.

We will use two different sources of data in our exploration of the effects of heterogeneity on redistribution (see details in Chapter 1). As was the case in Chapter 4, we begin by analyzing regional data from the

[11] A similar point could be made about the argument relating income and ethnic identity in Huber (2017). We come back to this issue in the next chapter.

European Social Survey (ESS). Our sample once again covers 129 regions in 14 countries between 2002 and early 2009.[12] We then use data from the General Social Survey (GSS) covering three decades (from 1978 to 2010). We limit our population to those who are of working age (20–65), not currently in full-time education. After removing individuals with missing values on covariates our sample consists of 19,025 individuals.

We summarized the ESS and GSS measures of relative income and redistribution preferences in Chapter 1, and readers should return to the description in those pages to get an intuitive sense of the data. Moreover, in the previous section we used the ESS data to present a figure (Figure 4.2) with a more concrete first illustration of the two things our argument is about: the existence of regional variation in support for redistribution among the rich and the poor. The figure captured the average level of support (i.e., the mean of the five-point scale) for redistribution in each of the regions in the ESS sample. First among the rich (those with household incomes 30,000 PPP-adjusted 2005 US dollars above the mean, the ninetieth percentile in the sample's income distribution) and then among the poor (with household incomes 25,000 PPP-adjusted 2005 US dollars below the country-year mean, the tenth percentile).

We now can do the same with our American data. As a reminder, we capture redistribution preferences using a commonly used measure (e.g., Alesina and Angeletos, 2005), available repeatedly in the GSS. It presents respondents with the following statement: "the government should reduce income differences between the rich and the poor, perhaps by raising the taxes of wealthy families or by giving income assistance to the poor." Answers are recorded on a seven-point scale, with labeled endpoints "1 – should" and "7 = should not," which we reverse for ease of interpretation. Figure 6.3 represents our first effort to illustrate the preferences for redistribution among the rich and poor in the United States. The rich are those at the ninetieth percentile of the income distribution in our GSS sample (around $53,000 above the mean in constant dollars), and the poor are those at the tenth percentile (around $37,000 below the mean).

As was the case in the previous analysis of Western European and British data, Figure 6.3 strongly suggest the existence of a general relative-income effect in the United States. By looking at the two panels, we can easily see that the support for redistribution of the poor is almost always

---

[12] For a detailed list of countries and years included, see Table 4.1 on page 95.

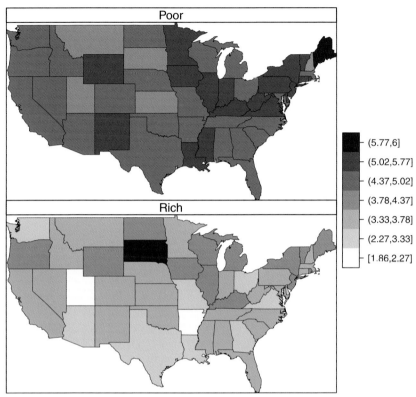

FIGURE 6.3 Preferences for redistribution among rich and poor, GSS

higher than that of the rich (the only exception is South Dakota, where support for redistribution is high for both groups and unusually so for the affluent). While in all states the poor's average support for redistribution is close to 5 in our 7-point reverse scale, the average for the rich is around 1.3. As was the case with the European data, a remarkable amount of regional variation is contained in Figure 6.3. The lowest support for redistribution among the rich (lower than 3 on the 7-point scale) can be found in Arkansas, Utah, Delaware, and Louisiana. On the other hand, the highest support for redistribution among the rich (higher than 4 on the 7-point scale) are in Maine, Vermont, Iowa, Washington DC, and (as mentioned before) South Dakota. For the poor, the lowest support for redistribution (around 4 on the 7-point scale) can be found in Utah, Montana, and New Hampshire. The poor's highest support (more than 5.5) is in Vermont, Maine, and Washington DC. Perhaps more relevantly for the arguments in this chapter, the biggest differences in the redistribution preferences of rich and poor (more than 2 on the 7-point scale) are in Maine, Utah, Virginia, Louisiana, Delaware, and Arkansas.

6.2.1 Heterogeneity and Redistribution

There are many types of heterogeneity in a society. Our choice of the particular measures of heterogeneity to be used in the analysis is determined by their importance to support for redistribution.

Heterogeneity as Immigration

With a changing societal composition due to increasing inflows of immigrants in the last decades, perhaps the most obvious challenge facing European welfare states is connected to this particular kind of population heterogeneity. It is impossible to ignore the importance of immigration in the Western European debate whether one looks at academic research, media reports, political debates or public opinion. Many Western European governments have been under pressure to provide welfare benefits only to their native population (De Koster et al., 2013) but immigration poses a challenge especially to Social Democratic parties, who are faced with a "progressive dilemma" (Kymlicka, 2015): how to preserve a comprehensive welfare state and create a multicultural society without losing public support, especially in times of economic austerity (see, for example, Jurado et al., 2013).[13]

There are several ways in which immigration and redistribution preferences are connected. Individual attitudes toward immigration can be affected by economic and non-economic (cultural) factors. On the one hand, a number of scholars show that economic factors affect preferences toward immigration (Scheve and Slaughter, 2001; Mayda, 2006; O'Rourke and Sinnott, 2006; Hanson et al., 2007; Facchini and Mayda, 2012; Ortega and Polavieja, 2012; Malhotra et al., 2013). Three facets of this economic approach should be distinguished. There is first a labor market competition argument. Individuals are expected to oppose immigration of workers with similar skills to their own (which would compete with them for jobs and underbid their wages)

---

[13] On the other hand, some populist Right parties have taken up "welfare chauvinism" as a way to appeal to poor voters (see, for example, De Koster et al., 2013). We return to the role played by redistribution preferences on voting for Left and populist parties in the next section of the book.

but support immigrants with different skill levels (who would increase competitiveness and lower the prices of the products and services they consume). There is then a fiscal burden argument. Immigrants are considered potential welfare beneficiaries that compete for limited fiscal benefits. They are believed to have lower education and employment levels, and a potentially higher reliance (without equivalent contributions) on welfare benefits, than natives. More immigration could therefore lead to lower support for redistribution because of the increasing costs of the welfare system (Burgoon et al., 2012). And there is also a compensation argument, proposing that immigration would lead to higher support for redistribution (rather than less). Some studies examine whether immigration-induced diversity actually contributes to higher support for redistribution because natives seek to be compensated for the higher economic risks of income loss or unemployment (see Van Oorschot and Uunk, 2007; Finseraas, 2008b; Van Oorschot, 2008; Burgoon et al., 2012).

On the other hand, several studies emphasize the role of noneconomic factors, especially cultural ones, over immigration attitudes (Citrin et al., 1997; Burns and Gimpel, 2000; Hainmueller and Hiscox, 2007, 2010). These authors argue that preferences are driven by cultural factors, and economic interests do not play as significant a role. The evidence so far, however, has not been conclusive. Hainmueller and Hiscox (2007) find that the link between education and attitudes toward immigrants is driven largely by differences among individuals in cultural values and beliefs. In contrast to less-educated respondents, more-educated individuals are less racist and value cultural diversity, and they are more likely to believe that immigration leads to benefits for the host country overall. But a number of findings in the aforementioned studies indicate immigration preferences are shaped by economic self-interest: anti-immigrant sentiment can arise among citizens who are concerned about competing for jobs with immigrants willing to work for lower wages (and under worse conditions) or about concerns with welfare benefit competition. Analyzing immigration specifically, Malhotra et al. (2013) find that economic factors trump cultural ones (concerns about labor market competition are more important for individuals than those concerning cultural identities).

As we have indicated earlier, our argument is quite specific about the role of immigration. We propose that any economic implication of immigration will be contained in the individual relative income effect while any noneconomic implication will be in-group altruism related and thus more significant to the rich. Following this line of reasoning, our analysis of ESS data uses a measure of the share of foreign-born population in each region.[14]

We hasten to add that the measure of heterogeneity used for our ESS analysis is not ideal. As should be clear from our argument above, we are conceptually interested in how different the poor (as potential beneficiaries of redistributive policies) are from the majority population. While it is reasonable to expect foreign-born individuals to be concentrated among the poor in most European countries, an ideal measure would capture this concentration directly. If we were interested in the level of heterogeneity at the national level (instead of the regional level), it would be possible to use the ESS surveys to assess the percentage of self-defined foreign-born individuals below the income mean. This survey-based measure of national share of foreign-born population among the poor would in fact be highly correlated with a national measure of the stocks of foreign-born population.[15] Because the regional number of foreign-born individuals below the mean income (whether using the ESS surveys or EU-LFS data) is very low, we cannot follow this strategy. We consider the benefits of regional data (both in terms of being the appropriate level for the altruism-identity nexus and of maximizing the amount of macro variation) to outweigh the costs of assuming that foreign-born individuals are concentrated among the poor in these regions. But we are able to produce a better measure for our American GSS analysis, as we explain later.

Heterogeneity as Race

The importance of race in debates about redistribution in the United States can hardly be overstated. For arguments about population heterogeneity and support for the welfare state (as the one in this chapter) it would indeed be strange to consider anything but racial diversity as our first port of call. Race permeates politics in America. In the words of King and Smith, in all policy arenas, ranging from employment to housing, from immigration to education, debates in the United States are dominated by race and vulnerable to the criticism of being either race-targeted or race insensitive (2011: 13). Or, in the more pessimistic words of legal scholar and civil rights activist Derrick Bell, "racism is an integral, permanent, and indestructible component of this society" (1992: ix).

---

[14] See a more detailed explanation of this measure in the next chapter.
[15] Rueda (2018) finds the correlation coefficient between these two measures to be .80. He uses the stocks of foreign-born population from the OECD International Migration Outlook 2012 statistical annex Table A.4.

A number of influential contributions in political economy have emphasized the relationship between racial diversity and decreasing levels of support for redistribution. Gilens convincingly shows that most Americans believe that the government should help the poor and even that this help should include cash assistance. He argues, however, that racial attitudes (particularly perceptions of African Americans as lazy and welfare recipients as undeserving) are "central elements in generating public opposition to welfare" (Gilens, 2009: 92).[16]

In a similar vein, Alesina and Glaeser (2004) argue that ethnic fractionalization is consistently associated with less support for redistribution not only in the United States but also in other industrialized democracies. The logic is perhaps best summarized by Alesina et al.:

> Racial discord plays a critical role in determining beliefs about the poor. Since minorities are highly over-represented amongst the poorest Americans, any income-based redistribution measures will redistribute particularly to minorities. The opponents of redistribution have regularly used race based rhetoric to fight left-wing policies. Across countries, racial fragmentation is a powerful predictor of redistribution. Within the US, race is the single most important predictor of support for welfare. America's troubled race relations are clearly a major reason for the absence of an American welfare state (2001: 4).[17]

It is important to emphasize that the crucial variable of interest in this literature is not population heterogeneity per se, but rather the coincidence of poverty and minority status. In Alesina and Glaeser's words, the focus is on whether "there are significant numbers of minorities among the poor," in which case "the majority population can be roused against transferring money to people who are different from themselves" (2004: 134). This concern very much affects our choice of the main heterogeneity measure in our analyses later. When analyzing redistribution preferences in the United States, we use the share of the African American population receiving welfare in each state. Our choice of heterogeneity measure follows Luttmer (2001), who uses race-specific welfare recipiency rates to explore whether support for the welfare state is not only affected by

---

[16] Other authors, on the other hand, would argue that race is not necessarily related to the demand for redistribution in the United States. Most notably, in a recent and influential contribution Cramer (2016) argues that rural consciousness (and not race) is the main factor in the identity politics emphasized earlier.

[17] But see a more recent contribution (Hersh and Nall, 2016) that finds income-based voting to be less important than racial context.

racial group loyalty but also by exposure to welfare recipients.[18] The logic behind our choice of measure is clear. The higher the number of out-group members receiving benefits, the less likely in-group members will be to support redistribution (because the identity of the poor contributes to a decline of the moral benefits of altruism).[19] Our measure also provides a connection with the findings by Hersh and Nall (2016), who, using geocoded registration records and precinct election returns, find the correlation between income and partisanship to be strong in heavily black areas of the Old South and other areas with a history of racialized poverty, but weaker elsewhere, including in urbanized areas of the South. They argue this shows the primacy of race over income, while we will emphasize the importance of heterogeneity within the poor.

6.2.2 Regional Heterogeneity in Western Europe and the United States

Figure 6.4 reflects the average regional levels of foreign-born population in our Western European sample. The figure makes clear the location of some regions with very high levels of heterogeneity. Foreign-born populations surpass the 30 percent share in London, West Sweden, South Sweden, Ticino (in Switzerland), Lake Geneva (also in Switzerland), Brussels-Capital in Belgium, and Île de France. Some regions in Western Europe have very low levels of heterogeneity. In the figure, the share of the population that is foreign born is less than 5 percent in some regions in Finland (North, East and West Finland) and Portugal (Alentejo and Norte), but also in the UK (North East England and Wales) or Spain (Extremadura and Asturias).

Perhaps more importantly, the figure also illustrates a high degree of within country cross-regional variation in the levels of foreign-born population. Both Spain and the UK have similar levels of *national* foreign-born populations (around 8.5 percent). These national levels, however, hide dramatic regional differences. As mentioned earlier, some of the regions with the highest levels of heterogeneity are in these two countries (London, Madrid, or the Valencian Region). But so are too some of

---

[18] Of course the rate of welfare recipiency among African Americans is determined in part by the characteristics of welfare program (e.g., eligibility criteria and sanction strictness). We analyze this issue in more detail in the next chapter.

[19] In the more systematic analysis in the next chapter, we also analyze the effects of heterogeneity defined more widely (as state-level share of African Americans in the population), and we do examine in more detail the relationship between these measures.

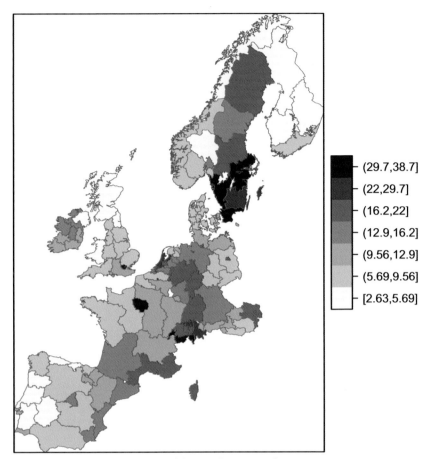

FIGURE 6.4 Average share of foreign-born population in Western Europe

the regions with the lowest levels of heterogeneity (North East England, Wales, Extremadura, or Asturias).

Figure 6.5 turns our attention to the equally important degree of temporal variation within West European regions. The shares of foreign-born population increase dramatically in some regions from 2002 to 2008. The average wave-to-wave change is greatest in three regions in Sweden (Stockholm, East Middle Sweden, and North Middle Sweden), one region in France (Île de France), in most of Ireland (all regions experience around a 4 percent average increase), and some regions in Spain (Aragon, Catalonia, Madrid, Valencian Region, and Murcia). Some regions, on the other hand, experience significant *decreases*. The most dramatic declines

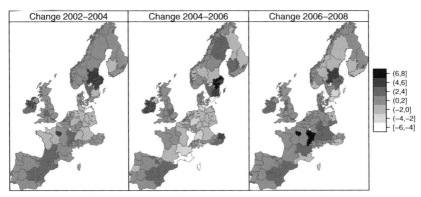

FIGURE 6.5 Change in share of foreign-born population in Western Europe

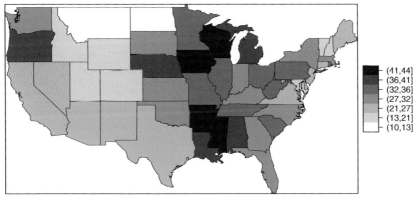

FIGURE 6.6 Average share of African American population on welfare in the United States, 1972–2008

take place in Germany (especially Mecklenburg Vorpommern, Saarland, Brandenburg, and Nordrhein-Westfalen) and France (Méditerranée and Nord Pas-de-Calais).

When looking at state-level heterogeneity in the United States, averaged over the entire period under analysis, the kinds of patterns a casual observer would expect emerge from Figure 6.6. The share of the African American population receiving welfare is more than 40 percent in Louisiana, Iowa, Mississippi, Wisconsin, and Arkansas. The share of the African American population receiving welfare, however, is less than 18 percent in Vermont, Utah, New Hampshire, Montana, and North Dakota.

For the analysis that we will develop in the next chapter, however, these state-level averages (which are influenced by a number of state-

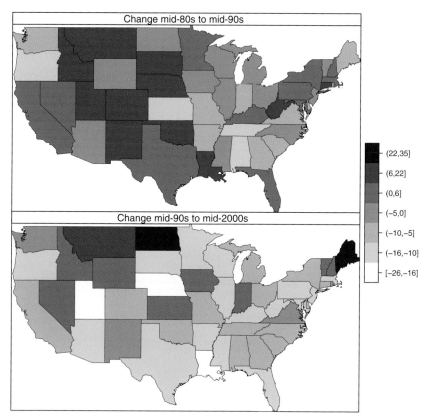

FIGURE 6.7   Change in share of African American population on welfare

specific factors) are not as important as the within-state temporal variation we can observe in Figure 6.7. Unlike the ESS data (limited to one decade, the 2000s), the GSS allows us to analyze a longer time period (from 1976 to 2008). We present this within-state temporal evolution by disaggregating it into changes from the mid-1980s to the 1990s and changes from the mid-1990s to the mid-2000s. In the first period (the upper panel), the greatest increases in the share of the African American population receiving welfare took place in Oklahoma, Louisiana, Utah, West Virginia, Montana, and South Dakota. All these states experienced increases of more than ten percentage points (and in Montana and South Dakota, more than fifteen points). The greatest decreases in the share of the African American population receiving welfare (more than 10 percent) took place in Alabama, Tennessee, Kansas, and Oregon. In the period from the mid-1990s to the mid-2000s (the lower panel in Figure 6.7), changes were more moderate (as indicated by the lighter colors when comparing the upper and the lower panels). Only three states experienced increases greater than 7 percent in the share of African Americans receiving welfare: Montana, Maine, and North Dakota (but these last two states had extreme increases of more than 20 percent). The greatest decreases in the share of the African American population receiving welfare (more than 15 percent) took place in Arizona, South Dakota, Louisiana, Nebraska, and Utah.

7

Analysis of Heterogeneity

To test the argument made in the previous chapter, we will examine the effects of income distance at the individual level and of the macrolevel of heterogeneity (while controlling for expected future income and a number of other factors, including fear of crime). As in other parts of the book, our first expectation is that income distance will be a significant determinant of redistribution preferences. We also expect, however, that increasing levels of regional heterogeneity will make the rich less likely to support redistribution.

7.1 CROSS-SECTIONAL EVIDENCE: EUROPE

As in Chapter 5, we use data from the European Social Survey (ESS). We select countries who participated in at least two rounds (to obtain usable regional sample sizes) and that provide consistent regional identifiers over time. As in Part II, we limit our analyses to surveys collected between September 2002 and January 2009. Thus, our data covers 129 regions in 14 countries: Austria, Belgium, Germany, Denmark, Spain, Finland, France, Great Britain, Ireland, Netherlands, Norway, Portugal, Sweden, and Switzerland, surveyed between 2002 and early 2009.[1]

7.1.1 Variable Definitions

The definition of variables included in the models to be developed later follows our description in Section 5.1.1. What is new here is our measure

---

[1] For a detailed list of countries and years included, see Table 4.1 on page 95.

of heterogeneity. We measure regional-level heterogeneity as the share of foreign-born individuals among the total population. We calculate yearly shares of foreign-born using information from the European Union Labor Force Survey (EU-LFS). The EU-LFS is a large household sample survey providing quarterly information on social characteristics and labor market outcomes of (noninstitutionalized) households and its members in European Union member states. Individuals are defined as foreign-born if they were born in a country different from the one they are currently living in.[2] Note that this implies a wider notion of heterogeneity than a measure based on citizenship because the number of foreign-born outnumbers the number of foreign-born citizens. Our earliest yearly observation available to use based on EU-LFS is from 2004.[3] In order to use all available individual-level survey data, we interpolate values for 2002 using a weighted combination of a linear and quadratic region-time trends (see Appendix A.4 for details).

7.1.2 Statistical Specifications

As in the previous part of this book, we model redistribution preferences as a function of income distance, population heterogeneity, their interaction, and a number of control variables. In contrast to our previous analysis, we use both cross-sectional information on differences between regions as well as information on regional change over time. Thus, we model redistribution preferences of individual i living in region j at time t, denoted by R_{ji}^* via the following specification:[1]

---

[2] EU-LFS provides lists of respondents' country of birth with varying detail. Due to confidentiality reasons some countries only report a coarse classification scheme. However, because we only need to separate individuals born in their country of residence from those who are not, this coarseness does not pose any further problems. In two extreme cases – Germany and Denmark – we only have information on whether a respondent was born in that country or not. Here we assume that the share of foreign-born is one minus the share of native-born. We also lack usable LFS data on the Netherlands. Here, we calculate the regional share of foreign-born population from published local population tables of the Dutch Central Bureau of Statistics (CBS, 2002, 2004, 2006, 2008).

[3] Exceptions are Germany and Denmark, whose observations start in 2005 and 2007, respectively.

[4] In this chapter, we use a simplified model setup compared to Chapter 5 and dichotomize our dependent variable into an indicator variable equal to one if a respondent indicates support for redistribution ("strongly agree" and "agree" categories). Redistribution preferences R_i^* are a latent construct obtained from observed categorical survey responses R_i via a simple probit formulation (i.e., we set the scale by fixing the error variance to one and fix the model's location by setting the threshold to zero).

$$R_{ijt}^* = \alpha \left(v_{it} - \bar{v}_t \right) + \beta h_{jt} + \gamma h_{jt}(v_{it} - \bar{v}_t) + \delta' x_{ijt} + \xi_j + \lambda_t + \epsilon_{it}. \quad (7.1)$$

Here α captures the effect of relative income, the difference between an individual's income in survey year t, v_{it}, and country-year average income $\bar{v}_t$. The (time-varying) effect of regional population heterogeneity h_{jt} is captured by β. As our argument stresses that heterogeneity matters more for the rich than the poor, we include an interaction between heterogeneity and individual income, with associated effect coefficient γ. We also include a range of individual and regional level controls x_{ijt} whose effects are represented by δ (these include, in some models, expected future income and fear of crime). Common shocks affecting all regions and individuals, such as aggregated changes in economic conditions, are captured by time fixed effects λ_t. Systematic differences between regions are captured by region-specific constants, ξ_j. These capture all time-constant, unobserved regional characteristics that shift preferences. We specify these as random effects, which implies that regional effects are drawn from a common normal distribution with estimated variance. In an alternative model we specify them as fixed effects as well.

7.1.3 Results

Table 7.1 shows estimates from several model specifications. In (1) we find the expected effects of income and heterogeneity on preferences. The direct effects of present income and heterogeneity (when their interaction is zero) indicate that individuals further above the national mean prefer less redistribution, as do those who live in regions with a large share of foreign-born. We also find clear evidence that the effect of income is conditional on population heterogeneity. In regions with lower levels of homogeneity, the effect of income on redistribution preferences is more negative. Because it is hard to gauge the true magnitude and meaning of this interaction from estimated coefficients alone, we will calculate quantities of interest (the effect of heterogeneity among rich and poor individuals). First, however, we turn to two further model specifications. In specification (2) we add country fixed effects to account for unobserved country-level factors (that are not already captured by regional effects) and find little substantive changes to our results. In specification (3) we account for the difference in our measure of the share of foreign born and the share of foreign born in the lower half of the income distribution (which would be our ideal measure, but is unavailable in some years). In Appendix A.4.1 (where we discuss the issue in greater detail), we calculate

TABLE 7.1 *Population heterogeneity, income, and redistribution preferences in Western Europe*

	(1)	(2)	(3)	(4)	(5)
Income distance	−0.048	−0.049	−0.052	−0.050	−0.017
	(0.003)	(0.003)	(0.003)	(0.003)	(0.001)
Foreign share[a]	−0.634	−0.706	−0.707	−0.649	−0.231
	(0.245)	(0.178)	(0.178)	(0.184)	(0.115)
Income × foreign	−0.081	−0.079	−0.073	−0.082	−0.036
	(0.018)	(0.018)	(0.018)	(0.019)	(0.006)
Income expectations				−0.083	−0.028
				(0.018)	(0.006)
Controls					
Individual + regional[b]	Yes	Yes	Yes	Yes	Yes
Time dummies	Yes	Yes	Yes	Yes	Yes
Country dummies	No	Yes	Yes	Yes	–
Region effects	Random	Random	Random	Random	Fixed

Note: ESS data 2002–2008. Specification (5) is a linear probability model.
[a]Foreign share adjusted by δ_c, the country-specific difference to the share of foreign-born with lower income. Calculated based on a post-2009 subsample of EU-LFS. See Appendix A.4.1 for details.
[b]Controls include age, education, household size, indicator variables for being unemployed, self-employed, not in the labor force.

a country-specific shift parameter, which captures the average difference between both measures, and use it to adjust our measure of foreign-born. Using this adjusted measure induces little change in our results, save for a minor reduction in the income-heterogeneity interaction.

We add our measure of expected income in specification (4). As in the previous chapter, we find that respondents who have higher lifetime expected income prefer less redistribution. Note that adding income expectations does little to alter our interpretation of the interplay between heterogeneity and (present-day) income. Before we turn to a more explicit examination of the conditional effect of heterogeneity, our final specification (5) presents a greater deviation from our previous models. We estimate a linear probability model and specify regional effects as fixed instead of random.[5] Note that this specification is a lot more stringent: we only use the over-time variation in heterogeneity

---

[5] We estimate this model as linear probability model because unconditional (or dummy variable) fixed-effects estimators for probit models are biased due to the problem of incidental parameters (Greene, 2004).

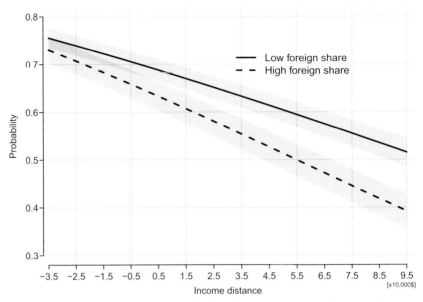

FIGURE 7.1 Predicted probabilities of redistribution support as function of income distance and regional-level heterogeneity in Western Europe

within regions to estimate its direct effect and its interaction with income. Even here we find clear evidence for the conditional effect of income. We now explore the substantive magnitude of this effect.

As in the previous section of the book, Figure 7.1 provides a more intuitive picture of the relationship between income and heterogeneity by showing average predicted probabilities for supporting redistribution for individuals living in regions with low and high shares of foreign-born population.[6] A high share of foreign-born refers to the nintieth percentile of the regional distribution, while a low share refers to the tenth. We calculate predicted redistribution support over the range of income in our sample and plot predicted values together with 90 percent confidence intervals. Figure 7.1 reveals a pattern close to our theoretical expectation (compare with Figure 6.2).

Also as in the previous part of the book, Table 7.2 shows average marginal effects of population heterogeneity on the probability of redistribution support among the rich and the poor (defined as those at the tenth and ninetieth percentiles of the income distribution). Comparing

---

[6] We use specification (1) in Table 7.1 for these estimates.

TABLE 7.2 *Average marginal effect of population heterogeneity on predicted support of redistribution among the rich and poor*

	Est.	s.e.	95% CI	
Poor	−0.149	0.083	−0.311	0.013
Rich	−0.345	0.094	−0.529	−0.160

Note: Based on specification (1) in Table 7.1.

estimates reveals that the effect of a marginal increase in heterogeneity is more than twice as large among the rich than among the poor. In fact, in line with our argument (refer again to Figure 6.2), a marginal increase in regional heterogeneity does not have a clearly systematic effect on the poor's support for redistribution: the confidence interval of the average marginal effect includes zero. In contrast, the negative effect of an increase in heterogeneity is substantively large and statistically significant among the rich.

WHAT ABOUT INEQUALITY?. Before moving on to check the robustness of our results, it is germane to ask what bearing the results in the previous part of this book have on our findings here. We have argued that increases in inequality may promote support for redistribution as a way to reduce the negative externalities of inequality. To the extent that macroinequality is related to levels of ethnic heterogeneity, the relationships proposed in both sections of this book have similar empirical implications.[7] We address this issue in more detail in the next chapter, where we estimate a joint model of expected income, inequality, and heterogeneity. Note that there is no clear relation between heterogeneity and inequality in the data we analyze (as we show in the next chapter), and we thus expect that the income-dependent effect of heterogeneity is separable from the impact of inequality. This is confirmed in our analysis (see Section 8.1), where we find that our results still obtain after conditioning on existing levels of inequality.

[7] For an argument connecting inequality and ethnic identity, see Huber (2017). Note that in our analyses of fear of crime as a visible externality of inequality in the previous part of the book, we do include the share of foreign-born as a control. There we find that crime fears are systematically shaped by local inequality, but not by local levels of foreign born. See Section A.3.1 in the appendix for estimates.

TABLE 7.3 *Overview of robustness checks; effect of heterogeneity among the rich in Western Europe*

Specification		Est.	s.e.
(1)	Social spending (national)	−0.077	0.022
(2a)	Social spending (regional)	−0.080	0.022
(2b)	Federalism	−0.082	0.021
(3a)	Population density	−0.079	0.022
(3b)	Urban area	−0.079	0.022
(3c)	Urban region	−0.082	0.022
(4)	Regional economic performance	−0.062	0.021
(5)	Foreign-born ($\pi = 0.6$)	−0.080	0.022
(6)	Religion	−0.080	0.022
(7)	Social class	−0.078	0.022
(8)	Skill specificity	−0.077	0.022
(9)	Wage earner sample	−0.080	0.022
(10)	Ideology	−0.069	0.021
(11)	Income imputed	−0.067	0.016

Note: Displayed are first differences in average predicted probabilities of moving from low to high heterogeneity among the rich.

7.1.4 Robustness Tests

We have estimated different statistical specifications for the same set of core variables. In this section we subject our analysis to a variety of robustness checks resulting from the inclusion of different variables based on further theoretical considerations. Table 7.3 shows first differences in average predicted probabilities of moving from low to high heterogeneity among the rich (again defined as ninetieth percentile of the income distribution). We use specification (1) in Table 7.1 as our baseline for comparison, where changing from a low to high foreign-population region is associated with a decrease equal to −0.079 in the average predicted probability of supporting redistribution for the rich (those with household incomes 30,000 PPP-adjusted 2005 US dollars above the mean).

SOCIAL SPENDING. As in previous chapters, we include existing levels of social spending in our estimation.[8] We do this to test alternatives implying that individuals take into consideration the levels of redistribu-

---

[8] Spending data are total public social spending (in cash and in kind), per head, in constant 2000 prices and PPP US dollars from OECD's SOCX database. The main social policy areas covered are: Old age, Survivors, Incapacity-related benefits, Health, Family, Active labor market programs, Unemployment, and Housing.

tion when answering the survey questions; that support for redistribution would fall when the existing levels of redistribution are high; or that high levels of redistribution are connected with encompassing welfare and labor market institutions that provide the poor and the rich with more information about redistributive issues. The results in specification (1) show our main findings are not affected by controlling for existing levels of social spending.

NATIONAL VERSUS REGIONAL REDISTRIBUTION. We consider the measure of redistribution preferences in this chapter's analysis to (mostly) capture national redistribution. However, as we argued in Part II, it is possible that in federal systems, where regional governments have a greater role in providing redistribution, respondents consider both national and regional redistribution policy. We address this issue in two ways. First, we create a measure of regional social spending. The regional measure weights national expenditure by the regional share of the recipient population. Second, we use a measure of federalism by creating an indicator variable that equals one if, within a country, regions are an autonomous source of government spending.[9] Specifications (2a) and (2b) in Table 7.3 show that our results are robust to these changes.

POPULATION DENSITY AND URBAN AREAS. In order to test if individuals living in high-density urban areas have distinct preferences (e.g., Cho et al., 2006) due to neighborhood sorting (Rodden, 2010: 322), we estimate three specifications. First, we include regional population density (data from Eurostat) in specification (3a). Second, we include an individual-level survey variable, which indicates if the respondent lives in an urban region in specification (3b). Third, in specification (3c) we use this survey variable to construct a measure of the regional degree of urbanization. Results of all three specifications are quite unequivocal: accounting for urban differences does not change the fact that the effect of heterogeneity is large and significant for the rich.

REGIONAL ECONOMIC PERFORMANCE. Our main model includes region-specific effects intended to capture regional differences. In specifi-

[9] We use regionally weighted national spending data because comparable region-specific spending data are only available for a very limited number of countries in our sample. We calculate the regional share of the recipient population from our available survey data as the population share of the unemployed, the disabled, and those in retirement. Information on regional sources of government spending is from Eurostat's government revenue and expenditure database.

cation (4) we include a set of covariates capturing regional economic conditions, namely regional gross domestic product and unemployment rates. We find that the interaction effect between income and heterogeneity is slightly reduced. However, we still find strong evidence for our theoretical predictions: the effect of heterogeneity on the predicted probability of redistribution support is large and significant for the rich (the difference between high- and low-heterogeneity regions is 6 percentage points with a standard error of 2).

REGIONAL SHARE OF FOREIGN-BORN POPULATION . Our share of foreign-born population measure, calculated from LFS data, is based on interpolated values for 2002. In Appendix A.4 we present additional details on our interpolation procedure, which is based on a weighted combination of linear and quadratic regional time trends. In our main model we weight the quadratic component more heavily (which amounts to setting a linear-to-quadratic weight parameter, π, to 0.4). In this robustness test, we estimate an interpolation model that puts more weight on a linear trend component (setting π to 0.6). Specification (5) shows that this does not change our core finding.

RELIGION AND SOCIAL CLASS. For reasons of parsimony we exclude a number of social factors such as religion and social class from our main model. While clearly important, we argue that these factors are orthogonal to the income-heterogeneity nexus. Specifications (6) and (7) in Table 7.3 show that including a five-category social class measure as well as religiosity (contrasting Seculars with Catholics and Protestants) in the model leaves our results unchanged.

SKILL SPECIFICITY. As in previous chapters, we return to the arguments that understand redistribution as insurance against an uncertain future (Moene and Wallerstein, 2001; Iversen and Soskice, 2009; Rehm, 2009). We have argued that expected future income encapsulates risk/insurance/mobility mechanisms (and we already controlled for the effects of this variable in our main results), but we also introduce an explicit measure of labor market risk into the analysis. In specification (8) we use the measure of skill specificity proposed by Iversen and Soskice (2001) (we calculate it following Cusack et al., 2006). We find our core results unchanged.

WAGE EARNERS. As in the previous section of the book, we test the robustness of our results to changes in the sample composition of income earners. This is partly to address the possibility that high levels of support for redistribution have to do with the low probability for tax compliance by non–wage earners in some countries in our sample. Specification (9) only includes respondents who currently obtain labor income. This does not change our core result.

IDEOLOGY. In specification (10) we include a measure to examine if ideological positions (as an independent source of redistribution preferences, see Margalit, 2013) alter our results. Our estimates show that the conditional (on income) effect of heterogeneity is still present.

INCOME IMPUTED. As a final robustness test we consider the problem of missing data. Our analyses in this part of the book were performed on data sets where we removed missing observations using listwise deletion. The incidence of item nonresponse is generally low, and robustness tests in the previous part of the book showed little difference between imputed and complete-case analysis results. However, for one of our central variables – income – nonresponses are much more likely. In this robustness test, we impute missing income using predictive mean matching (Rubin, 1986; Schenker and Taylor, 1996) from five nearest neighbors creating ten imputed data sets. The marginal effects reported here are averages over those imputations with multiple imputation corrected standard errors.[10] We find that our substantive findings do not depend on this choice.

7.1.5 Additional Microlevel Implication: Immigration Attitudes

We mentioned in the previous chapter that the measure of heterogeneity in our analysis of ESS data is not perfect. While it is reasonable to expect foreign-born individuals to be concentrated among the poor in most European countries, an ideal measure would capture this concentration directly. In specification (3) of Table 7.1, we accounted for the difference in our measure of the share of foreign-born and the share of foreign-born in the lower half of the income distribution (which would be our ideal measure, but is unavailable in some years). In this section, we provide a complementary test using an alternative measure of heterogeneity based on the implication our model has on the microlevel. The individual-level manifestation of an income-dependent effect of heterogeneity is a difference in how attitudes about immigration (whether it is perceived

---

[10] Addressing missing income is difficult because it is likely that nonresponse depends on income itself. The assumption underlying multiple imputation is that the missingness process is "missing at random," i.e., that the incidence of missing values is ignorable conditional on a set of covariates. We use the covariates included in our analysis model and add variables that are likely helpful predictors for income, such as urbanization of respondent's region of residence, divorce status, and household size.

as positive or negative) are translated into preferences for redistribution by the rich and the poor. Thus, we expect that attitudes toward migrants have a stronger impact on redistribution preferences among the rich than among the poor. This holds whether immigration attitudes are shaped by economic issues (such as competition) or purely cultural ones (such as symbolic threats). While it is certainly possible that the poor hold strong antimigrant sentiments, their present material interests (if our argument is correct) should keep them from translating these sentiments into lower redistribution preferences. The rich, however, should be able to "afford" the translation of pro-immigrant sentiments into higher redistribution preferences.

To address this issue, we use a question in the ESS asking respondents whether their country "is made a worse or a better place to live by people coming to live here from other countries." Answers range from 0 ("Worse place to live") to 10 ("Better place to live"). We consider this a difficult test for our hypotheses. We have argued that a high level of population heterogeneity will make the affluent less likely to support redistribution (because of the decrease in the moral gains in their altruism). At a general level, this could of course still be the case whether the affluent think that immigration is a good or a bad thing (the out-group distinction could still be relevant and affect altruism, even when the out-group is recognized as valuable). In this section, therefore, we explore an extension of our argument. It would imply that the utility of other-regarding preferences is connected to the nature of the out-group. If the perception of the out-group is a negative one, the general argument still applies. If the perception of the out-group is a positive one (as reflected in the ESS question), then we would not expect a lack of support for redistribution to follow.

The estimates in Table 7.4 compare the changes in average predicted probabilities for those in the 10 percent and 90 percent percentiles in the

TABLE 7.4 *Relationship between immigration attitudes and redistribution preferences among the poor and rich*

	Est.	s.e.	95% CI	
Poor	0.023	0.007	0.010	0.036
Rich	0.064	0.009	0.048	0.081

Note: ESS data 2002–2008. Entries are differences in average predicted probabilities at tenth and ninetieth percentiles of immigration attitudes distribution. Parameter estimates for this and alternative specifications are available in Appendix A.4.6.

distribution of attitudes about immigration.[11] The results are remarkably similar to those in our analysis of heterogeneity. For the poor, having positive or negative attitudes toward immigration makes much less of a difference in their redistribution preferences than for the rich. A large change in immigration attitudes increases the expected value of redistribution preferences by only 0.2 points among the poor. The effect is almost three times as large among the rich, where it increases support for redistribution by 0.6 points. The symmetry of these results shows that whether we analyze objective immigration levels or individual attitudes toward immigration, we reach the same conclusions.

7.2 REPEATED CROSS-SECTIONAL EVIDENCE: UNITED STATES

To subject our theoretical claims to another set of tests, we turn to a completely different context. We analyze the effect of heterogeneity in the United States over a span of thirty years (from 1978 to 2010). To do so we rely on data from the General Social Survey, which has been used in previous research to study redistribution preferences (e.g., Alesina and La Ferrara, 2005).[12] As we mentioned in the previous chapter, a number of influential contributions in the American Politics literature have focused on the relationship (or lack thereof) between racial diversity and support for redistribution (Luttmer, 2001; Alesina and Glaeser, 2004; Gilens, 2009; Cramer, 2016; Hersh and Nall, 2016). Our income-dependent arguments about population heterogeneity challenge some of these contributions, and we go about presenting some supporting empirical evidence below.

7.2.1 Variable Definitions

MEASURE OF HETEROGENEITY. We construct two different measures of racial heterogeneity based on data from 2.1 million households sampled in the Annual Social and Economic Supplement of the Current Population Survey. The first is the ratio of the share of African American welfare recipients to the share of the African American population in a state in a given year. African American welfare recipients are defined

---

[11] The 10 percent percentile of the attitudes about immigration corresponds to a 2 answer and the 90 percent to an 8 answer. The results presented are calculated from estimates of a probit model with income × attitudes interaction, region random effects, country and year fixed effects, and a full set of controls.

[12] For a more detailed description of the GSS see Chapter 1.

as (self-identified) Blacks who live in a household receiving welfare. We classify a household as welfare receiving if at least one of its members receives income from welfare programs (such as AFDC/TANF), supplemental social security payments, or food stamps (SNAP).[13] We label individuals as "Black" based on their racial self-identification.[14] From now on we refer to this measure as *Black welfare recipiency rate* for brevity. Our second measure is constructed similarly, but captures African American poverty instead. We define a household as poor if its total household income is below the official poverty threshold for this type of household in a state in a given year.[15] This is similar in construction to the measure used by Luttmer (2001), who uses "the product of the race-specific rates of poverty and single motherhood" in a particular geographic area as a measure of the welfare recipiency rate (Luttmer, 2001: 501). We refer to this as *Black poverty rate* for brevity. We calculate both measures from detailed information on incomes and poverty provided in the Current Population Survey (CPS) Annual Social and Economic Supplement.[16]

7.2.2 Statistical Specifications

We analyze Americans' preferences for redistribution via the same basic specification as in Section 7.1.2. However, due to the nature of our data, there are two important changes. First, we treat the dependent variable, which in the GSS is comprised of seven categories, as continuous instead of estimating a large number of ordered probit thresholds. Second, and more important, the fact that we have more than thirty years of observations for each state allows us to employ a full *within-geographic unit* design. Thus, we estimate models with state fixed effects, which rely solely

---

[13] The characteristics of these programs evolve over time, most notably after the Personal Responsibility and Work Opportunity Reconciliation Act. We conduct an analysis of these changes later in this chapter.

[14] While the number of racial categories used in our data evolves together with societal interpretations of the concept, until and including 2002 there is one (and only one) clear category identifying African Americans ("Black"). After 2002 it includes "mixed" categories, such as "Black-Asian" (in accordance with the US census of 2010). We classify all categories that include "Black" as African American.

[15] Poverty thresholds take into account family size, the number of children, and age of the family householder. They are updated every year to reflect changes in consumer prices.

[16] The Census data used in Luttmer (2001) provide greater geographic resolution, but they are only available decennially requiring interpolation over long periods. We thus prefer annual CPS data. Furthermore, Luttmer (1999) shows that measures based on CPS and Census Summary Tape Files are in close agreement.

on within-state changes over time. Alternatively, because the number of sampled cases is low for some states, we pool (some) cross-state information using random effects model specifications.[17]

7.2.3 Results

The results of our analyses are displayed in Table 7.5, which shows estimates and standard errors for six model specifications. The first two columns show models using our measure of the Black welfare share estimated using fixed and random effects specifications, respectively. Columns (3) and (4) do the same, but use our poverty-based measure. The final two columns show models that explicitly account for income expectations.[18]

In order to conserve some space, we do not display estimates of covariates. Suffice it to say that they point in the expected directions: on average, women support redistribution more than men, as do the unemployed and union members. In contrast, the self-employed and those with higher levels of education prefer less redistribution. Note that we did not include a measure of an individual's race. A simple race dummy variable (separating African American respondents) does not capture adequately the multiplicity of ways in which race shapes both economic and political outcomes. Rather, we will analyze the link between income, heterogeneity, and preferences separately for African Americans below.

Turning to the estimates of our core variables, we find that, as expected, respondents' income is a strong determinant of their preferred levels of redistribution. The greater someone's distance above the mean income is, the less she supports redistribution, all else equal. We find that the main effect estimates for Black welfare recipiency and poverty rates carry quite a large standard error. They are not statistically distinguishable from zero (remember that these estimates refer to their interaction with income being zero), indicating a high level of heterogeneity between states. However, in specifications (1) and (2) we do find a clear and systematic

---

[17] Note that we also estimate a covariate measurement error model (Wansbeek and Meijer, 2000) to account explicitly for the fact that our measure of heterogeneity is an estimate carrying more uncertainty in states where either the nominator or the denominator of our measure is small. As we find that this correction does not change our substantive results, we opt for using simpler model specifications in the main text. For more details see Appendix A.4.2 and Table A.8.

[18] The following analyses are conducted on a pooled sample of the US (GSS) population. See Subsection 7.2.7 for an analysis separated by respondents' race.

TABLE 7.5 *Population heterogeneity, income, and redistribution preferences in the United States*

	(1)	(2)	(3)	(4)	(5)	(6)
Income distance	-0.064	-0.062	-0.071	-0.070	-0.066	-0.071
	(0.011)	(0.011)	(0.012)	(0.012)	(0.012)	(0.012)
Black welfare recipiency rate	-0.163	-0.050			-0.260	
	(0.161)	(0.147)			(0.169)	
Income × Welfare	-0.118	-0.120			-0.103	
	(0.035)	(0.035)			(0.037)	
Black poverty rate			-0.076	-0.156		-0.168
			(0.163)	(0.150)		(0.174)
Income × Poverty			-0.090	-0.092		-0.085
			(0.038)	(0.037)		(0.039)
Expected income					-0.162	-0.162
					(0.014)	(0.014)
Controls[a]						
Individual & regional	Yes	Yes	Yes	Yes	Yes	Yes
State effects[b]	Fixed	Random	Fixed	Random	Fixed	Fixed

Note: General Social Survey data 1978–2010. N = 19,025 (models with expected income N = 18,013). Appendix A.4.3 provides an analysis accounting for measurement error in Black welfare recipiency rate. Expected income is obtained from age × education-specific Mincer wage regressions.

[a] Individual and regional controls are age, education, indicator variables for female part-time work, unemployment, self-employment, living in a city, being a union member, and state-level unemployment rate.

[b] Fixed effects are within-state least-squares estimates, random effects are ML estimates assuming normally distributed state random effects.

TABLE 7.6 *Average marginal effects of Black welfare recipiency rate and Black poverty rates on redistribution preferences of the rich and poor*

		Est.	s.e.	95% CI	
(A) Black	Poor	0.275	0.212	−0.140	0.689
welfare recipiency	Rich	−0.787	0.241	−1.260	−0.314
(B) Black	Poor	0.264	0.214	−0.155	0.684
poverty rate	Rich	−0.563	0.258	−1.068	−0.058

Note: Based on specification (1) and (3) in Table 7.5. Random-effects based marginal effects for the rich are −0.686 (0.233) in specification (2) and −0.643 (0.250) in specification (4).

estimate of their interaction with income. This finding holds in both fixed (within-state) and random (partially pooled) effects specifications. The sign of the interaction points in the expected direction: as the Black welfare recipiency rate increases, richer individuals are less likely to support redistribution. These results are confirmed with our alternative measure of poverty (rather than welfare recipiency) in specifications (3) and (4): as the Black poverty rate increases, richer respondents shy away from expressing support for income redistribution. As in our previous analyses, extended models that include respondents' income expectations show that they systematically shape preferences. Higher levels of expected future income are associated with less support of redistribution. And, like in our analysis of Western Europe, including expectations does not alter our substantive conclusion about the (present-day) income-conditional effect of heterogeneity.

We cannot make definitive statements about the correspondence between our theoretical argument and the results of our statistical analysis from the estimated coefficients alone. Therefore, we calculate the effect of the Black welfare recipiency rate and the Black poverty rate on redistribution preferences for the rich and the poor. As before, we define rich and poor as those at the tenth and ninetieth percentiles of the income distribution.[19] Table 7.6 shows first differences in average expected values of redistribution preferences for a change from low heterogeneity (the tenth percentile of the state heterogeneity distribution) to high heterogeneity (the ninetieth percentile). We find that, for both

---

[19] These values are defined as averages over all years. Remember that we deflate our measure of income.

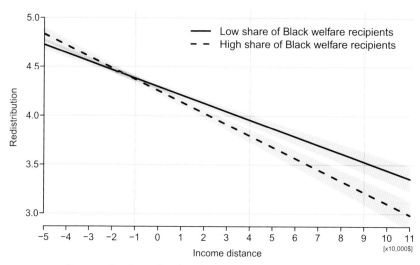

FIGURE 7.2 Expected values of redistribution support as function of income distance and state-level heterogeneity in the United States

measures, the effect of increasing heterogeneity is fairly small among the poor as well as statistically indistinguishable from zero. In contrast, increasing heterogeneity has a marked impacts on the rich. Holding all else equal, we find that a marginal increase in Black welfare recipiency rates significantly reduces rich individuals' redistribution preferences. The same holds when using our Black poverty rate measure.[20]

While marginal effects provide a useful "one number summary," Figure 7.2 provides a more intuitive appraisal of the substantive implication of our findings. It plots expected values of redistribution preferences for individuals at varying points of the income distribution living in states with low or high Black welfare recipiency rates (defined, as before, as the tenth and ninetieth percentiles). First, Figure 7.2 stresses once more the relevance of the Meltzer–Richards model as a starting point of an analysis of redistribution preference formation. Individuals further away from the mean of the income distribution are far less likely to support redistribution. The differences between individuals at different positions in the income spectrum are large and statistically significant.

---

[20] Second differences – the difference between the first differences – are also statistically different from zero. This is important to note because the difference between two effects being not significant and significant might not itself be statistically significant (Gelman and Stern, 2006).

Second, Figure 7.2 confirms our theoretical argument that low levels of homogeneity decrease support for redistributive policies among the rich, whereas population homogeneity does not really matter to the poor.

INEQUALITY. As in our analysis of European data earlier, one might ask what our results look like when including state-level inequality. Do inequality and heterogeneity capture distinct characteristics of states? Or are we explaining the same variance in redistribution preferences with different variables? In the next chapter of this book (see Section 8.1), we show that inequality and heterogeneity are not strongly related in the United States (both across-states and within-states over time). After estimating a joint model of inequality and heterogeneity, we do find a separable impact of heterogeneity in line with our results in this chapter.

7.2.4 Robustness Checks

Our use of state-specific effects (both fixed and random) implies that state-level confounders can be ruled out as alternative explanations, as long as they are time-constant. Thus, in the following paragraphs we focus on either alternative individual-level factors or explanations that involve *time-varying* state-level variables.

SOCIAL SPENDING. In the context of this analysis, accounting for existing levels of social spending means we need a state-specific measure. We calculate per capita transfer receipts (in constant 1999 dollars) for each state-year using income data from the Regional Economic Accounts of the Bureau of Economic Analysis.[21] We include this measure in specification (1) in Table 7.7, which shows that our core result changes very little.

STATE WEALTH. Following the work of McCarty et al. (2008) and Gelman et al. (2008), we account for a state's wealth as a time-varying covariate influencing preferences. We include both state gross domestic product (from the Bureau of Economic Analysis) as a broad indicator, and state median household income (in constant 1999 dollars, calculated from March CPS files) in specifications (2) and (3). Accounting for different rates of changing household income (which is negatively correlated with

---

[21] They include income maintenance benefits, unemployment insurance compensation, retirement and disability insurance benefits, medical benefits, veterans' benefits, education and training assistance, and other transfer receipts of individuals from governments.

TABLE 7.7 *Overview of robustness checks; effect of heterogeneity among the rich in the United States*

Specification	Est.	s.e.
State-level variables		
(1) Federal social transfers	−0.724	0.246
(2) Gross-domestic product	−0.670	0.245
(3) Median HH income	−0.656	0.251
(4a) Population density	−0.692	0.244
(4b) Urban region	−0.677	0.244
(5) Ethnic fractionalization	−0.701	0.245
(6) Residential segregation	−0.720	0.246
(7) Deindustrialization	−0.686	0.248
(8a) State ideology	−0.661	0.242
(8b) Share of liberals	−0.783	0.242
(9a) State linear time trends	−0.727	0.255
(9b) State nonlinear time trends[a]	−0.881	0.277
Individual-level variables		
(10) Occupational risk	−0.688	0.260
(11) Industry effects	−0.777	0.242
(12) Religion	−0.750	0.260
(13) Social class	−0.767	0.242
(14) Ideology	−0.714	0.241
(15) Income imputed	−0.747	0.241

Note: Displayed are average marginal effects.
[a]Restricted cubic time splines with 4 knots (at 0.05, 0.35, 0.65, and 0.95 percentile).

increases in heterogeneity) does weaken our result; however, we still find a clear effect of heterogeneity for the rich.

POPULATION DENSITY AND URBAN AREAS. As in the previous section, we include regional population density (people per square-mile, calculated from the Census Bureaus' intercensal population estimates) in specification (4a) and the state-level degree of urbanization, measured as the share of a state's population living in an urban area (as defined by the Census; data are from CPS) in specification (4b). In both cases we find that even after accounting for changing levels of urbanization the rich behave appreciably differently in more heterogeneous states.

ETHNIC FRACTIONALIZATION. We account for over-time changes in ethnic fractionalization in specification (5). In their seminal study Alesina and Glaeser (2004: 11) observe that increasing ethnic fractionalization reduces the redistributive effort of the welfare system. On the individual level this implies a negative relationship between (macro) fractionalization and (micro) preferences (see the survey in Alesina and La Ferrara, 2005). Using CPS data for each state-year, we calculate the share of individuals identifying as either White, Black, Asian, or Other and use these to construct the ethnic fractionalization index of Alesina et al. (2003). Our results show that accounting for fractionalization does not affect our main result.

RESIDENTIAL SEGREGATION. Are our main findings simply a reflection of changes in residential segregation? As was the case in our analysis of ESS data, the relationship between individual preferences and neighborhood sorting needs to be addressed. If the rich increasingly select themselves into segregated neighborhoods, their experience of heterogeneity mechanically decreases. To account for this possibility, we measure racial residential segregation in each state in each year using tract-level Census data (following Chetty et al., 2014). We create a multigroup segregation index based on a Theil index (Iceland, 2004). More details are available in Appendix A.4.5. Interestingly, including racial residential segregation (which is weakly positively correlated with heterogeneity) in specification (6) increases the magnitude of the effects of heterogeneity for the rich in the United States.

DEINDUSTRIALIZATION. Another source of substantial temporal change is the process of regional deindustrialization (Lawrence, 1984: 43).[22] We capture state-specific deindustrialization trends by the relative decline of the manufacturing sector.[23] Our results in specification (7) show that accounting for the secular decline in manufacturing does not change our core finding.

STATE IDEOLOGY. Another possible concern is the omission of ideology from our analysis. As in all previous analyses in this book, our main model does not include individuals' ideology because we conceptualize redistribution preferences as an intrinsic part of ideological positions.

---

[22] For a comparative approach, see Iversen and Cusack (2000).
[23] We measure employment in manufacturing as a share of total private employment in a state in a given year. Historical data on employment by industrial sector are available from the Bureau of Labor Statistics' State and Area Current Employment Statistics Series. The series reaches back to 1990, thus we need to extrapolate values for previous years. We do so by fitting flexible ARIMA models to each state series and calculate backwards predictions based on model estimates. Details on our extrapolation models and descriptives of state-specific trends are available in Appendix A.4.4. In line with the literature on deindustrialization, we find that the last thirty years are marked by a strong secular decline in manufacturing. However, there are marked differences in the rate of decline among states.

However, this issue might have less to do with *individual* ideology (which we evaluate later), than with a changing general ideological predisposition of a state's citizens. When accounting for the fact that citizens of some states (say on the coasts) become increasingly liberal over time, we might see our findings based on changing heterogeneity disappear. We use two measures of state-level ideology to address this concern. Our first one is the share of individuals in each state in each year classified as liberal computed from NYT/CBS poll responses using a dynamic multilevel poststratification model (see Pacheco, 2011). Our second measure uses an indirect strategy to capture *citizen ideology* (or policy mood) on a liberal-conservative continuum. Following the strategy pioneered by Rabinowitz et al. (1984), Berry et al. (1998) calculate citizens' ideology using interest group ratings of the ideological position of each state's member of congress and their challenger in each district. These district ratings are then averaged for each state and year. See Berry et al. (2010) for an extended discussion of the reliability of their measure. We include both variants in specifications (8a) and (8b). Notably, ideology based on legislators' and challengers' positions has a somewhat more marked impact on our income-dependent heterogeneity effect, which nonetheless remains substantively large and statistically different from zero. This robustness test is of particular relevance because ideology is also a factor shaping the generosity or *strictness* of welfare policy, which affects one of our heterogeneity measures (the share of African Americans receiving welfare). We elaborate on this point later.

TIME-TRENDING STATE UNOBSERVABLES. We mentioned earlier that our inclusion of state-specific effects accounts for time-constant unobservables. However, even after the extensive set of time-varying state-level covariates included in our robustness test, one may be concerned that unobserved time-varying unobservables shape both the evolution of welfare recipiency/poverty rates and welfare preferences. We can (partially) address this concern by estimating robustness checks with state-specific time trends. Specification (9a) rules out linearly time-varying unobserved state-level confounders by estimating a linear time trend for each state. Specification (9b) is more extensive and allows for nonlinear time trends, estimated via state-specific restricted cubic splines. In both specifications we find our core results confirmed. When allowing for possibly nonlinear influences of state unobservables, we find the average marginal effect of heterogeneity among the rich is even more pronounced.

EMPLOYMENT CHARACTERISTICS. Turning to individual-level characteristics, as in our previous analysis of European data, we return to arguments that understand redistribution as insurance against an uncertain future. An important literature stresses the role of occupational characteristics, such as skills specificity or unemployment risk, as well as more generally painting one's workplace as a site of preference formation (e.g., Cusack et al., 2006; Kitschelt and Rehm, 2014). An alternative approach emphasizes the nature of an individual's industry as the most important determinant of her demand for redistribution – even if there is no agreement about which sectoral characteristics matter (Iversen and Cusack, 2000; for a discussion, see Rehm, 2009). We include a direct measure of occupational unemployment risk, following Rehm (2011), as well as more general industry fixed effects in specifications (10) and (11).[24] Accounting for occupational risk brings about little change, while accounting for unobserved industry effects slightly increases the heterogeneity effect among the rich.

SOCIAL CHARACTERISTICS AND IDEOLOGY. As before, we include religion and social class, as well as a respondent's ideology (see the previous section for a more detailed discussion). We capture religion via respondents' church attendance and social class position using the five-category version of the Erikson and Goldthorpe (1992) class scheme. Ideology is a respondent's self-rating on a seven-point liberal–conservative scale. The inclusion of these individual level characteristics does not alter our core finding.

INCOME IMPUTED. Finally, we again estimate a specification where we impute missing income. The details are the same as in our European analysis. Again, we find that our core results are not substantially altered.

7.2.3 The 1996 PRWORA Reform

We now turn to a more pressing concern. One of our two measures of heterogeneity is based on households' welfare receipts, which is not just determined by the incidence of welfare demand (i.e., a mother of two becoming unemployed) but also by welfare program characteristics, such as eligibility rules, waiting periods, and work requirements. If states have the freedom to set and alter welfare rules, therefore inducing changes in our heterogeneity measure, one has to worry that these changes are

---

[24] Our risk measure is the occupational unemployment rate matched to GSS respondents' DOT occupations. We thank Philip Rehm for providing us with his data. Industry effects are on the one-digit industry level.

endogenous to characteristics of states' citizenry. If these characteristics include citizens' preferences for redistribution, our results are subject to bias.[25]

The 1996 Personal Responsibility and Work Opportunity Reconciliation Act (PRWORA) marked a major change in the role individual states play in the design of welfare programs. Significantly for the focus of this chapter, the federal Aid to Families with Dependent Children program was transformed into a block grant-based system, Temporary Assistance for Needy Families, which grants states considerable authority over program rules.[26] As a result, post-reform welfare program characteristics vary widely between states (Weil and Finegold, 2002). Thus, in order to study the possible endogeneity of reform intensity between states, we can examine if pre-reform preferences (and ideology) influence welfare program characteristics after PRWORA. We can then further explore whether it is macro welfare recipiency levels that affect individual preferences or the other way around by exploring the nature of the changes in citizens' support for redistribution before and after welfare reform.

We consider four central welfare program characteristics (following Soss et al., 2001). First, we consider the *strictness of sanctions* imposed on recipients who do not comply with TANF's requirement to work. State differences in sanctions can be placed in three categories: (1) weak, sanctioning only the adult portion of the benefit, thus leaving most family benefits intact; (2) moderate, involving a partial benefit cut, which rises progressively with non-compliance; and (3) harsh sanctions, entailing the loss of the full family benefit after the first violation (Burke and Gish, 1999; Soss et al., 2001). Second, we use an indicator for the existence of *immediate work requirements*, capturing state work trigger time limits (Burke and Gish, 1999) that are tougher than federally mandated. Our third program measure is an indicator for the existence of a *family cap* limiting or denying additional benefits for children born to families already receiving cash assistance (Rector and Youssef, 1999). Fourth, PRWORA introduced a welfare lifetime limit of 60 months, but some states set a

---

[25] To the extent that households' incomes are affected by welfare payments, our second measure capturing African American poverty rates is also affected by this endogeneity issue.

[26] For a concise comparison of pre- and post reform welfare programs see Department of Health and Human Services (2003).

TABLE 7.8 *Relationship between pre-reform ideology and preferences on post-PRWORA program characteristics; average marginal effects*

	Post-reform program characteristics			
	Sanction strictness	Work requirement	Family cap	Lifetime limit
(1) Pre-reform state ideology	−0.011 (0.003)	−0.002 (0.006)	−0.002 (0.006)	−0.008 (0.008)
(2) Pre-reform preferences	0.227 (0.183)	−0.319 (0.304)	0.084 (0.265)	−0.081 (0.311)

Note: Pre-reform ideology and preferences are 1985–1994 averages. Model for sanction strictness is ordered probit; marginal effects refer to probability of strictest sanction. Other models are probit.

lower level, such as Arkansas, where the lifetime limit is 24 months.[27] We use an indicator variable equal to one if a state's limit is below the federal maximum. Finally, we calculate, for the pre-reform period from 1985 to 1994, average state-level redistribution preferences and state citizen ideology. The former is based on our GSS sample, the latter from Berry et al. (1998) – see the previous robustness section for details.

Table 7.8 shows results from several models regressing program characteristics on pre-reform redistribution preferences and pre-reform ideology, respectively. Starting with the strictness of sanctions, we find that in states with more liberal citizens' ideology the probability of strict sanctions is indeed slightly lower. However, we find no systematic effect of redistributive preferences on sanction strictness. In fact, preferences are not systematically related to *any* of the four reform characteristics studied here (a finding that is broadly in line with Lee et al., 2002). Of course, we cannot claim that our results are not affected by endogeneity issues. But we have at least ruled out that welfare rules are shaped in large part by citizens' redistribution preferences. While citizen ideology does matter for the strictness of sanction imposed on noncomplying recipients (although for no other program characteristic), accounting for this does not substantively alter our core finding, as we have shown in specification (8a) in Table 7.7.

[27] Data are from the Urban Institute's welfare rules database, which codes detailed welfare rules from caseworkers handbooks. They refer to 1998, the first year where all states had switched to TANF.

TABLE 7.9 *Redistribution preferences in states implementing strict versus weak/moderate reforms; average preferences before and after passing of PRWORA; means and adjusted means with standard errors in parentheses*

State's sanction rules	Pre-reform years		Post-reform years	
	Raw	Adj.	Raw	Adj.
Weak or moderate	4.32	4.33	4.36	4.36
sanctions	(0.03)	(0.03)	(0.03)	(0.03)
Strict sanctions	4.30	4.27	4.15	4.16
	(0.05)	(0.05)	(0.05)	(0.05)
Difference	−0.02	−0.05	−0.21	−0.20
	(0.06)	(0.05)	(0.06)	(0.06)

Note: Pre-reform refers to GSS survey years 1987–1994 ($N = 5,838$), post-reform refers to GSS years 2000–2010 ($N = 5,430$). Adjusted means account for age, gender, race, and urban location. Heteroscedasticity-consistent standard errors.

Table 7.9 relates changes in citizens' support for redistribution to the strictness of welfare reform. It displays mean preferences, both unadjusted and adjusted for basic individual characteristics, before and after the reform and distinguishes states that implemented weak or moderate sanctions from states that implemented strict sanctions for noncompliance with welfare rules. To calculate average citizen preferences before and after the reform we use GSS surveys from 1987 to 1994, and 2000 to 2010, respectively. This yields two samples of approximately similar size divided by the passing of PRWORA in August 1996 and its implementation in 1997 and 1998.[28] Comparing weak to strict sanction states in pre-reform years, we find that average preferences are 4.32 and 4.30, respectively, indicating no systematic differences in preferences between both types of states, a fact that is confirmed by a difference in means test, which is not statistically different from zero. This conclusion also holds when adjusting means for differences in citizens' characteristics, such as age, gender, and race. Turning to preferences in years after the reform, the picture changes. In states that passed weak or moderate sanctions, average preferences for redistribution remain essentially unchanged. In contrast, in states that implement strict welfare sanctions, average preferences declined to 4.15. This constitutes a tenfold

---

[28] Both samples comprise over 5,000 individuals. Note that using different start and end years does not appreciably influence our substantive results.

increase in the difference between citizens' preferences in weak and strict sanction states, increasing from −0.02 in pre-reform years to 0.21 post reform. Accordingly, this difference is now statistically different from zero. In a preliminary way, therefore, our exploration of PRWORA indicates that, as assumed in our main models, it is macrowelfare recipiency levels (as a measure of heterogeneity) that affect individual preferences for redistribution, and not the other way around.

7.2.6 Additional Microlevel Implications: Racial Attitudes

Just as we did when analyzing European data, in this section we provide a complementary test using an alternative measure of heterogeneity based on the implication our model has on the microlevel. In the American context, the individual-level implication of the income-dependent effect of heterogeneity we hypothesize is a difference in how attitudes about race (whether it is perceived as positive or negative) are translated into preferences for redistribution by the rich and the poor. As before, we expect that attitudes toward African Americans will have a stronger impact on redistribution preferences among the rich than among the poor (because the rich can "afford" the translation of positive racial sentiments into higher redistribution preferences). As in the previous section in this chapter, we consider this a difficult test for our hypotheses. It moves away from the general argument that a high level of population heterogeneity will make the affluent less likely to support redistribution (because of the decrease in the moral gains in their altruism), to the more concrete implication that the utility of other-regarding preferences is connected to particular perceptions of the out-group.

Table 7.10 shows first differences in expected redistribution preferences for a *ceteris paribus* change from negative to positive attitudes toward African Americans among the rich and the poor. These results

TABLE 7.10 *Effect of positive change in racial attitude on redistribution preferences among the poor and rich*

	Est.	s.e.	95% CI	
Poor	0.769	0.056	0.659	0.879
Rich	1.572	0.073	1.429	1.716

Note: Effect represents change in expected value of redistribution preference when moving from "too much" to "too little." Parameter estimates for this and alternative specifications are available in Appendix A.4.6.

are based on a linear model including an interaction between income and attitudes, as well as a full set of individual controls and state-fixed effects. Our measure of attitudes toward African Americans is an item asking respondents if more resources should be spent to improve their living conditions.[29] We find that a positive change in racial attitudes generally increases support for redistribution, but that its effect is decidedly larger among the rich. A unit change in attitudes toward improving Black living conditions increases the expected value of redistribution preferences by roughly 0.8 points among the poor. Its effect is twice as large among the rich, where it increases support for redistribution by 1.6 points.[30]

7.2.7 The Crucial Role of Race

We finally turn to our delayed discussion of the role of race in the United States. As discussed earlier, we did not include an indicator of race in our previous analysis of preferences because we argued that a simple dummy variable does not adequately capture many channels of economic disadvantage for African Americans. We employ a stricter statistical specification in this section. We reestimate our model separately for respondents (self-)classified as Black versus all others. This amounts to a specification where the coefficients on income distance and on state-level shares of Black welfare recipients, as well as on all covariates, are allowed to differ for African American respondents. We then calculate expected values of redistribution support like in Figure 7.2 on page 170. The results of this analysis are plotted in Figure 7.3. It immediately conveys two stark findings. First, we find our core prediction confirmed even when limiting our sample to non-Black respondents. The left panel in Figure 7.3 clearly shows effects of heterogeneity conditional on income that are very similar to our main results. Second, this effect is not present among the African American subset of our sample, although the point estimates suggest a pattern in the expected direction. While poor African Americans, too,

---

[29] The full question wording is "We are faced with many problems in this country, none of which can be solved easily or inexpensively. I'm going to name some of these problems, and for each one I'd like you to name some of these problems, and for each one I'd like you to tell me whether you think we're spending too much money on it: Improving the conditions of Blacks." Answer options are "too little, about right, too much." We will not enter here into the debate in American politics on whether racial prejudice is best understood as "old-fashioned racism" (see, for example, Sniderman and Tetlock, 1986) or as "symbolic racism" (Kinder and Sears, 1981).

[30] The difference between these two effects is statistically different from zero.

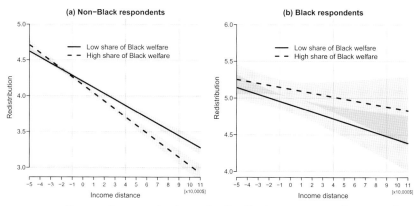

FIGURE 7.3 Race and expected values of redistribution support as function of income distance and state-level heterogeneity in the United States: Panel (a) shows results for the subset of non-Black respondents, panel (b) for the subset of Black respondents

show little reaction to changes in population heterogeneity, the rich living in areas with more heterogeneity are more supportive of redistributive policy.[31] While the rather large confidence intervals indicate that no statistically significant conclusions can be drawn from that particular (small) sample, this result is compatible with our main arguments. In effect, by dividing the sample, we are redefining in-group and out-group in a more meaningful way for Black respondents. Affluent African Americans would experience an increase in the altruism effect (rather than a decline as non-Black respondents) when the share of in-group individuals as welfare recipients grows.

[31] Note also that the relationship between income and demand for redistribution is weaker for African Americans, as reflected on the flatter slopes in panel (b). Affluent African Americans have more similar preferences to those of poor African American, and this could be relate to a sense of linked fate (see Dawson, 1995).

PART IV

FROM PREFERENCES TO VOTING

8

The Political Consequences of Redistribution Demands

In the introduction to this book we asked why we should care about redistribution preferences. When discussing Figure 1.1, we argued that the (often implicit) model behind much of the comparative politics and political economy literature starts with redistribution preferences. These redistribution preferences affect how individuals behave politically and their political behavior (whether it is voting or other less-conventional forms of political participation) then affects, and is in turn affected by, the actions of political parties (and other political agents). In this concluding section of the book we will focus on perhaps the most momentous potential consequence of redistribution preferences: voting. This is not a trivial topic. Not only because of the importance of the outcome itself, but also because, while a significant literature in political economy has recently focused on the relationship between inequality and redistribution preferences, it is unclear that these preferences have in fact any influence over political behavior.

Inequality and redistribution have seen a resurgence in academic interest in recent times. This is particularly the case in the United States, where Bartels (2009) has shown the spectacular increase in inequality over the past thirty-five years to be the product of policy choices in a political system dominated by partisanship and particularly receptive to the preferences of the wealthy. Hacker and Pierson (2011) coincide not only in the appreciation of the attention that policy-makers pay to the rich but also about the fact that politics is the main factor behind inequality ("American politics did it"). This chapter's analysis addresses one of the implications of most arguments about the importance of economic circumstances to political outcomes. If income (and inequality) matter to individual political behavior, it seems reasonable to assume that they do so through their influence on redistribution preferences. These redistribution preferences may (or may not) then be reflected on party positions and, eventually, government policy. In the United States, rising inequality has become a visible feature of the economy (e.g., Levy and Murnane, 1992; Gottschalk, 1997; Piketty and Saez, 2003) as well as of mainstream political debates. The same can be said about immigration or race in political debates all over Western Europe and America. At the same time, as we will show later (but also as observed by Gelman et al., 2008 for the case of the United States), affluent people in some regions and states are much more likely to vote for redistributive parties than in others (while for the poor, this difference is much less pronounced). Are these two issues (one concerning the demand for redistribution, the other electoral outcomes) related?

The connection between inequality and political behavior remains unclear. A number of observers would deny that income and inequality are significant determinants of voting.[1] We agree with McCarty et al. when they contend that:

Although much recent work in comparative political economy has sought to link inequality to political conflict and back to economic policy, few of these insights have been applied to American politics. [...] Perhaps one reason for the dearth of interest is that income or wealth has not been seen as a reliable predictor of political beliefs and partisanship in the mass public, especially in comparison to other cleavages, such as race and region, or in comparison to other democracies. (McCarty et al., 2008: 73)

Some analysts would agree that an individual's income affects her political behavior,[2] but they would not necessarily agree on the reasons why this is the case. This chapter therefore returns to one of our motivating questions and addresses one of the implications of most arguments about the importance of economic circumstances to political outcomes. Income, inequality, and altruism, as we have shown in the previous sections of this book, significantly influence redistribution preferences. But do they matter to individual political behavior?

---

[1] See, for example, Green et al. (2004) and Lewis-Beck (2009) or, more recently, Achen and Bartels (2016).

[2] There is an influential literature in political science on how pocketbook issues and class (both closely related to income) influence voting. See Downs (1957), Key (1966), or Fiorina (1981) on pocketbook issues and Lipset (1983), Evans (1999), or Brooks and Manza (1997) on class.

In this chapter, the final substantive analysis before moving on to the conclusions, we want to make three related points. The first one revisits our main arguments about the determinants of redistribution preferences and offers a joint model for the impact of present and expected income, inequality, and heterogeneity. The second one is that inequality and heterogeneity matter more to the voting behavior of the rich than that of the poor. Our third and most important point is that redistribution preferences do indeed matter to voting and that these voting patterns can (in a significant part) be explained by the fact that the preferences of rich voters in high-inequality and high-heterogeneity regions are systematically different from those of rich voters in low-inequality and low-heterogeneity regions. Our arguments add to those prevalent in the literature in two important ways. First, most political economy models link individual characteristics to behavioral outcomes making the essential assumption that there is a relationship between preferences and voting. We specify explicitly the theoretical mechanisms that determine preferences and party choice and test them empirically. Second, an important debate about the lack of redistributive policies in industrialized democracies after the "golden age of social democracy" has centered around the perception that second-dimension issues have become disproportionately important to the poor. As we have mentioned in previous chapters, a good example of this is the contention that cultural, religious, and social values outweigh economic concerns for the American working class in some states (see Frank, 2004 and, more recently, Hersh and Nall, 2016). The implication of these arguments is that the solution to the puzzle affecting (the lack of) redistribution in these countries concerns demand. We show in this chapter that this may not be the case. We find the poor to be uniformly in favor of redistribution and therefore uniformly more likely to vote for redistributive parties. The puzzle of redistribution may have more to do with supply (what parties do, the effects of electoral institutions, etc.) than with demand.

8.1 INCOME, INEQUALITY, HETEROGENEITY, AND REDISTRIBUTION PREFERENCES

Little needs to be written by now about the relationship between, on the one hand, income, inequality, and heterogeneity and, on the other hand, redistribution preferences. The previous three sections in the book have presented a cumulative picture of (1) the influence of expected future income as a good measure capturing risk/insurance/mobility motivations;

(2) the importance of the negative externalities connected to macro levels of inequality; and (3) the other-regarding motivations underlying the effects of population heterogeneity. While we have provided evidence in previous chapter that the effects of any one of our variables of interest are robust to controlling for rest, we go a step further in this section of the book. We provide a joint model for the influence of these three effects that allows us to consider their substantive importance simultaneously.

We have mentioned before that, to the extent that macro inequality is related to levels of population heterogeneity, the relationships proposed in Parts II and III of this book have similar empirical implications. We can show, however, that this is not the case. We do this in two ways, by illustrating the lack of a relationship in our estimation sample and by describing more generally the evolution of inequality and heterogeneity in Western Europe and the United States.

Figure 8.1 reflects the lack of a clear relationship between heterogeneity and inequality. In the figure, we use our estimation sample to plot average levels of inequality and heterogeneity by state and region. Focusing on the American data, panel (a) in the figure shows high variation in inequality corresponding to both low and high levels of Black welfare recipiency rates. There are states with low average inequality and low-black welfare recipiency rates (like New Hampshire and Maryland). And there are states with high inequality and low Black welfare recipiency rates (like Montana and Wyoming). The same, however, can be said when we look at states with high rates of Black welfare recipiency.

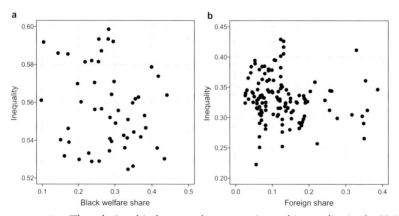

FIGURE 8.1 The relationship between heterogeneity and inequality in the United States (panel a) and Western Europe (panel b)

There are some with low inequality (like Wisconsin and West Virginia) and some with high inequality (like Mississippi and Louisiana). It is difficult to discern a systematic relationship between inequality and black welfare recipiency rates from the figure. A similar conclusion follows a visual inspection of the relationship between inequality and foreign-born population in the Western European regions in our sample. Panel (b) shows European regions with low shares of foreign-born population and both low levels of inequality (Cantabria and Vorarlberg) and high levels of inequality (like the Mid West of Ireland or Northern Ireland). At the highest levels of foreign-born population, we still can see regions with low levels of inequality (such as the Ticino canton and South Sweden) and with high levels of inequality (like London and the Brussels region).

Figure 8.2 focuses on over-time variation and shows the development of inequality and heterogeneity in the United States and Western Europe.[3] Several patterns are noteworthy. First, the levels of inequality are generally higher in the American states that in our Western European nations (even if the variation at any given point in time in Western Europe and the United States is similar). Over time, moreover, there is secular increase in inequality in most American states that is much less visible in Western Europe (this is the case even when we focus on the post-1990 period). In regard to population heterogeneity (and keeping in mind that these are two very different measures), there is larger geographic variation in heterogeneity in the United States than in Western Europe. Over time, there is a secular increase in the share of foreign-born population in Western Europe while there is a general decrease in the Black welfare recipiency rates in the United States (there is lower heterogeneity in many US states in 2010 when compared to the 1980s). Again, then, there is little concern from the evidence reflected in Figure 8.2 about inequality and heterogeneity being highly correlated.[4]

We therefore model the joint impact of income, inequality, and heterogeneity on citizens' redistribution preferences and revisit some of the main findings from the previous sections of the book. We estimate sepa-

---

[3] In order to display information for a larger time span, this figure does not use our estimation sample. Instead, we use information from the OECD migration database on the (national) share of the non-native-born population, and Gini indices calculated by Solt (2016).

[4] There is, however, the possibility that inequality and heterogeneity have interactive effects over redistributive voting, as suggested by Huber (2017). We come back to this issue in Section 8.4.

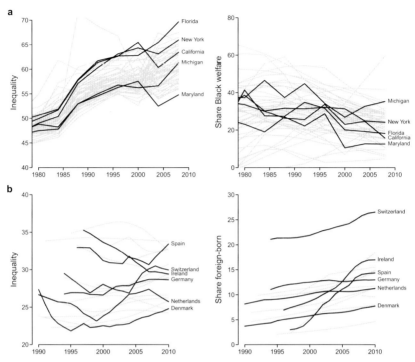

FIGURE 8.2 Inequality and heterogeneity in the United States (panel a) and Western Europe (panel b)

rate models for the United States and Western Europe that include our measures of local heterogeneity and inequality, as well as respondents' expected income. In order to make results from both models and different variables easier to compare, we estimate linear models and standardize preferences to have unit standard deviation. We then express all effects in terms of an increase from the tenth to the ninetieth percentile of the respective distribution of each variable. The results of this analysis are shown in Table 8.1.

Starting with expected income, we confirm the highly similar pattern in the United States and Western Europe shown in Chapter 3. An increase in expected income reduces preferences for redistribution in the United States by 0.26 standard deviations, while an equally sized increase in Western Europe reduces preferences by 0.28 standard deviations. As shown in Part 1, individual expected income concerns (whether related to insurance, risk, mobility, or other factors) influences the present demand for redistribution in a very substantive way. The estimates in Table 8.1

TABLE 8.1 *Joint models for the impact of expected and present income, inequality, and heterogeneity on preferences for redistribution in Western Europe and the United States*

	United States[a]	Western Europe[b]
A: Expected income	−0.261	−0.282
	(0.033)	(0.024)
B: Inequality × present income		
Poor	−0.010	0.113
	(0.046)	(0.055)
Rich	0.193	0.202
	(0.035)	(0.073)
C: Heterogeneity × present income		
Poor	0.033	0.004
	(0.027)	(0.051)
Rich	−0.081	−0.103
	(0.033)	(0.050)

Note: Entries are effects of moving from tenth to ninetieth percentile of the respective variable, holding everything else at observed values. Preferences are in standard deviation units. Expected income matched based on age × education-specific Mincer wage regressions. Age and education controls are net of expected income. Heteroscedasticity-consistent standard errors in parentheses.
[a]General Social Survey, 1978–2010. Linear model with fixed effects for 49 states, controlling for age, education, indicator variables for female part-time work, unemployment, self-employment, living in a city, being a union member, and state level unemployment rate.
[b]European Social Survey (ESS), 2002–2008. Linear model with random effects for 129 regions, controlling for household size, age, education. Indicator variables for survey years, being unemployed, self-employed, not in the labor force, and living in an urban area.

also confirm the conclusions in Part II about the income-dependent effects of the negative externalities of inequality. In the United States, an increase in inequality from the tenth to the ninetieth percentile of the state distribution increases the redistribution preferences of the rich by 0.19 standard deviations, but it has no discernible effects on the demands of the poor. In Western Europe, an increase in inequality from the tenth to the ninetieth percentile of the regional distribution increases the redistribution preferences of both the poor and the rich. But this increase is much more substantial for the rich (0.20 standard deviations, almost double the effect for the poor). Focusing on population heterogeneity, the estimates in Table 8.1 show it to be irrelevant to the demand for redistribution of the poor whether we look at the data from the United States or from Western Europe. An increase in population heterogeneity from the tenth to the ninetieth percentile of either the state or regional distributions, however, decreases the support for redistribution by the rich in important and similar ways in both our ESS and GSS analyses. In the United States and Europe, the rich demand less redistribution by more than 0.08 and almost 0.10 standard deviations, respectively. As in Part III, we find the altruism of the affluent to be severely limited by immigration and racial diversity.

8.2 REDISTRIBUTION PREFERENCES AND POLITICAL BEHAVIOR

In this chapter we argue for the unequivocal relevance of redistribution preferences to voting. Our starting point here is the assumption that economic factors affect individual preferences and, therefore, voting behavior. We follow a well-established literature on the relationship between income and political behavior. As mentioned at previous points in the book, the assumption that an individual's position in the income distribution contributes to her redistributive political preferences is widely extended. The literature on economic voting and class voting are based on similar arguments. Like authors in the economic voting tradition (e.g., Duch and Stevenson, 2008), our argument posits that there is a relationship between an individual's economic interests and her likelihood to vote for a particular party. Class voting analyses (e.g., Evans, 1999; Evans and de Graaf, 2013) emphasize the effects of socioeconomic cleavages on political preferences, but their focus on occupational factors is largely compatible with our arguments. Our approach is also related to a recent literature that emphasizes risks and skills as determinants of preferences. While this literature associates unemployment vulnerability with skill profiles (e.g., Cusack et al., 2006), we highlight the importance of redistribution preferences (regardless of skills).

Like the traditional economic voting literature (Downs, 1957), we conceive of voters as instrumental rational actors. Individuals will vote following a comparison of what they gain or lose from the policies proposed by each party. In the words of Duch and Stevenson, we assume that "voters rationally derive expected utilities for competing political parties and that these determine their vote choice" (2008: 9). As in the pioneering work of Kramer (1971) and Fair (1978), we consider that economic well-being (and therefore redistribution and insurance) is a significant factor affecting a voter's utility function.

As an aside, an important literature would disagree with the starting point we described earlier and posit that the poor are diverted from the pursuit of their material self-interest. We can revisit here one of the arguments mentioned in several of the previous chapters: the contention that second-dimension issues (particularly cultural and social ones) outweigh economic ones for the American working class. Frank (2004) and the critique in Bartels (2006) are good illustrations of this debate, but so is the emphasis on cosmopolitanism as a determinant of voting in Gelman et al. (2008). More comparatively, De La O and Rodden (2008) argued that religion distracts the poor from their material interests and that there is a moral values dimension that explains the vote of the poor better than income, especially in countries with multiparty systems.[5] In his contribution to the political economy of identity formation, Shayo (2009) follows a related logic. His theoretical model emphasizes two identity dimensions: economic class and nationality. As a result of status differences, the poor are more likely than the rich to identify with the nation rather than their class in high inequality countries. Because they take group interests into account, moreover, the poor who identify with the nation are less supportive of redistribution than the poor who identify with their class.

While not denying that moral, cultural, or national-status issues are important to voting in industrialized democracies, we emphasize the importance of redistribution preferences. We will show later that the effects of income, inequality, and heterogeneity *through* redistribution preferences are a powerful determinant of voting even when allowing for other channels of influence (such as values).

A substantial literature debates the issue of how exactly economic considerations enter into the voter's utility function. Two main approaches can be distinguished, one emphasizing *sanctioning* and the other focusing on *selection* (here, we follow the analysis provided in Duch and Stevenson, 2008). The *sanctioning model* is characterized by the consideration that voters are narrowly retrospective and mostly motivated by punishing or rewarding incumbents (see the classic works of Key, 1966; Kramer, 1971; Fiorina, 1981). Focusing on moral hazard, i.e., the risk of rent-seeking by incumbents if not punished for bad economic outcomes,

---

[5] But see Stegmueller (2013b) for evidence that the redistributive vote of religious individuals is primarily based on economic not moral preferences. For the United States, see McCarty et al. (2008: 100–101), who show that income is an extraordinarily good predictor of partisanship and voting even among conservative Christians.

Barro (1973) and Ferejohn (1986) also belong within this tradition. The *selection/competency model* argues that voters gather more information to assess the likely economic outcomes associated with competing political alternatives. Downs (1957) and Stigler (1973) are classical examples of this approach, but we would argue that this is also the understanding of voting underlying Meltzer and Richard (1981) and subsequent political economy treatments of redistribution and voting (Persson and Tabellini, 2000). While the sanctioning model has dominated the economic voting literature, it is clear that our argument implies a selection logic. We propose that individuals who are in favor of redistribution will identify Left parties as more likely to promote equality and therefore be more likely to vote for it.[6]

More specifically, we consider voting to be a discrete choice. By this we mean a decision made over a set of exclusive and exhaustive choices (see Duch and Stevenson, 2008: 39). Each voting choice (i.e., the parties a voter can select) offers some utility with regard to the voter's redistribution preferences. It is the contribution of these individual redistributive preferences to the voting choice that matters to the main focus of this chapter, but our approach can be described in more general terms. Like Alvarez et al. (2000: 240), we assume that each individual obtains some utility from each party and that the individual votes for the party offering the highest utility. The utility of each party is understood to be a function of a set of systematic components (specific to the voter, to the party and to the election) and a random disturbance. The parameters in these random utility models are often estimated with multinomial probit techniques using distance variables as the predictors. These variables reflect the spatial distance between a respondent's position on an issue (in our case, redistribution) and the respondent's view of each party's position on the same issue (for examples of this approach, see Alvarez and Nagler, 1995, 1998). In the analyses that follow, we lack information on the respondent's views of each party's position, and we use party labels and party manifesto information on party positions instead.[7] Using both American and European data, we explore individual vote choice as an unobserved vector of probabilities associated to the redistributive positions of different parties.

---

[6] The selection logic, as it applies to the focus of our analysis, of course, depends on Left parties actually supporting redistributive policies. We return to this issue later when exploring alternative measures of vote choice.

[7] We sacrifice an explicit measure of spatial distance on redistribution here to maximize the coverage of countries and years in our analysis.

While these intuitions are pretty straightforward, they have arguably not received enough attention in the existing Comparative Politics literature. Two clear illustrations of this are major recent works on partisan identification and voting in the United States by Green et al. (2004) and Lewis-Beck (2009).[8] Both analyses underplay the importance of income (and, even more so, of its connection to redistribution preferences). To the extent that income and redistribution preferences are considered in this literature, it is often through the prism of "class voting" (see, for example, Evans, 1999; Evans and de Graaf, 2013).[9] But this approach is quite distinct from the political economy arguments that we present in this book.

Even though income does not emerge from the previous chapters in this book as the only determinant of redistribution preferences, perhaps the approaches that are most similar to the one we attempt later are those exploring a link between income and voting. In Comparative Politics, this means the work on economic voting (as in Duch and Stevenson, 2008), some versions of issue voting (see, for example, Ansolabehere et al., 2008), but also some work on religion and redistributive voting (like De La O and Rodden, 2008 or Stegmueller, 2013b). In American Politics, McCarty et al. (2008),[10] and their finding that voting in presidential elections is increasingly linked to income, is compatible with our arguments. But the equilibrium in most political economy models is achieved by individuals deriving their preferences over optimal fiscal policy based on their income position, which are then "aggregated into an economywide policy via the collective choice mechanism in place" (Drazen, 2000: 312). Thus the two central concepts are citizens' redistribution preferences (or ideal points) and vote choices (the collective choice mechanism). Moreover, the traditional mode of empirical analysis has also been to relate income to economy-wide outcomes, such as spending (see, e.g., the summaries of empirical research in Persson and Tabellini, 2000; Mueller, 2003). This, however, simply assumes that our central argument – the relationship between preferences and voting – is indeed the mechanism at work (whether looking at the

---

[8] The more recent contribution by Achen and Bartels (2016) could also be added here. Our book challenges their argument that political loyalties (typically acquired in childhood) and economic myopia determine political behavior.

[9] In the American case, Lewis-Beck (2009) finds class to have become less significant a determinant of voting in presidential elections, while Manza and Brooks (1999) find the class cleavage to be stable from 1952 to 1996. In a more recent contribution, Hersh and Nall (2016) find income-based voting to be less important than racial context.

[10] But see also Brooks and Brady (1999), who argue that income shapes voting behavior indirectly (by affecting evaluations of social welfare and government size).

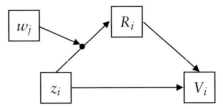

FIGURE 8.3 Illustration of joint model of preferences and vote choice

effects of income on voting or policy as an outcome). Our contribution here is to specify explicitly the theoretical mechanisms that determine preferences and party choice and to test them empirically.

Figure 8.3 summarizes the main claims in this chapter. The first one is that inequality and heterogeneity matter more to the voting behavior of the rich than that of the poor. We expect to observe a positive interaction effect between income distance and macro-levels of inequality and heterogeneity. Our second point is that these voting patterns can be (partly) explained by the fact that the preferences of rich voters in high-inequality and high-heterogeneity contexts are systematically different. The figure illustrates the structure of the empirical model implied by our arguments. In its lower half it illustrates that an individual's vote choice, V_i, is shaped by his or her income distance, denoted z_i, but that this relationship is influenced by the existing macro-level context, w_j (representing inequality or heterogeneity). The upper half of Figure 8.3 illustrates a key part of this chapter's analysis. It shows how preferences, R_i, are introduced as an intermediary variable, mediating the impact of the interaction between income distance and inequality and heterogeneity on vote choice. The quantity of interest is a decomposition of the income-dependent effects of inequality and heterogeneity into "direct" and "indirect" paths, that is, to which extent their effect on vote choice is due to preferences for redistribution (the path to V_i going through R_i) as opposed to many other possible channels (general ideology, second dimension concerns, etc.: the path going directly to V_i).

8.2.1 Decomposing Direct and Indirect Effects

To give a more precise description of the quantities we want to estimate, we define them in the potential outcomes framework (Robins, 2003; VanderWeele and Vansteelandt, 2009; Imai et al., 2011). This does, of course, not entail the claim that the quantities we estimate are automatically causal. Rather, we argue that an explicit definition lays bare what it is that we want to know, and what assumptions are needed to know it (VanderWeele, 2010; see also Pearl, 2001 on the necessity of a clear operational definition of indirect effects). In the best of circumstances (which are unlikely to be met in an observational analysis), estimating these quantities does produce a causal estimate of direct and indirect effects. In the second-best version, an analysis needs to acknowledge untested assumptions and find ways to demonstrate empirically the quantitative impact of their violation.[11] Following the strategy of Imai et al. (2010), we conduct sensitivity analyses to see how robust our results are against violations.

Let us describe the decomposition of *direct* and *indirect* effects. To illustrate what we mean, we use the relationship between relative income and inequality, but the explanation would equally apply to the effects of population heterogeneity. Following the setup depicted in Figure 8.3, denote by z_i the income distance (to the national mean) of individual i living in a state or region with level of inequality w_j. She prefers a certain level of redistribution, which is a function of her income and the level of inequality, which we write as $R_i(z_i, w_j | x_{1i})$. Possibly confounding variables (individual and contextual characteristics) are denoted by x_{1i}. At election time she casts her vote based on her redistribution preferences and on a number of other factors. We write this vote function as $V_i(z_i, w_j, R_i(z_i, w_j | x_{1i}) | x_{2i})$. Again, we allow for a set of possible confounders, x_{2i}. Note that inequality appears twice (corresponding to the two possible paths in Figure 8.3): as a factor changing preferences (which in turn shape vote choice) and as a factor directly shaping vote choice (via possibly infinitely many other possible channels).

---

[11] Importantly, the usual assumptions of standard regression models still apply. What we focus on now are additional assumptions needed to decompose different mechanisms. The first assumption is that, after conditioning on included observables, there are no unobserved confounders that change with treatment (e.g., income) and affect vote choice (V_i) or preferences (R_i). The second assumption concerns the mediating variable, namely redistribution preferences. It requires that no unobserved confounders affect both V_i and R_i after conditioning on observables (x_{1i}, x_{2i}). Clearly, much weight rests on the set of covariates to be correctly specified. In our empirical application, as in any analysis having to rely on observational data, we accept that these conditions are likely to be violated to some degree. We therefore use sensitivity analyses (discussed in Appendix A.5.2) to gauge how increasingly severe violations of these identifying assumptions influence our results.

To understand the role of, say, inequality, examine a counterfactual shift in inequality from w_j to w'_j. The *total effect* of this change in inequality on vote choice is given by (we omit covariates for clarity):

$$TE \equiv V_i(z_i, w_j, R_i(z_i, w_j)) - V_i(z_i, w'_j, R_i(z_i, w'_j)). \qquad (8.1)$$

This is the expected difference in the probability of voting for a redistributive party as a result of changing inequality. It results from the combination of the systematic effects of changing preferences, as well as of all other factors not relevant to our argument. As emphasized earlier, we are interested in decomposing the total effect into two components: the effect due to preferences and the effect due to other factors.[12] To get the former, we define the effect that a (counterfactual) change in inequality has on vote choice through redistribution preferences *alone* (Pearl, 2001). By fixing inequality and only changing preferences, we isolate our preference mechanism and eliminate the impact of competing mechanisms (Imai et al., 2011: 769). Thus, the effect channeled via redistribution preferences, termed the *indirect effect*, is given by:

$$IE \equiv V_i(z_i, w_j, R_i(z_i, w_j)) - V_i(z_i, w_j, R_i(z_i, w'_j)). \qquad (8.2)$$

This is a strict statistical expression of our hypothesized inequality–preference nexus *net* of alternative channels (such as, for example, second dimension concerns).

The remaining effect of changes in inequality on vote choice *not* transmitted via preferences is termed the *direct effect*, defined by changing levels of inequality in the vote function, but keeping it fixed in the preference function:

$$DE \equiv V_i(z_i, w_j, R_i(z_i, w_j)) - V_i(z_i, w'_j, R_i(z_i, w_j)). \qquad (8.3)$$

It thus represents how inequality affects vote choice in ways that are not considered in our model (i.e., through all mechanisms other than preferences).

We now describe the statistical model used to estimate the quantities described. Let y_{1ijt} be the observed vote choice of individual i ($i = 1, \ldots, n_{jt}$) in state or region j ($j = 1, \ldots, J$) at time point (year) t ($t = 1, \ldots, T$). We model choices in terms of an underlying latent index, y^*, such that $y_{1ijt} = 1$ if $y^*_{1ijt} > 0$ and zero otherwise. Let y_{2ijt} denote

---

[12] To understand *how* inequality shapes the vote via preferences it is not enough to look at disparate sets of regression coefficients (of, say, inequality on preferences, and preferences on voting).

redistribution preferences of the same individual, which we treat as continuous for simplicity.[13] Our model consists of the following jointly estimated two equations:

$$y^*_{1ijt} = x'_{ijt}\boldsymbol{\alpha}_1 + \lambda y_{2ijt} + \delta_1 z_{ijt} + \beta^I w^I_{jt} + \beta^H w^H_{jt} + \xi_j + \epsilon_{1ijt} \tag{8.4}$$

$$y_{2ijt} = x'_{ijt}\boldsymbol{\alpha}_2 + \delta_2 z_{ijt} + \gamma^I_1 w^I_{jt} + \gamma^I_2 w^I_{jt} z_{ijt} + \gamma^H_1 w^H_{jt} + \gamma^H_2 w^H_{jt} z_{ijt} + \zeta_j + \epsilon_{2ijt} \tag{8.5}$$

The first equation describes vote choice as a function of income distance z_{ijt}, inequality, w^I_{jt} and heterogeneity, w^H_{jt}. Endogenous preferences for redistribution, y_{2ijt}, influence vote choice via λ. Preferences are modeled as a function of covariates, income distance and its interaction with inequality and heterogeneity. Both equations include a vector of both individual and regional covariates (also including our measure of expected income), x_{ijt}, with associated coefficients $\boldsymbol{\alpha}_1$ and $\boldsymbol{\alpha}_2$. We also account for (time-constant) unobserved state or region effects affecting preferences and choices (via ζ_j and ξ_j). Note that the income-dependent effects of inequality and heterogeneity reach vote choice in two ways: via their coefficients in the first equation and via their effect on preferences, which in turn affect choices.

With estimates from our joint preference and vote model in hand, we can calculate the direct and indirect (counterfactual) effects specified in equations (8.2) and (8.3).[14]

8.3 DATA AND MEASUREMENT OF VOTE CHOICE

To explore the hypotheses explained earlier, we again use data from the European and General Social Surveys (as in Chapter 5). Our analysis of US elections covers nine presidential races between 1976 and 2008. We limit our sample to those who did cast a vote in a presidential election, leaving us with 10,215 observations. After removing individuals with missing values on covariates our final sample is comprised of 9,071 individuals.[15] Our Western European analysis covers elections between 1999 and 2009,

---

[13] Using a more complex latent variable model does not make a substantive difference to our results.

[14] See, for example, the discussion in Muthén and Asparouhov (2015).

[15] Due to the complexity of the model used, we opted not to use multiple imputation for missing covariates in the analyses reported in the main text. We also removed individuals for which we observe neither vote choice nor preferences. The redistribution item is only presented to a subset of respondents; we impute these missing-at-random responses as part of the MCMC sampler. Note that we obtain qualitatively identical results when we omit these cases instead (for a sample of 5,012 cases). The majority of missing cases are

which we match to the corresponding waves from the ESS. If multiple survey waves matched one election, we use the one closest in time. Table A.11 in the appendix shows survey fieldwork periods and election dates for waves included in our analysis.

The influence of redistribution preferences is the main focus in this chapter's analysis of voting. For this reason, it is of paramount importance that the voting data coincides with the redistribution preferences data. As explained in more detail later, respondents self-report the party they voted for in the previous national election. At the time of the survey, these elections have taken place in the past while redistribution preferences are measured in the present. It is important, therefore, to restrict the analysis to ESS waves when this coincidence of data is reasonable.[16] This also requires special attention to when the surveys were actually conducted. The ESS surveys are fielded over a period of months, often starting at the end of the wave year and running into the following one. In the following analysis, we try to minimize the time between the date when the national election has been held and when the ESS survey was conducted (so that redistribution preferences are plausibly connected with voting behavior). We also eliminate surveys that were conducted in months that include an election (and therefore may contain voting choices for different elections depending on the respondent's interview date). In practical terms, this means the analysis matches macro-micro data for twenty-four elections held in fifteen countries, namely Austria, Belgium, Germany, Denmark, Spain, Finland, France, Great Britain, Ireland, Luxembourg, the Netherlands, Norway, Portugal, Sweden, and Switzerland.

Vote Choice in the United States

Recall from our theoretical intuitions earlier that we model voting as a discrete choice influenced by the distance between an individual's redistribution preferences and the redistributive positions of the parties she can vote for. This approach requires us to define whether a party is redistributive or not. In the US context, this is straightforward enough. Our dependent variable translates into a respondent choosing the Democratic Party (which consistently offers relatively more redistributive policy positions) over the Republican alternative.

---

due to missing income information. In Appendix A.5.3 we discuss this issue and provide an analysis where we impute income.

[16] The same considerations apply to measures of relative income, inequality, and heterogeneity, which are part of the redistribution preferences estimation.

Our vote choice variable is based on the retrospective self-report of GSS respondents (which party did they vote for in the last presidential election?).[17] We create a simple indicator variable equal to 1 if a vote was cast for the Democrats and 0 if the Republican Party was chosen. As in other analyses of voting in the United States (see Gelman et al., 2008 or Hersh and Nall, 2016), respondents who abstained or chose a third candidate (such as Anderson in 1980 or Perot in 1992/96) are not included in the sample, to allow us to make meaningful "two-party choice" comparisons.[18]

We have argued earlier that rich individuals who live in unequal or homogeneous states will be more likely to support redistribution and, therefore, to vote Democrat. The first stage of our argument involves the relationship between relative income and voting. As Gelman et al. (2008) have noted, affluent people in some states are much more likely to vote for the Democratic Party than in other states (while for the poor, this difference is much less pronounced). Figure 8.4 presents data on the average percentage of Democratic vote among the poor and the rich in presidential elections from 1976 to 2008. The poor are defined as those $32,590 below the national income mean, the rich are those $26,953 above the mean (these correspond to the ninetieth and tenth percentiles in the national income distribution). It is important to mention that these are averages over time, not reflecting the temporal variation that will be captured by the analysis in the following sections. Nevertheless, the figure confirms the general findings in Gelman et al. (2008), the poor are generally highly likely to vote Democrat. The states in the upper panel are uniformly dark. There are a couple of exceptions (Montana and Maine) where the percentage of Democratic voters among the poor is unusually low (around 20 percent). But the rest of states have uniformly high levels of Democratic vote (in thirty-six states, the percentage is higher than 50 percent; in thirty states, it is higher than 60 percent).

---

[17] There are well-known issues with misreporting of turnout and vote choice in academic surveys (see Selb and Munzert, 2013 for an excellent discussion). This raises concerns, especially because our survey interviews often occur more than one year after the act of casting a vote. Wright (1990) argues that respondents are more likely to state that they have voted for the winner as time passes (cf. the debate between Gronke, 1992 and Wright, 1992). To account for this possibility we estimate models that include the time (in days) between election and survey interview. Rainey and Jackson (2013) show that this strategy often works well to capture misreporting. We find that our results are little affected. See Appendix A.5.4 for more details.

[18] In further work we will incorporate a full model for abstention. Note, however, that a proper unified model of turnout and party choice is a lot more complex than simply including abstention as another "party" (see, e.g., Adams et al., 2006).

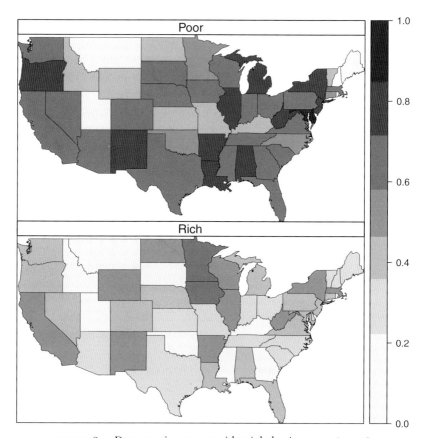

FIGURE 8.4 Democratic vote, presidential elections 1976–2008

Voting Democrat among the rich, however, exhibits much higher state variance. There are states with very low percentages (below 20): Kentucky, Oklahoma, and Mississippi. There are states with low percentages (between 20 and 30): Idaho, Montana, Georgia, New Hampshire, Ohio, Delaware, and Texas. There are a number of states with percentages of Democratic votes between 30 and 40: Arizona, Kansas, Indiana, North Carolina, Tennessee, Vermont, Maine, South Carolina, Florida, Missouri, and Virginia. There are then 20 states with percentages of Democratic vote between 40 and 50 and 5 states where these percentages are higher than 50: Massachusetts, Minnesota, Iowa, and DC.

Vote Choice in Western Europe

In the Western European multiparty context, defining what constitutes a redistributive party is more complex than in the US case. On the one hand, we could use a party "label" as the indicator of redistributive position. In this approach, a "Left" party would be considered a redistributive party by virtue of its ideology and its commitments to historically meaningful groups of voters. The existence of stable ideological and historical connections between parties and some social groups "not only creates easily identifiable choices for citizens, it also makes it easier for parties to seek out their probable supporters and mobilize them at election time" (Powell, 1982: 116). To the extent that party labels are used as information shortcuts by voters to capture a party's redistributive position, this is an attractive strategy. In the analysis later, we classify parties as "Left" (and therefore "redistributive") if their party family is either socialist/social democratic or communist as recorded by the Comparative Manifesto Project (CMP).[19]

Labels, ideology, and history, however, are not enough. Elections need to be contested, and they inevitably revolve around issues, like redistribution, that give political meaning to partisan attachments and social divisions (Dalton, 2002: 195). Moreover, in our analysis of Western Europe, simply classifying parties based on their label might not constitute a proper operationalization of the concept of redistributive voting because country- as well as election-specific factors influence parties' position on redistribution.

We therefore construct an alternative dependent variable based on of how much redistribution a party proposes in its electoral platform.[20] Using data from the Comparative Manifesto Project (Budge et al., 2001) and its 2016 update (Volkens et al., 2016), we calculate the extent to which parties favor state involvement in the economy — a measure of redistributive politics proposed by Benoit and Laver (2006, 2007).[21] It is calculated from parties' statements on multiple economic topics (represented by "quasi sentences" in the CMP data set), which are combined into a measure of a party's policy position as the balance of negative (N) to positive (P) statements[22] following Lowe et al. (2011): $\theta = \log \frac{N+.5}{P+.5}$. Parties can occupy any position on this scale, but more extreme positions need

---

[19] For a more detailed review of party families, see Mair and Mudde (1998).

[20] For an alternative approach, see Huber (2017), who identifies the location of parties in the left–right redistributive continuum as the mean of the redistributive preferences for voters of that party.

[21] One should note that using the CMP's simple "left–right" measure is misleading because it carries surplus meaning that is not related to redistribution, such as positions on "traditional morality" (Huber and Stanig, 2008).

[22] Positive statements include those referring to market regulation, economic planning, protectionism, controlled economy, nationalization, welfare, education, and labor groups.

considerably more relative emphasis, yielding a magnitude scaling of policy positions.[23] This yields interval level information on the redistributive
policies of almost all European parties, where smaller values indicate a
more pro-redistributive position.[24]

For the following analyses, we create a binary variable indicating if a
party favors redistributive policies. We classify a party as redistributive if
it takes a policy position below (or "to the left of") the country-election
specific redistribution policy mean, and thus proposing more redistribution than the (hypothetical) average party. Taking the mean as a reference
point is the preferred strategy because the interval level measure of party
policy does not imply that zero is a centrist position (cf. Lowe et al., 2011:
131). It also makes clear that this reference point changes (endogenously)
with each new election in each country.

As we show in Figure 8.5, the distinction between "redistributive"
and "Left" parties turns out to be a significant one. This is the case
both when we consider the effects on the redistribution mean of the
electoral success of parties that are more redistributive than traditional
Left parties and also when we consider the recent influence of populist
parties.[25] We have chosen two countries (the UK and Spain) and present
both the redistributive positions and the vote percentages of some
selected parties.[26] The figure conveys several interesting ideas. First, it
illustrates which selected parties are more or less redistributive compared
to the country-election mean (indicated by the dashed line). Using our
first classification of redistributive parties based on the "Left" party
label (socialist/social democratic or communist families), Labour, PSOE,
and Podemos (but not its related regional parties like En Marea) are
considered redistributive throughout the period under analysis. The figure
makes clear, however, that when using the second classification, which is
based on parties occupying more redistributive positions than the country-

Negative statements refer to free market economy, incentives, (against) protectionism,
economic orthodoxy, and (against) welfare.

[23] Lowe et al. (2011) add a small constant (0.5) to prevent problems with low numbers of
quasi sentences.

[24] Some small, extreme parties are not represented in the data set because the CMP
contains no information on their position. An example is the National Democratic Party
(NPD) in Germany, a nationalistic, extreme right party. However, the number of survey
respondents that chose those parties is generally negligible.

[25] We return to this second issue in the Conclusions.

[26] While the following analysis considers all parties in the CMP data, we use only a sample
here to illustrate our points.

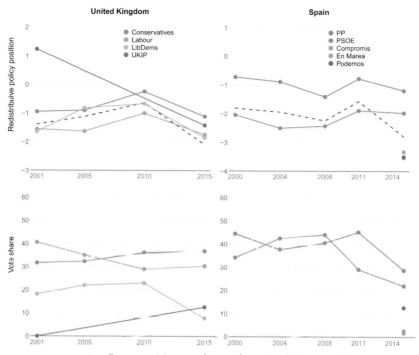

FIGURE 8.5 Party positions and vote shares in the UK and Spain

election mean, both Labour and PSOE are not considered redistributive in the 2015 elections. In Spain, the more redistributive positions of Izquierda Unida, Podemos, and related regional parties pull down the country-election mean, which makes PSOE propose less redistribution than the (hypothetical) average party in that election.[27] Second, the relatively stable and not particularly redistributive positions of the main "Left" parties (Labour and PSOE) are correlated with decreasing levels of electoral support after the beginning of the Great Recession. In the UK, Labour reaches its highest vote percent during our period of analysis in 2010. In Spain, PSOE does the same in the 2010 election. Third, in the 2015 Spanish election, the more redistributive Podemos-related parties obtain a significant amount of electoral support. In the UK, UKIP becomes much more redistributive from 2001 to 2015, even though it still does not cross the threshold to be considered a redistributive party. In an unsystematic but suggestive manner, UKIP's redistributive switch is

[27] The same could be said about the influence of the Green Party in the UK's 2015 election.

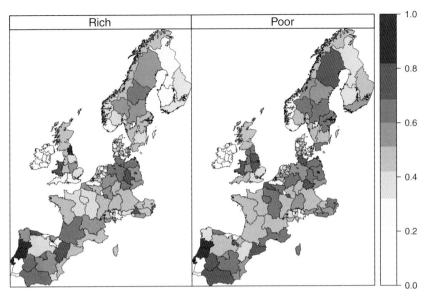

FIGURE 8.6 Vote share for Left parties in Western European regions

associated with a move from negligible voter support in 2001 to more than 12 percent of votes in 2015.

As was the case in our analysis of the US data, we are once again interested in the relationship between relative income and voting. Figure 8.6 presents data on the average vote share for Left parties in the Western European regions in our sample, among both the rich and the poor. The figure is meant as an illustration and uses only one of our alternative measures of "redistributive" parties. Given the limited number of observations in some regions, in this figure we have defined the rich and the poor differently from other parts of the book, as those above the eightieth and below the twentieth percentiles of the national (as opposed to regional) income distributions. The figure shows that as in the United States, the poor are generally highly likely to vote for this kind of redistributive parties. The regions in the right panel of the figure are generally darker than those in the left panel (although the exceptions are more numerous that in the American data).

In the figure, regions in the South and East of Spain, in England, or in Southern Sweden, for example, are a good illustration of the more general pattern we found in the United States (where the poor's vote share for Left parties is homogeneously higher than that of the rich). Regions in Ireland (where differences among parties have been long recognized not to follow a clear left–right dimension), exhibit a much less clear pattern. It is, of course, important to emphasize that this is not an accurate test of our hypotheses. For the conditional probabilities implied by our income-dependent claims, we now turn to a more systematic analysis of the relationships linking relative income, redistribution preferences, and voting.

8.4 REDISTRIBUTION PREFERENCES AND VOTE CHOICE

8.4.1 An Illustration

Before we delve into the full-fledged analysis decomposing the effects of income, heterogeneity, and inequality, we start with a simpler question: Are redistribution preferences related to individual vote choices at all? While we have put redistribution preferences front and center in this book, their status in models of voting is less clear. As we mentioned in more detail earlier, a number of scholars (both in the Comparative and the American Politics literature) would argue that the demand for redistribution is not among the most important determinants of voting.

To illustrate this relationship, we estimate models for our Western European and US samples in which we relate the probability of voting for a "Left" or redistributive party (as defined earlier) to the preferences over redistributive policies held by individuals.[28] In Figure 8.7, we plot average the predicted probability of respondents reporting having voted Democrat (in the US case) and having voted for a party labelled as "Left" or defined as redistributive based on its stated policy position (in the Western European case) as a function of preferences for redistribution. As shown in Tables A.1 and A.1 in the Appendix, the mean for the redistribution preferences question in our GSS sample is 4 (the standard deviation is 2). The mean in our ESS sample is 4 (the standard deviation is 1). The left panel in the figure therefore shows that a change in the demand for redistribution from 3 to 5 (a standard deviation around the mean), increases the likelihood of voting Democrat from around 40 percent to 60 percent for an American respondent. A similar change using the Western European data (from 3.5 to 4.5, a standard deviation around

---

[28] We specify probit models with state- or country-year fixed effects, basic demographic characteristics (age, gender, and education), and heteroscedasticity-consistent standard errors. Based on these estimates, we calculate average the predicted probabilities over the observed range of redistribution preferences.

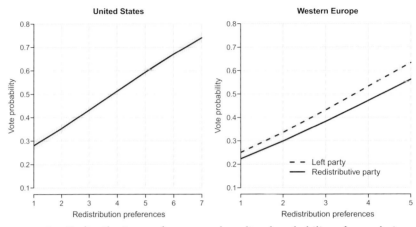

FIGURE 8.7 Redistribution preferences and predicted probability of vote choice in the United States and Western Europe

the mean of 4), increases the likelihood of voting for a redistributive party from around 40 percent to 50 percent and the likelihood of voting for a "Left" party from around 47 percent to 58 percent. These are substantively important effects that can easily affect the outcome of elections. Do they hold up in an analysis decomposing the effects of income, heterogeneity, and inequality?

8.4.2 Results

Table 8.2 shows, for our US sample, estimates of the total effect of expected income and the income-dependent effects of heterogeneity and inequality, as well as the decomposition of their effects into components due to preferences and other possible channels.

Beginning with a discussion of total effects, panel (A) of Table 8.2 shows that a unit increase in expected income raises the probability of voting for the Democratic Party candidate by 0.79 percentage points. The sign of this relationship is the opposite of what we found in previous chapters relating income expectations to preferences. However, one should note that the standard error of this change is quite large (0.45), raising the possibility that the total effect of expected income on party choice is indistinguishable from zero. The next two columns display the decomposition into indirect and direct effects. They make clear that a change in income expectations has two counterbalancing effects on the party choices of the American electorate. An increase in expected future income

TABLE 8.2 *Joint model of income, inequality, heterogeneity, endogenous preferences, and Democratic Party choice in the United States; total effects, indirect, and direct effects; estimates and standard errors*

	Total	IE	DE
(A): Expected income	0.788	−0.614	1.402
	(0.454)	(0.138)	(0.444)
(B): Income × inequality			
Low inequality	−5.182	−2.618	−2.565
	(0.642)	(0.337)	(0.558)
High inequality	−3.588	−1.433	−2.155
	(0.532)	(0.224)	(0.485)
(C): Income × heterogeneity			
Low heterogeneity	−3.883	−1.549	−2.334
	(0.561)	(0.240)	(0.517)
High heterogeneity	−4.670	−2.309	−2.361
	(0.576)	(0.254)	(0.520)

Note: Based on 40,000 MCMC samples. Derived from joint model of vote choice and endogenous preferences (for formulas used see Appendix A.5) with random effects for preferences and choices. Covariates included are age, education, regional unemployment rate, indicators for being female, Black, other non-white, member of a trade union, and living in a city

has a negative effect on voting Democrat *via preferences*, while its effect via all other (unmodeled) channels is positive. This underscores the value of the analysis undertaken in this section. While we are also interested in the overall relationship between our key variables and vote choice, the key quantity of interest in the context of this book's arguments is, specifically, how they impact choices via preferences. Thus, while the total effect of an increase in expected income is statistically uncertain, it has a clear statistically significant negative effect on the probability of voting for the Democratic Party through the influence of preferences for redistribution.

Panel (B) displays the estimated impact of a unit change in income distance at low and high levels of inequality (the tenth and ninetieth percentiles of the overall macro inequality distribution). We find that an increase in income (relative to the national mean) has a clear and statistically significant effect on the probability of voting for the Democratic Party. In line with our argument, the strength of this relationship is moderated by context. Where income inequality is low, a unit increase in income reduces the vote probability by five percentage points. In high-inequality contexts, the same change in income reduces the probability of a Democratic vote by only three and a half percentage points. How much of this relationship is due to preferences? Column "IE" shows that the effect of increasing income via preferences on vote choice in a low-inequality state is −2.6 percentage points. As before, this relationship is clearly weaker for individuals in high-inequality states, where the change in the probability of voting Democrat is −1.4 percentage points. When looking at the final column, which shows the impact of increasing income on vote choices not due to changing redistribution preferences, we find the difference between low- and high-inequality contexts to be far less pronounced. An increase in income is related to a decrease in the probability of voting Democrat of, respectively, 2.6 and 2.2 percentage points. Thus, the impact of income on voting for the Democratic Party is in large part due to preferences: About 40 percent to 50 percent of the total effect of changes in income is via changes in individuals' preferences for redistribution. Preferences are also largely responsible for the finding that the relationship between income and voting varies with levels of inequality (the difference between contexts is almost three times as large for indirect effects compared to direct effects).

Panel (C) displays again estimates of a unit change in income now calculated at low and high levels of heterogeneity (the tenth and ninetieth percentiles of the state-level distribution of black welfare recipiency rates). It, too, shows that an increase in income has a negative impact on the probability of voting for the Democratic Party candidate. A unit increase in income in a state with a low Black welfare recipiency rate reduces this probability by 3.9 percentage points, while the same change in a state with a high Black welfare recipiency rate reduces it by 4.7 percentage points. As with inequality, about 50 percent of this total effect is due to changes in preferences. In a low-heterogeneity context, we find that an increase in income decreases the probability of voting Democrat via decreasing preferences for redistribution by about 1.5 percentage points. In high-heterogeneity contexts the decrease in probability is 2.3 percentage points. Both effects via preferences are clearly significantly different from zero. There is also a sizeable remaining direct effect, which represents all channels other than redistribution preferences. However, these (unmeasured) variables are less sensitive to heterogeneity: the decrease in probability of voting Democrat not due to preferences is 2.3 and 2.4 percentage points in states with low versus high rates of Black welfare recipiency.

Table 8.3 shows the same set of calculations for our Western European sample. Here, we present two sets of results corresponding to the two possible conceptualizations of vote choice discussed earlier: casting one's vote for a party with a left label, and voting for a party proposing more

TABLE 8.3 *Joint models of income, inequality, heterogeneity, endogenous preferences, and party choice in Western Europe; total effects, indirect, and direct effects; estimates and standard errors.*

	Left party			Redistributive party		
	Total	IE	DE	Total	IE	DE
(A): Expected income	−1.118	−0.895	−0.222	−0.077	−0.985	0.908
	(0.330)	(0.070)	(0.313)	(0.405)	(0.082)	(0.391)
(B): Income × inequality						
Low inequality	−1.732	−0.975	−0.757	−3.306	−1.205	−2.101
	(0.280)	(0.088)	(0.254)	(0.377)	(0.108)	(0.349)
High inequality	−1.471	−0.733	−0.738	−2.602	−0.806	−1.796
	(0.275)	(0.086)	(0.249)	(0.360)	(0.100)	(0.321)
(C): Income × heterogeneity						
Low heterogeneity	−1.477	−0.717	−0.760	−2.910	−0.864	−2.046
	(0.275)	(0.077)	(0.255)	(0.365)	(0.093)	(0.342)
High heterogeneity	−1.822	−1.091	−0.731	3.105	−1.245	−1.860
	(0.285)	(0.102)	(0.247)	(0.393)	(0.125)	(0.334)

Note: Based on 40,000 MCMC samples. Derived from joint model of vote choice and endogenous preferences (for formulas used see Appendix A.5) with random effects for preferences and choices. Covariates included are age, education, household size, regional unemployment rate, indicators for being female, not in the labor force, unemployed, member of a trade union, and living in an urban area.

redistributive policies than the average for a particular election. Beginning with the role of income expectations, panel (A) shows that a unit increase in expected income decreases the probability to vote for a Left party by 1.1 percentage points. In contrast to our findings for the US sample, the size of the estimate and its standard error indicate that this relationship is statistically different from zero. Remarkably, the impact of expectations on Left party choice is almost completely due to changes in redistribution preferences. Our estimate for the indirect effect is −0.9 percentage points, while the remaining direct effect of −0.2 is indistinguishable from zero. At first blush, the relationship between expected income and voting for a party characterized by a relatively redistributive policy position looks rather different. We find that a unit change in expected income barely decreases the probability of a vote (estimated with a large standard error). However, when turning to the impact of expected income channeled by redistributive preferences, we find that a unit change in expected income decreases the probability of a vote for a redistributive party by about 1 percentage point. This estimate is similar in magnitude to the one we obtain when considering votes for parties labeled as Left. What is different here is the size of the direct effect, which indicates that factors other than preferences have a large influence in the opposite direction.

Panel (B) shows the role of macro-level inequality in Western Europe. A unit increase in income decreases the probability of voting for redistributive as well as for Left parties. Notably, the size of the effect is almost twice as large in the case of redistributive vote choice. But in both cases the relationship is statistically significant. Compared to our analysis of American data, we find somewhat less variation between high- and low-inequality contexts. In regions with low levels of inequality, an increase in income is associated with a decrease in the probability of voting for a redistributive party of 3.3 percentage points, while in a high-inequality region the same change is associated with a decrease of 2.6 percentage points. The impact of income on Left party choice channeled via preferences for redistribution in low- and high-inequality regions is -1 and -0.7 percentage points, while the corresponding estimates for redistributive party choice are -1.2 and -0.8. This underscores that, as was the case in our US analysis, preferences are a significant channel linking economic conditions to political behavior. On average, about 50 percent of the total effect of income and inequality on voting for a Left party is due to changing preferences for redistribution, while the proportion is closer to 30 percent in the cases of voting for a party offering redistributive policies.

Panel (C) shows estimates of the role of heterogeneity measured as the regional share of foreign-born individuals. As before, we find that the extent to which an increase in income changes the probability of voting for a Left or redistributive party varies positively with the prevailing level of heterogeneity. In regions with low shares of foreign-born population a unit increase in income decreases the probability of voting for a Left party by 1.5 percentage points, while in regions with high shares of foreign-born the estimated decrease is 1.8. In case of redistributive party choice, the overall magnitude of the effect is larger, but the difference between high and low levels of heterogeneity is smaller. Interestingly, when turning to indirect effect estimates, we find that they vary more strongly with regional levels of heterogeneity: in regions with low levels the impact of income on redistributive voting via preferences is -0.86, while it is -1.2 in regions with high levels. This preferences channel is highly statistical significant (as is the case for Left party choice). These results emphasize, again, the relevance of preferences in linking economic conditions to party

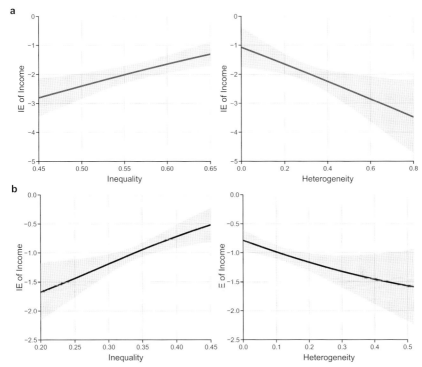

FIGURE 8.8 Indirect effect of income distance on vote choice via preferences moderated by inequality and heterogeneity; Panel (a) United States, and panel (b) Western Europe (redistributive party choice)

choice: at least one-third of the total variation is due to changes in individuals' redistribution preferences.

Figure 8.8 shows marginal effects of a change in income (relative to the national mean) at varying levels of inequality and heterogeneity in the United States and Western Europe. Before looking at specific results, we want to emphasize the similarity of the patterns displayed. While many idiosyncrasies divide both continents, the role of inequality and heterogeneity in shaping their citizens' political preferences and party choices seems remarkably similar (although note the reduced scale of the Western European panel). The left half of Figure 8.8 illustrates how inequality conditions the effect of income on vote choice via preferences. In the United States, an increase in inequality from a Gini coefficient of 0.5 (Connecticut in 1980) to 0.6 (Connecticut in 2002) decreases the negative indirect effect of income from −2.5 to −1.7. In Western Europe, a similar increase, from 0.3 (West Sweden or Schleswig-Holstein) to 0.4 (Algarve or the South West of Ireland) decreases the negative indirect effect from −1.4 to −0.7. The right half of Figure 8.8 shows the corresponding indirect effects of income for varying levels of heterogeneity. Remember that in the United States, we capture heterogeneity via the rate at which African Americans in a state receive welfare, while in Western Europe we capture it via the foreign-born share of a region's population. An increase in the Black welfare recipiency rate from 0.1 percent (New Hampshire in 2003) to 0.4 percent (Connecticut in 1979 or Nebraska in 2011) increases the negative indirect effect of income from −1.3 to −2.2 percentage points. In Western European regions, an increase in the share of foreign born from 0.1 (Wallonia in 2002) to 0.35 (West Sweden in 2008) increases the negative indirect effect of income on redistributive voting from −1 to −1.4 percentage points.

Robustness Test

A number of robustness tests are summarized in Table 8.4. We do not repeat the large number of tests pertaining to redistribution preferences that we have carried out in previous chapters. Rather, we examine factors relevant for vote choices and likely confounding of the preferences–outcome relationship. Focusing on the role of indirect effects, we calculate all tests for both our Western European and US sample, save for a test specific to the European case. Table 8.4 displays five columns representing the indirect effect of expected income (EI) and that of income at low (L) and high (H) levels of inequality and heterogeneity.

The literature on social class and voting is too large to summarize here (for a recent contribution, see Evans, 1999; Evans and de Graaf, 2013), but its central critique to our analysis would be that focusing on income and its subsequent effect on vote choices via preferences excludes the role of class in shaping party preferences unrelated to material self-interest (e.g., via patterns of socialization). The variation of income within class categories is high enough to allow us to assess whether our main results are robust to controlling for the effects of class as we do in specification (1). In Western Europe we once again use the six-category version of the Erikson–Goldthorpe social class scheme (Erikson and Goldthorpe, 1992), while in the United States we use a five-category version.

Following a similar line of argument, we control for religion in specification (2). The importance of religion for preferences and voting has been well-documented for both Western Europe and the United States

TABLE 8.4 *Robustness tests; indirect effect estimates*

	EI	Inequality		Heterogeneity	
		L	H	L	H
A: United States					
(1) Social class	−0.453	−2.582	−1.361	−1.494	−2.249
	(0.149)	(0.335)	(0.225)	(0.241)	(0.253)
(2) Religion	−0.807	−2.306	−1.256	−1.543	−1.886
	(0.149)	(0.335)	(0.243)	(0.260)	(0.256)
(3) Population density	−0.655	−2.589	−1.423	−1.544	−2.278
	(0.140)	(0.334)	(0.223)	(0.238)	(0.251)
(4) Social transfers	−0.569	−3.094	−1.381	−1.769	−2.409
	(0.153)	(0.422)	(0.255)	(0.280)	(0.275)
(5a) Ideology	−0.684	−1.539	−0.998	−1.058	−1.400
	(0.117)	(0.257)	(0.176)	(0.186)	(0.200)
(5b) Share liberals	−0.603	−3.227	−1.339	−1.780	−2.428
	(0.153)	(0.431)	(0.236)	(0.279)	(0.275)
(6) Model specification[a]	−0.783	−3.001	−2.101	−1.783	−2.822
	(0.199)	(0.420)	(0.316)	(0.374)	(0.292)
B: Western Europe					
(1) Social class	−0.743	−1.112	−0.720	−0.769	−1.160
	(0.081)	(0.106)	(0.097)	(0.091)	(0.121)
(2) Religion	−1.001	−1.221	−0.789	−0.858	−1.266
	(0.082)	(0.108)	(0.099)	(0.092)	(0.125)
(3) Population density	−0.983	−1.228	−0.774	−0.890	−1.166
	(0.082)	(0.109)	(0.098)	(0.096)	(0.129)
(4) Social spending	1.074	1.114	0.790	0.805	1.193
	(0.092)	(0.108)	(0.126)	(0.099)	(0.129)
(5a) Ideology	−0.794	−0.784	−0.530	0.557	−0.851
	(0.070)	(0.081)	(0.069)	(0.068)	(0.085)
(5b) Share liberals	−0.965	−1.236	−0.798	0.865	1.295
	(0.081)	(0.109)	(0.099)	(0.093)	(0.126)
(6) Model specification[a]	−0.850	−1.123	−0.790	−0.829	−1.199
	(0.084)	(0.095)	(0.091)	(0.084)	(0.101)
(7) Federalism	−0.975	−1.121	−0.894	−0.879	−1.200
	(0.081)	(0.104)	(0.105)	(0.094)	(0.122)

Note: EI: expected income. L: low levels of inequality or heterogeneity, H: high levels
(refers to tenth and ninetieth percentiles, respectively).
[a] Alternative, extended model specification with country fixed effects and
context-preference interaction in vote choice equation.

(e.g., De La O and Rodden, 2008; Evans and de Graaf, 2013; Stegmueller, 2013b, 2014). We capture religion via respondents' frequency of church attendance and their denomination (Protestant, Catholic, and others).

Going back to at least the seminal work of Lipset and Rokkan (1967), students of voting have stressed the division in preferences and behavior of individuals living in urban versus rural settings. This line of reasoning is also echoed in the recent political economy literature that stresses the sorting of individuals with distinct preferences (and voting choices) into more urban contexts (e.g., Cho et al., 2006; Rodden, 2010). We partly tackled this issue by including an individual-level indicator of living in an urban area in the main analysis. In specification (3) we additionally include a macro-level measure of urbanization: the population density of a state or region.

In specification (4) we account for the possibility that some respondents take existing levels of redistribution into account when deciding to vote for a party offering redistributive policies. We include existing levels of social expenditures in our estimation. In the Western European sample, we use social spending calculated from OECD data; in the US sample we use state-level per capita federal transfer receipts calculated from the Regional Economic Accounts of the Bureau of Economic Analysis (as in Chapter 5).

As in other analyses in this book, our main models do not include a measure of ideology or left–right self-placement. This is because our objective is to explain economic preferences as a key constituent of ideology, and it therefore should not be an "explanatory" variable in a vote choice equation. However, individuals' self-declared ideological positions can represent noneconomic sources of vote choice (or proxy for them). We therefore conduct robustness tests including ideology in two ways. In specification (5a) we include individuals' ideology in our model equations, while in specification (5b) we capture the ideological leanings of respondents' regions or states. Individual ideology is measured by individuals' self-placement on a left–right scale. In the United States, we measure state-level ideology via the share of individuals in each state in each year classified as liberal computed from NYT/CBS poll responses (see Pacheco, 2011). In Western Europe, we lack external data with complete coverage and thus calculate the regional share of voters placing themselves on the "Left" part of the ideological spectrum from our ESS data.[29]

Specification (6) differs from previous ones in that we do not add new variables, but instead substantively change some model assumptions.

---

[29] The ESS presents respondents with an eleven-point left–right scale. We classify respondents as left if they choose values left of the midpoint.

We allow for an interaction between inequality and heterogeneity and unobserved "nonpreference" channels from income to vote choice. Our indirect effect decomposition is now calculated under this more flexible specification. Furthermore, we include country or state fixed effects instead of random effects allowing for an arbitrary correlation between (time-constant) country-level unobservables and covariates.

Finally, we conclude with a specification unique to the Western European context, addressing the possibility that in federal countries (where regional government has more of a role in providing redistribution), respondents integrate a combination of national and regional policy into their assessment of redistribution and vote choices. In specification (7) we include a measure of federalism via an indicator variable that equals one if, within a country, regions are an autonomous source of government spending (based on Eurostat's government revenue and expenditure database).

To summarize a large amount of information, our results appear to be quite robust to the inclusion of these additional variables in both the United States and Western European samples. In general, the level of indirect effect estimates is reduced, but they remain statistically different from zero. Individuals with higher levels of lifetime expected income have preferences for less redistribution and are thus less likely to vote for parties offering redistributive policies. We also still find that the preferences–choices nexus is shaped by the inequality and heterogeneity contexts. In states and regions where income inequality increases, it reduces the negative impact of income on voting for a redistributive option mediated through preferences. Increasing population heterogeneity has the opposite effect. Where heterogeneity increases, it increases the negative impact of rising income on redistributive voting (mediated through preferences).

We consider two sets of robustness tests especially noteworthy. First, we include individual and contextual ideology in specification (5). Accounting for an individual's ideology in a model of preferences and choices provides a rather strict test for our argument as it pits a clearly defined measure of economic preferences against an omnibus measure that captures a conglomeration of economic, cultural, and moral aspects of policy preferences. Even when including ideology we find substantial effects of expected income via preferences on vote choice, as well as income effects dependent on context (albeit reduced in levels by almost 50 percent). Including voters' ideological *context* strengthens our conclusion that the extent to which an increase in (present-day) income is translated into political choices depends on prevailing levels of inequality and heterogeneity. In states with low levels of inequality, the effect of an increase in income (translated via preferences for redistribution) on the probability of voting Democrat is −3.2 percentage points, while in high-inequality states it is only −1.3. In Western Europe the change from our main results is less pronounced. The indirect effect estimate in low- vs. high-inequality regions is −1.2 vs. −0.8.

Second, changing the basic structure of the model in specification (6) allows us to account for more complex situations, in which inequality and heterogeneity interact with income to shape vote choice directly (not via preferences). At the beginning of this chapter, we showed that macro inequality is not correlated to levels of population heterogeneity (neither in our estimation sample or when looking at the evolution of inequality and heterogeneity in Western Europe and the United States). However, we recognized the possibility that inequality and heterogeneity could have interactive effects over redistributive voting. Huber (2017) argues that inequality can foster the success of parties that focus on creating electoral coalitions based on noneconomic identities, such as ethnicity. If these coalitions based on noneconomic identities succeed electorally, the policies needed to redress inequality will be less likely than when coalitions based on economic identities succeed.[30] While not addressing its effects directly, the results from specification (6) in Table 8.4 show that the main findings in this chapter are robust to the inclusion of this interaction.

---

[30] Paradoxically, this is the case when inequality is low relative to ethnic polarization.

9

Conclusion

We started this book with the objective of addressing some of the assumptions underlying most arguments about the importance of economic circumstances to political outcomes. The demand for redistribution, we argued, matters to politics, but its effects are highly variable, and we don't know enough about how economic self-interest combines with other concerns (about the negative externalities of inequality or about in-group solidarity) to influence individual redistribution preferences. It is appropriate to conclude by reemphasizing the importance of our main results and exploring their implications to three essential themes in political science: democratization, the welfare state, and electoral politics.

9.1 MAIN FINDINGS: INCOME, CONTEXT, AND VOTING

We have mentioned in different parts of this book that most analysts would agree that an individual's relative income (i.e., whether she is rich or poor) affects her political behavior. Regarding the preferences and political behavior of Americans, however, this is not an uncontroversial view. In a widely referenced work, Citrin and Green (1990) conclude that calculations of personal cost and benefit play only a limited role in determining the preferences of the American public. In an equally influential book, Gilens (2009) agrees and de-emphasizes self-interest as good predictor of support for the Welfare State in the United States. In the literature on Comparative Politics, the well-known finding that redistribution seems to increase with market income equality (rather than inequality) when comparing across industrialized democracies (see, for example, Moene and

Wallerstein, 2003 or Lindert, 2004) has been taken as powerful evidence against the Meltzer–Richard approach.

The first thing to note, therefore, is that we find otherwise. The systematic analyses of very diverse data sets in the book all point in one direction: the Meltzer–Richard baseline is a good starting point to understand the redistribution preferences of individuals in industrialized democracies. This is as much the case in Western Europe as it is in the United States. Our findings using GSS data in fact support the seminal work in Campbell et al.'s *The American Voter*, arguing that self-interest alone was perhaps the best explanation of Americans' social policy preferences.

We argued in Part I that, although very useful, the common political economy approach to material self-interest as a motivation for redistribution preferences is too limiting. Focusing exclusively on present income as the main determinant of support for redistribution is constraining and nonintuitive. It is natural to think that life-cycle income concerns would matter to redistribution preferences as much as the position an individual presently holds in the income distribution. Using a well-established labor economics literature as our inspiration, we provided a simple way of operationalizing expected future income and proposed that this is an effective way of unifying different (and often disconnected) political economy approaches emphasizing risk, insurance, and mobility. Using European cross-country survey data and individual-level panel data from Germany and the United Kingdom, we presented convincing evidence that our hypotheses contribute to a better understanding of the material self-interested side of the individual demand for redistribution.

In Part II, we argued that, once separated from its individual income–tax–transfer component, macro inequality is connected to negative externalities that are most important to the rich. We proposed that poor people (regardless of their expected future income) value redistribution for its immediate tax and transfer consequences. The redistributive preferences of the rich, on the other hand, are less significantly affected by current tax and transfer considerations. For the rich, fear of crime (as a most visible negative externality of inequality) becomes a significant justification for greater redistribution. In our empirical analyses, we showed that the association between inequality and redistribution preferences proposed in our main argument is extraordinarily robust. Our evidence, based on both cross-sectional and panel data analyses, demonstrates that for the poor, noneconomic concerns are trumped by immediate disposable income incentives and that redistribution preferences converge regardless of the level of inequality as income declines. By contrast, inequality promotes concerns for its negative externalities for the rich. We showed that the redistribution preferences of a rich individual in a low-income region differ starkly from those in a high-inequality region and that this difference depends on fear of crime.

In some ways, this is a profoundly unintuitive result (the rich are more supportive of redistribution in those regions where inequality is highest). We do provide an intuitive solution for this puzzle (the concern for crime by the rich) but it is germane to ask whether our results emerge from the idiosyncrasies of our particular sample. We mentioned in Chapter 4 that the rich, if concerned about the externalities of inequality, could do (at least) two things: reduce inequality through redistribution, or reduce its potential consequences by demanding more protection (through policing, incarceration, etc.). We argued that demands for redistribution and protection can be complementary, but it is tempting to think that the rich in Western Europe may be more likely than the rich in other regions to think of redistribution as a good option. We return to this topic when we analyze voting for redistributive parties in Part IV (both in Western Europe and, more importantly in the United States), but we will mention here that our findings connect with a significant literature of the consequences of inequality in the United States. Using American data, Gelman et al. (2008) find, like us, that the poor (whether in Connecticut or Mississippi) vote in similar ways. In a project related to this book, Dimick et al. (2016) find that, just as in Western Europe, the rich are more supportive of redistribution in the more unequal states.[1]

Going back to the unintuitive nature of the findings in Part II, one might also ask why we do find more inequality in precisely the places where the rich are more supportive of redistribution. After all, a growing literature has argued that, in the American case at least, policy outcomes tend to reflect the preferences of the rich, rather than those of the poor.[2] While we would argue that a number of variables exogenous to redistribution affect inequality, here we must also fall back into one of the starting statements in our Introduction. In this book we have focused on the demand for redistribution and ignored the many factors (some of which we emphasized when discussing Figure 1.1) that transform that demand into redistributive policy. We hope that the arguments in this part

---

[1] Although fear of crime does not seem to be as relevant an externality concern for the rich in the United States.

[2] See Schattschneider (1960), Schlozman (1984), or Gilens and Page (2014) on the bias in American politics in favor of business and the well-off.

of the book clarify the role of preferences as an essential first step for an accurate understanding of the supply of redistribution.

In the discussion of altruism and identity that is the main thrust of Part III of the book, we once again suggested that lower stakes and longer time-horizons mean that altruistic concerns are more important for the rich. We also argued that parochial altruism would be conditional on the identity of the poor. This section's results showed that "moral" gains from supporting redistribution are most obvious to the rich in regions characterized by low levels of heterogeneity (whether we measure it as foreign-born population in Western Europe or the share of African Americans living in a household receiving welfare in the United States).

These findings regarding group heterogeneity are important in two respects. First, in some ways they confirm the conventional wisdom about the effects of heterogeneity. More heterogeneous areas do exhibit less-aggregate support for redistribution. Second, and more important, they question the logic behind this conventional wisdom. As we mentioned in Chapter 6, many of these arguments rely on the assumption that heterogeneity diverts low-income individuals from pursuing their material self-interest. The poor know that they gain from redistribution, but they may not support it if they do not share an identity with other poor individuals (this is the argument underlying much of the debate about welfare and race in the United States and about welfare and immigration in Europe). We have argued for an alternative explanation that integrates identity considerations into a general altruism logic. In doing so, we have also offered evidence showing that these differences have in fact little to do with the poor. It is the parochial altruism of the rich that is affected by heterogeneity. As issues related to population heterogeneity (immigration, ethnicity, race) come to dominate electoral politics in industrialized democracies, our argument and findings should transform the way we think about the demand for redistribution in industrialized democracies.

In Part IV, we returned to the three main arguments in the book and explicitly connected them to voting for redistributive parties. Income, inequality, and heterogeneity, as we showed in previous sections, significantly influence redistribution preferences. But do they matter to individual political behavior? This chapter's analysis argued that, while most political economy models link individual characteristics to policy outcomes, they make the essential assumption that there is a relationship between preferences and voting. We specified explicitly the theoretical mechanisms that determine preferences and party choice and tested them empirically.

We showed that, when focusing on the impact of expected income channeled by redistributive preferences, an increase in expected income decreases the probability to vote for a Left or redistributive party in Western Europe and in the United States. We also showed the marginal effects of a change in income (relative to the national mean) at varying levels of inequality and heterogeneity in the United States and Western Europe. In both analyses, an increase in inequality decreases the negative indirect effect of income on voting for a Left or redistributive party in a substantively important way. An increase in the Black welfare recipiency rate in the United States or an increase in the share of foreign-born in Western European regions, on the other hand, increases the negative indirect effect of income again in a substantively meaningful way. We argued that an important debate about the lack of redistributive policies in industrialized democracies after the "golden age of social democracy" has centered around the perception that second-dimension issues have become disproportionately important to the poor. The implication of these arguments is that the solution to the puzzle affecting (the lack of) redistribution in these countries concerns demand. We showed in this chapter that this may not be the case. We find the poor to be more consistently in favor of redistribution and therefore more likely to vote for redistributive parties (than the rich). The puzzle of redistribution may have more to do with supply (what parties do, the effects of electoral institutions, etc.) than with demand.

9.2 REDISTRIBUTION PREFERENCES AND DEMOCRACY

The arguments presented in this book have significant implications for our understanding of the political economy of democratization. Scholarship on the political economy of transitions from autocracy to democracy has experienced a resurgence in the last twenty years. The most influential of these studies share a common approach based on the existence of a fundamental redistributive conflict between the rich and the poor. Acemoglu and Robinson, in their highly influential *Economic Origins of Dictatorship and Democracy*, express the foundations of these approaches as follows:

To facilitate the initial exposition of our ideas, it is useful to conceive of society as consisting of two groups – the elites and the citizens – in which the latter are more numerous. Our framework emphasizes that social choices are inherently conflictual. For example, if the elites are the relatively rich individuals – for short, the rich – they will be opposed to redistributive taxation; whereas the citizens, who will be relatively poor – for short, the poor – will be in favor of taxation that would redistribute resources to them. More generally, policies or social choices that benefit the elites will be different from those that benefit the citizens. This conflict over social choices and policies is a central theme of our approach." (Acemoglu and Robinson, 2005: 15)

In these transitional accounts, individuals have relatively well-defined preferences that help them evaluate the choice between democracy and nondemocracy according to their assessments of their economic consequences. In almost all cases, the poor are understood to benefit from democracy (because it increases their political influence and allows them to promote more redistribution), while the rich elites fear democratic expropriation and are on the side of autocratic survival. In this general approach, a more equal distribution of income reduces the expropriation threat by the poor, and makes the rich autocratic elites more likely to tolerate democracy (see, for example, Boix, 2003: 10). While this is a common underlying thread about the autocratic elite's fear of democratic expropriation, different interpretations of the relationship between inequality and democratization exist in the literature.

For Acemoglu and Robinson, the relationship between inequality and the probability of democratization follows an inverted U-shaped curve (where democratization is most likely at intermediate levels of inequality). In relatively equal countries, the potential redistribution and expropriation gains are small, and therefore the population does not threaten to revolt. At intermediate levels of inequality, the gains from redistribution are higher, revolution becomes appealing to the poor, but the elites are unwilling to use repression (because redistribution is relatively inexpensive) When inequality is relatively high, the cost of redistribution surpasses that of repressing revolts, and elites are more likely to repress. For Boix, the distribution of assets is complemented by the nature of those assets. In this view, democracy prevails when either equality or capital mobility is high in a country. When the costs of moving capital away from its country of origin are low, the rich do not feel threatened by the possibility of expropriation (even when inequality is relatively high) because they would exit the country if taxes became too high. For Ansell and Samuels (2014), finally, regime change is not as much a function of the autocratic elite's fear that the poor will expropriate their assets under democracy. It is instead a function of the bourgeoisie's (the politically disenfranchised yet rising economic group) fear of expropriation by the autocratic governing elite.

The analysis in this book adds some important caveats to these redistributive approaches to the politics of democratization. Three factors emphasized in our arguments mitigate the affluent's fear of expropriation: expected future income, the negative externalities of inequality, and population homogeneity. Our expected future income chapters make clear that support for redistribution by the rich is not only affected by their present income (in which case there would be no material self-interested motivation for redistribution by those who are net contributors). Like other work emphasizing insurance, risk, and mobility, our argument about the importance of concerns about life-cycle income implies that fear of expropriation during a transition to democracy would be mitigated by the likelihood that the affluent could suffer a decline in income in the future and need redistribution. Similarly, the chapters on the negative externalities of inequality emphasize that there are potential costs to increasing inequality, even for those who pay for redistribution. The rich may be concerned about the possibility of expropriation by the poor in a democracy, but they are also concerned about crime (as a most visible negative externality of inequality), and this can become a significant justification for greater redistribution (and for the acceptance of a democratic transition). Through a different causal mechanism, population homogeneity finally also mitigates the fear of expropriation for the rich. We showed that altruism is conditional on the identity of the poor. Because the "moral" gains from supporting redistribution are most obvious to the rich when population heterogeneity is low, we expect the redistributive conflict inherent to a democratic transition to be less problematic in places characterized by high levels of ethnic (or any other identity-related) homogeneity.

9.3 REDISTRIBUTION PREFERENCES AND THE WELFARE STATE

An overview, even if cursory, of the literature on the welfare state would identify the same redistributive conflict emphasized in the previous section as an essential characteristic of the most influential approaches to its relation to inequality. The emergence of the welfare state was inevitably connected to both redistribution from the rich to the poor and the protection of individuals from labor market risks.[3] The influential "political class struggle" or "power resources" approach is perhaps most clear in its connection to redistributive conflicts. This view – associated most

---

[3] In the words of Peter Baldwin, "(s)ocial insurance provided the tools with which to reapportion and moderate the effects of natural and manmade misfortune" (1990: 3).

prominently with the work of Stephens (1979) and Korpi (1983), among others – posits that the strength and organization of the working class is associated with the likelihood of Left government and, therefore, of more expansive welfare state policy. A clear summary of the core of this argument is provided by Shalev. "The essential argument of this perspective on the welfare state," he notes, "is that the growth of reformist labor unions and parties which reflect the class divisions of capitalist society, and in particular the ascension of labor parties to executive power, have been the preeminent forces in the initiation and development of public policies for furthering justice and equality between the classes" (1983: 317). The "political class struggle" is a conflict about income and equality. The direct role of the welfare state in influencing the income losses associated with "manmade misfortune" (like unemployment) is quite straightforward. A more generous welfare state will minimize these losses both by having a high replacement rate for lost wages and by covering a large amount of the population under the blanket of social protection. Social benefits provide a way to redistribute wealth to the poor and to insure them against labor market risks (Moene and Wallerstein, 2003). As argued by Esping-Andersen (1990), by insuring the poor against labor market risks, welfare programs reduce people's dependence on employment as a source of income. According to this logic, the welfare state emerges as the result of a political exchange among actors concerned first and foremost with their own welfare. In "ideal type" terms, workers (through their unions) commit to wage moderation and social peace in return for the provision of a generous welfare state by social democratic governments. The affluent (and employers) finance the development of a large public insurance system in exchange for the unions' moderation and the availability of a well-qualified labor force. Employers also commit to stable investment and long-term growth in return for the social democratic government's promise not to tax their benefits to finance the welfare state (Cameron, 1984; Przeworski and Wallerstein, 1988; Cusack and Beramendi, 2006).

Welfare policy is complex and multifaceted. The preceding paragraphs make clear that we have a particular dimension of the welfare state in mind: labor market policy. This emphasis is justified for two main reasons. First, dealing with the labor market (whether by promoting employment or by mitigating the effects of unemployment) is one of the most redistributive roles of the welfare state. The generosity of labor market policy is targeted at a particularly vulnerable portion of the population and, unlike other more general policies of the welfare state, can therefore have significant effects over the distribution of income.[4] Second, it is this dimension that is most important to some influential theoretical frameworks exploring the political economy of industrialized democracies (for example, those emphasizing worlds of welfare capitalism, varieties of capitalism, or risk and redistribution).[5]

It is nevertheless clear that the arguments in this book complement these influential approaches to the welfare state. While a Meltzer–Richard oriented focus on the redistributive conflict surrounding social policy is still useful, our analysis emphasizes some important distinctions. Our argument about expected future income adds to recent work highlighting the insurance dimension of welfare policy. While the redistributive character of social policy affects interpersonal inequality, its insurance dimension puts the accent on inter-temporal risk. Something similar can be argued about the negative externalities of inequality. While other work in political economy has focused on the economic advantages of a generous welfare state (regarding individual investments on skills, social peace or low inflation), our argument about fear of crime as a negative externality of inequality provides another significant reason for (even completely selfish) affluent individuals to support social spending. The introduction of population homogeneity as a relevant factor influencing altruism, finally, harks back to an earlier sociological literature on the welfare state that underlined its ideological nature and the collective concern with fairness (see, for example, Wilensky, 1975 or Rothstein, 1998). In conjunction, the three main points in this book allow for a movement away from intergroup redistributive conflict and for the consideration of the potential cross-class coalitions that can support a more generous welfare state.

9.4 REDISTRIBUTION PREFERENCES, THE DECLINE OF MAIN LEFT PARTIES, AND THE RESURGENCE OF POPULISM

In this final section of our conclusions, we return to two important topics that we touched upon both in the introduction and in the analysis of

---

[4] See, for example, Korpi and Palme (2003).

[5] We recognize that the focus on traditional social policies leaves out other significant dimensions of the welfare state. Recent work has shown that education policy is an important determinant of inequality and is significantly connected to other parts of the welfare state (see, for example, Iversen and Stephens, 2008 or Ansell, 2010). Work–family policy as a response to "new social risks" is another area in which the welfare state has been transformed in recent years (Bonoli, 2005; Iversen and Rosenbluth, 2010).

voting provided in Chapter 8. The first one is the electoral decline of main Left parties. Traditional center-left parties seem to be on the back foot of late. If we survey the results of the most recent elections in industrialized democracies, this is the case whether we look at Hillary Clinton's defeat in 2016, the Labour Party having lost the last three elections in the UK, the historical loss of support by the PvdA in the Netherlands, the dramatic lack of success of the PS in France, the failure of the SPD in Germany, or the decline of the PSOE in Spain. The second topic is the reemergence of populism in many of these countries. In Chapter 1, we mentioned the populist undertones of the Brexit debate in the UK, the election of Donald Trump in the United States, the increased (but eventually fruitless) popularity of Marine Le Pen in France's most recent presidential election, and the recent success of Alternative for Germany. These developments do not only concern the support of the Left or populism as outcomes of interest on their own. They also very much affect fundamental issues regarding democracy. As Sheri Berman argues in an op-ed piece for *The New York Times*, the disastrous decline of the European center-left is a cause for concern because Social Democratic parties remain essential to democracy in Western Europe. Moreover, she continues, this decline "has created a space for a populist right whose commitment to liberalism, and even democracy, is questionable."[6]

The key question for our book is the extent to which redistribution preferences are part of the explanation for the decline of main Left parties and the upsurge in populism. We have shown in the previous chapter that redistribution preferences matter significantly to voting. There is also anecdotal evidence (as suggested in the Introduction) that: (1) increasing population heterogeneity is an electoral challenge for Left parties (particularly if they do not adopt redistributive positions), and (2) future expected income and a sense of deteriorating well-being are factors affecting support for the National Front in France, Trump in the United States, and Alternative for Germany. Given the contemporary nature of these developments and the consequent lack of systematic data, it is difficult (and beyond the scope of these conclusions) to analyze these relationships. One plausible explanation is that in recent times, Left parties have become less redistributive and populist parties more redistributive – and therefore more attractive to parts of the traditional core constituency of the Left. While the commitment of traditional main

[6] See https://tinyurl.com/y853n78p.

Left parties to redistribution has generally been assumed,[7] the preferred economic policies of populist Right parties are not particularly clear. In the pioneering work of Kitschelt and McGann (1995), the radical Right was considered a fusion of neoliberalism (on the traditional economic dimension) and authoritarianism (on the values/culture dimension). The free-market orientation of the populist Right, however, has been questioned (see Ivarsflaten, 2005; De Lange, 2007). Mudde (2007) (among others) argues that second dimension issues (ethno-nationalism, opposition to cosmopolitanism and globalization, etc.) more than economic policy define populist Right parties, and Rovny (2013) shows that these parties often aim to attract voters by blurring their position on the economic dimension. As argued by Afonso and Rennwald (2018), the redistributive strategies of populist Right parties span "from libertarian to socialist, with different shades of welfare chauvinism in-between."

Different redistributive electoral strategies have at times been combined with a shift from an emphasis on *more or less* redistribution (the focus of traditional Left parties) to *who should benefit from* redistribution. Cavaillé and Trump (2015) argue that in the UK there is stability in support for general redistribution, but increasingly restrictive attitudes about who the recipients of redistribution should be (not only immigrants, but also the unemployed or single mothers). As mentioned in the population heterogeneity section of this book, on the one hand Left parties face a "progressive dilemma" (Kymlicka, 2015): maintaining a comprehensive welfare state in increasingly multicultural society without losing public support. On the other hand, some populist Right parties have taken up "welfare chauvinism" as a way to appeal to poor voters (see, for example, De Koster et al., 2013).[8]

Two important issues are not fully resolved by our voting analysis. The first one concerns the calculus of winning and or losing votes from core and noncore constituencies, the second one concerns voting turnout itself. Regarding the first, we have explored in this book both the factors affecting the demand for redistribution and the connection to individual voting. A more explicit connection between our "bottom-up" political economy

---

[7] But see Rueda (2007) for an argument about how labor market dualization, and the interests of insiders as the core constituency of Social Democratic parties, can influence the nature of redistribution.

[8] It is, however, also possible that redistribution preferences are becoming less relevant for voting Left through time, while other preferences (potentially unrelated to redistribution) are making populist parties more attractive to the traditional core constituency of the Left.

approach and the general comparative politics literature on dynamic party competition[9] is a productive area for future research. A particularly relevant element in these arguments is the distinction between core and noncore voters. As Downs (1957) recognized long ago, political parties are torn between the incentives to seek the support of pivotal, centrist voters and the need to cater to the interests of core supporters. Dixit and Londregan (1996) express the logic for parties to cater to the interest of swing voters in the center, noting that groups "that are densely represented at the center will be the beneficiaries of redistributive politics," whereas individuals closer to the extremes "will be written off by one party and taken for granted by the other" (1996: 1143). Others (see, for example, Cox and McCubbins, 1986) argue that political parties have strong incentives to mobilize core voters by targeting benefits to those groups. Having clarified in this book how the redistributive preferences of individuals are connected to voting, a necessary next step is to explore the momentous consequences of the strategic choices regarding core and noncore potential voters for redistributive outcomes.

We will point out, finally, that while a transfer of votes to populist alternatives is a possible explanation for the decline of main Left parties, the implications of the connection between preferences and voter turnout are also important. In our analysis of voting in Chapter 8, like in much of the related literature, we excluded individuals who did not turn out to vote. We argued that a full model combining turnout and party choice is a lot more complex than simply including abstention as another "party" (see, e.g., Adams et al., 2006 for a more sophisticated approach). This issue has far-reaching implications. Let's assume the reader accepts the main arguments in this book (that voters' preferences for redistribution are a function of their relative income and the effects of expected future income, negative externalities, and population heterogeneity) and also the conceptualization of parties as strategic actors responding to voter preferences. As argued by Pontusson and Rueda (2010), among others, in this theoretical framework the extent to which income inequality is associated with political inequality conditions party responses to voter preferences. The issue of income skew in voter turnout is therefore central to the relationship between redistribution preferences and voting. As Meltzer and Richard (1981) themselves recognize, their prediction that inequality

---

[9] See, for example, Stimson et al. (1995), Adams et al. (2004, 2009), and Adams and Somer-Topcu (2009).

will be associated with more redistribution rests on the unrealistic assumption that all income earners vote. Under any other circumstance, we are required to distinguish between the income of the median voter and the median income (Nelson, 1999; Barnes, 2013). To the extent that political inequality rises with income inequality (Leighley, 1995; Schlozman et al., 2012), the effect of increasing income inequality on redistribution preferences and then voting might well be offset by a decline in electoral turnout among low-income citizens. This is once more a topic to which these conclusions cannot dedicate the attention it deserves, and a potentially productive area for future research.

A

Appendices

A.1.1 Distribution of Income

Figure A.1 plots the distribution of income distance in Western Europe using kernel density estimates. We average over available survey rounds. Kernel density estimates are calculated at a 100-point grid over the domain of income distance using a Gaussian kernel with bandwidth 1.5.

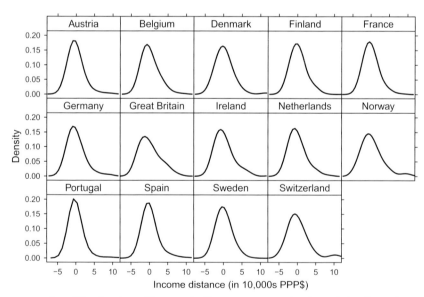

FIGURE A.1 Distribution of income in European countries; kernel density estimates

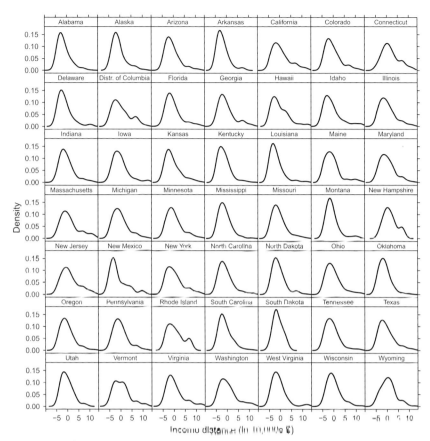

FIGURE A.2 Distribution of income in US states; kernel density estimates

Figure A.2 plots the distribution of income distance in US states averaged over time. We use kernel density estimates as described earlier, with a kernel bandwidth of 1.3.

Figure A.3 plots the distribution of income distance over two decades in the United Kingdom. We use kernel density estimates as described earlier, with a kernel bandwidth of 0.5.

A.1.2 Sample Characteristics

Tables A.1–A.3 show descriptive statistics for our European, American, and British samples, respectively. Note that all samples are limited to the working-age population.

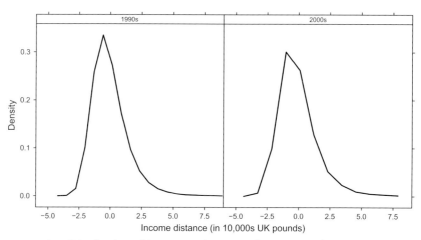

FIGURE A.3 Distribution of income in the UK in the 1990s and 2000s; kernel density estimates

TABLE A.1 *Sample characteristics, ESS; means (standard errors) and standard deviations*

	Mean	Std. dev.
Redistribution preferences	3.708 (0.004)	1.060
Income [1,000 US$]	37.550 (0.113)	28.302
Age [years]	42.915 (0.045)	12.589
Female	0.523 (0.002)	0.499
Education [years]	12.864 (0.015)	4.028
Unemployed	0.055 (0.001)	0.228
Not in labor force	0.165 (0.001)	0.371
Household size	2.772 (0.005)	1.358
Immigration attitude	5.033 (0.008)	2.192
Fear of crime	1.916 (0.003)	0.781
Victim of crime	0.220 (0.002)	0.414
Gini index	0.333 (0.000)	0.033
Share foreign born	0.133 (0.000)	0.105
Education (categories)[a]		
Lower secondary	0.139 (0.002)	0.346
Upper secondary	0.397 (0.003)	0.489
Postsecondary	0.085 (0.002)	0.279
Tertiary	0.300 (0.003)	0.458

Note: European Social Survey (ESS) data pooled over all waves. Working age population.
[a] Refers to male-only subsample.

TABLE A.2 *Sample characteristics, GSS; means (standard errors) and standard deviations*

	Mean	SD
Redistribution preferences	4.282 (0.013)	1.949
Income [1,000 US$]	48.854 (0.206)	36.898
Age [years]	40.067 (0.063)	11.854
Female	0.557 (0.003)	0.497
Education [years]	13.283 (0.016)	2.912
Unemployed	0.066 (0.001)	0.249
Part-time employed	0.119 (0.002)	0.323
Self-employed	0.119 (0.002)	0.323
Urban–rural	0.308 (0.002)	0.462
Union member	0.104 (0.002)	0.305
Percent unemployed	6.167 (0.011)	2.098
Black welfare recipiency rate	0.299 (0.001)	0.112
Black poverty rate	0.303 (0.001)	0.104
Racial attitudes	2.131 (0.004)	0.730

Note: General Social Survey (GSS) data pooled over all waves. Working age population.

TABLE A.3 *Sample characteristics, BHPS; means (standard errors) and standard deviations.*

	Mean	SD
Redistribution preferences	2.979 (0.008)	1.074
Labor income [1,000 £]	26.481 (0.128)	17.068
House value [10,000 £]	11.865 (0.106)	14.116
House owner	0.821 (0.003)	0.383
Age	42.791 (0.055)	7.300
Work experience	26.797 (0.070)	9.086
Female	0.514 (0.004)	0.500
Household size	3.125 (0.010)	1.286
Nonwhite	0.041 (0.001)	0.197
Union member	0.232 (0.003)	0.422
Divorced	0.074 (0.002)	0.263
Unemployed	0.032 (0.001)	0.177
Education		
O-levels	0.366 (0.004)	0.482
A-levels	0.170 (0.003)	0.376
Degree	0.218 (0.003)	0.413

Note: British Household Panel Survey (BHPS) data pooled over all waves. Working age population.

A.2 APPENDIX TO CHAPTER 3

A.2.1 Prior Details of BHPS Income Expectations–Preferences Model

To complete the Bayesian setup of our model, we need to specify priors for all free model parameters. All regression-type coefficients (including the coefficient for expected income) have vague normal priors with zero mean and a rather large prior variance of 100: $\alpha, \beta, \gamma, \delta_0, \delta_1 \sim N(0, 100)$. This ensures that their impact on inferences is minimal. The prior for the preference persistence parameter is centered over 1/2 with large prior variance, $\phi \sim N(0.5, 100)$. An alternative prior that is uniform on $(-1, 1)$ does not yield different conclusions. The individual effects variance–covariance matrix Σ has an inverse Wishart prior, $\Sigma \sim IW(S, \nu)$ with scale matrix $S = I * 0.05$ and $\nu = 3$ degrees of freedom, while each individual income variance parameter is assigned an inverse-Gamma prior: $\forall i : \psi_i \sim IG(0.001, 0.001)$. The prior for the variance of individual specific effects ξ_i is uniform on the standard deviation as suggested by Gelman (2006): $\sigma_\xi^2 \sim U(0, 20)$. An alternative specification with a larger upper threshold does not yield different results.

We estimate the model via Markov Chain Monte Carlo simulation, using two chains run for 30,000 iterations (thinned by a factor of 20 to save memory). We discard the first 10,000 iterations as transient phase of the sampler and use the remaining 20,000 posterior samples for inference. Nonconvergence tests do not point toward absence of convergence. Furthermore, following Gill (2008), we conducted an "insurance run" of 1e6 iterations, which lead to identical results.

A.3 APPENDIX TO CHAPTER 5

A.3.1 Complete Tables of Estimates

TABLE A.4 *Effect of externalities on redistribution preferences in Western Europe; complete table of estimates*

	(1)		(2)		(3)		(4)	
	Est.	s.e.	Est.	s.e.	Est.	s.e.	Est.	s.e.
Eq.: Redistribution preferences								
Income distance	−0.054	0.003	−0.056	0.003	−0.071	0.005	−0.069	0.006
Gini	1.508	0.771	1.297	0.635	0.720	0.770	0.237	0.666
Income × Inequality	0.217	0.104	0.237	0.102	0.179	0.089	0.207	0.101
Expected income			−0.173	0.032			−0.169	0.031
Fear of crime					0.235	0.075	0.312	0.075

(Continued)

	(1)		(2)		(3)		(4)	
	Est.	s.e.	Est.	s.e.	Est.	s.e.	Est.	s.e.
Income × fear				0.011	0.003	0.009	0.003	
Age	0.018	0.007	0.020	0.007	0.016	0.006	0.017	0.006
Female	0.163	0.014	0.161	0.014	0.067	0.034	0.033	0.036
Education	−0.032	0.002	−0.006	0.005	−0.028	0.003	−0.002	0.004
Unemployed	0.166	0.021	0.161	0.023	0.145	0.028	0.131	0.026
Not in LF	−0.052	0.012	−0.048	0.015	−0.064	0.014	−0.064	0.016
HH members	0.018	0.005	0.014	0.005	0.021	0.004	0.018	0.005
Share foreign-born	−0.244	0.349	0.483	0.411	0.035	0.007	0.028	0.007
Unemployment rate	0.036	0.008	0.029	0.008	−0.085	0.041	−0.103	0.033
High-tech region	−0.085	0.036	−0.104	0.034	−0.045	0.040	−0.018	0.043
GDP	−0.063	0.046	−0.043	0.045	−0.391	0.389	0.271	0.506
Eq.: Fear of crime								
Victimization					0.271	0.022	0.268	0.022
Income distance					−0.019	0.003	−0.019	0.003
Gini					4.884	0.770	4.882	0.832
Age					0.020	0.005	0.020	0.006
Female					0.610	0.020	0.610	0.021
Education					−0.023	0.003	−0.023	0.003
Unemployed					0.124	0.024	0.124	0.027
Not in LF					0.079	0.014	0.079	0.012
HH members					−0.021	0.007	−0.021	0.006
GDP					−0.129	0.047	−0.129	0.045
Share foreign-born					1.051	0.839	1.050	0.662

Note: Models (1) and (2) correspond with Table 5.1; (3) and (4) correspond to Table 5.4. ML estimates of ordered probit models, region-county bootstrapped, multiple overimputation standard errors.

A.3.2 Multiple Imputation and Measurement Error

We use multiple imputation to address missing values. It is well known that listwise deletion or various "value substitution" methods can produce biased estimates and standard errors that are too small (Allison, 2001; King et al., 2001; Little and Rubin, 2002). Using multiple imputation we not only obtain complete data sets, but (more important) generate conservative standard errors reflecting uncertainty due to missing data (Rubin, 1987, 1996). An additional advantage of using multiple imputation is that we can use auxiliary variables that are not used in our analyses to predict missing responses, yielding so called "superefficient" imputations (Rubin, 1996). As additional predictors we include a set of variables, which help us predict missing income, such as the number of dependent children, living in an urban or rural area, ideology, as well as questions on satisfaction with one's current income, assessment of subjective health, and general life satisfaction. Multiple imputations are created by random draws from a multivariate normal posterior distribution for the missing data conditional on the observed data (King et al., 2001). These draws are used to generate five complete (i.e., imputed) data sets. Our models are estimated on each of these five data sets and then averaged with standard error adjusted to reflect the uncertainty of the imputed values (Rubin, 1987).

As mentioned in the main text, decomposing Gini into regional values involves calculating the distance of individual household income from a regional income mean. These means can carry considerable uncertainty when calculated from survey data. Thus, Gini values are measured with error, a fact that is often ignored and leads to classical errors-in-variables bias in one's results. In our analyses we correct for measurement error following the methodology outlined by Blackwell et al. (2012, 2017), who propose to treat measurement error in the framework of missing data. One creates several (about 5) "multiply overimputed" data sets, in which the variable measured with error is drawn from a suitably specified distribution representing the variable's measurement error.

We implement this idea in three steps. First, we obtain the variance of our Gini estimator following Karagiannis and Kovacevic (2000). Thus, for each regional Gini value, we have a point estimate $\hat{w}_j$ and a standard error $\sqrt{\text{Var}(\hat{w}_j)}$. Second, we generate five overimputed data sets with Gini values for each data set drawn from $w_j \sim N\left(\hat{w}_j, \text{Var}(\hat{w}_j)\right)$. To illustrate the "penalty" incurred by this measurement error technique, we plot, in Figure A.4, three regions with similar Gini estimates, but different standard errors. Région lémanique (in Switzerland), Niedersachsen (in Germany), and Noord-Friesland (in the Netherlands) share an estimated regional Gini between around 0.31 and 0.32. For each region we show the Gini estimate as black dot and five random multiple-overimputation draws as gray diamonds. Figure A.4 clearly shows how larger Gini standard errors lead to a considerable increase in the variance of overimputed values. Third, we then estimate all our models five times and adjust standard errors as suggested in Blackwell et al. (2012) or Rubin (1987). In essence, we reflect the uncertainty of Gini estimates in our analyses and adjust our standard errors for the variance of our Gini estimates.

A.3.3 Additional Robustness Tests

We performed a number of additional robustness tests.

PRECRISIS YEARS. One might argue that survey interviews conducted in late 2008 are affected by the onset of the global economic

TABLE A.5 *Overview of additional robustness checks; average marginal effects among the rich from simple model and model including fear of crime; estimates whose 95 percent confidence interval includes zero are marked with †*

| | Simple model | | Model with endogenous fear | | | |
| | Gini | | Fear | | Gini | |
Robustness tests	Est.	s.e.	Est.	s.e.	Est.	s.e.
(10) Precrisis years	0.574	0.235	0.082	0.035	0.371	0.243
(11) Small N regions dropped	0.589	0.258	0.092	0.035	0.362	0.266
(12) Grouped Gini	0.569	0.253	0.094	0.035	0.342	0.260
(13) UK + Portugal dropped	0.547	0.272	0.118	0.045	0.326	0.277
(14) Listwise deletion	0.462	0.203	0.092	0.035	0.214	0.226

Note: Robust, multiple imputation standard errors clustered by 129 regions and penalized for 5 imputations (Rubin, 1987).

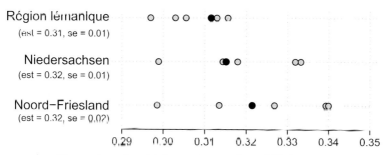

FIGURE A.4 Illustration of multiple overimputation of Gini measurement error

downturn. To check for this possibility we drop this entire wave from the analysis in specification (10) and use only interviews conducted before 2008. Results in Table A.5 show that this does not affect our results.

GINI FROM LIMITED SAMPLE SIZE AND GROUPED DATA. The next two robustness tests deal with the fact that we have to calculate our Gini index from limited survey data, in order to have full coverage of all regions. While we already adjust for the fact that our measure of inequality is calculated from relatively small samples (following Deltas, 2003), we perform an additional robustness test by dropping the 20 percent of regions with the smallest sample size in specification (11). We find that our main results are confirmed. Further problems might arise from the grouped nature of income measurement in the ESS. As we describe in the main text, incomes are asked in brackets, leading to coarse income measurements, which we treated as continuous in our calculation of the Gini coefficient. However, Gini calculations based on grouped data are known to exhibit (some) downward bias (Lerman and Yitzhaki, 1989; Davies et al., 2011). To check if this influences our results, specification (12) uses a first-order correction term proposed by Van Ourti and Clarke (2011) to adjust for the fact that we use group data. With this adjustment our main pattern of results is confirmed as well.

COUNTRY-SPECIFIC INCOME CONCENTRATION. It could be argued that the bulk of rich or poor people are concentrated in the wealthiest (or most unequal) countries. Although the transformation of local currencies into PPP-adjusted constant 2005 US dollars mitigates this potential problem (see Figure A.1 on page 232), we verify that the households with the greatest and lowest income differences are in fact not concentrated in a handful of countries. Table A.6 contains the number and percentages of individuals classified as rich and poor in our analysis (with standard errors in parentheses). It shows most countries to have significant amounts of individuals included in both the poor and rich groups. Confirming Figure A.1, no country seems to concentrate either an overwhelming number of poor or of rich people. Nevertheless, the two countries with the more unusual percentages of rich and poor are Portugal and the UK. The reasons for this are slightly different. In Portugal there is an unusually low number of poor people (we must keep in mind that incomes are measured as PPP-adjusted constant 2005 US dollars). In the UK (a highly unequal country), we have a high number of rich people and a high number of poor people. We therefore conduct an additional robustness test in Table A.5 by dropping simultaneously both countries from our analysis. Specification (13) shows our substantive results remain the same. We also address this concern in an alternative way by using country-specific definitions of "rich" and "poor" and calculating marginal effects of inequality by country. See Section A.3.4 for more details.

Finally, in specification (14) we show that our results do not depend on the assumptions underlying the (multivariate normal) imputation procedure used in the analysis.

TABLE A.6 *Individuals classified as rich and poor in our analysis; number of cases and percentages (standard errors in parentheses)*

	Poor		Rich	
	Percent	N	Percent	N
Austria	7.10 (0.14)	2,279	14.12 (0.19)	4,530
Belgium	5.19 (0.12)	1,657	15.99 (0.21)	5,104
Switzerland	11.09 (0.17)	3,939	14.28 (0.19)	5,072
Germany	9.48 (0.13)	4,809	12.23 (0.15)	6,209
Denmark	5.89 (0.16)	1,231	10.99 (0.22)	2,297
Spain	3.84 (0.11)	1,234	16.07 (0.20)	5,168
Finland	4.61 (0.16)	832	11.56 (0.24)	2,085
France	4.96 (0.12)	1,653	10.43 (0.17)	3,476
Great Britain	15.67 (0.19)	5,951	21.70 (0.21)	8,273
Ireland	5.08 (0.15)	1,031	16.80 (0.26)	3,410
Netherlands	9.35 (0.15)	3,418	13.03 (0.18)	4,764
Norway	12.53 (0.18)	4,227	14.11 (0.19)	4,759
Portugal	8.51 (0.04)	170	16.18 (0.20)	5,349
Sweden	3.00 (0.09)	1,030	10.52 (0.17)	3,617

Note: Calculated based on five multiply imputed data sets.

A.3.4 Classification of Rich and Poor and Country-Specific Effects

For predicted probability and marginal effects calculations in the main text we define poor and rich in terms of tenth and ninetieth percentiles of the overall distribution of incomes in our sample. A high concentration of rich and poor people in particular countries may emerge from this

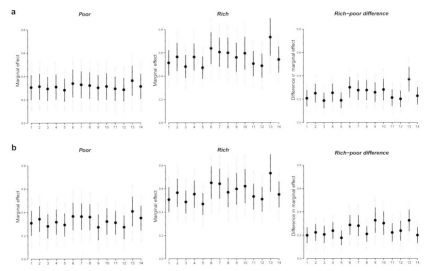

FIGURE A.5 Effects of inequality on preferences by country. Shown are marginal effects among the poor, the rich, as well as the difference between rich and poor. Panel (a) uses pooled sample percentiles, panel (b) uses country-specific percentiles

global definition of "poor" and "rich." In Figure A.5, we report results using both a common definition of poor and rich and a country-specific one. Panel (a) shows marginal effects of inequality among the poor (first plot), the rich (second plot), as well as the difference in marginal effects of poor and rich. The definition of poor and rich is the same as we use in the main text (the tenth and ninetieth percentile of the overall income distribution). Marginal effects are calculated for each country separately. Panel (b) repeats the same plots (poor, rich, difference) but uses the country-specific income distribution to define the tenth and ninetieth percentiles.

Figure A.5 shows both that the results are substantively the same when using these alternative definitions and that the country-specific marginal effects of inequality on preferences are remarkably similar. The marginal effect of inequality is always lower for the poor than for the rich. In a more systematic test, the difference in marginal effects between rich and poor is always significant (as indicated by the confidence intervals not including zero).

A.4 APPENDIX TO CHAPTER 7

A.4.1 Foreign-Born Share Details

As discussed in the main text, our measure of heterogeneity, the share of foreign-born, is "second best." Our ideal measure would be the share of foreign-born in the lower half of the income distribution, making them likely recipients of transfers. However, information on individuals' income position is only available in EU-LFS starting with 2009 and completely unavailable for some countries. We tackle this issue in two ways. First, we show that our simple measure of foreign-born correlates highly with an ideal measure of lower-income foreign-born in the years where we have data for both. Second, we calculate a country-specific shift parameter, which captures the average difference between both measures, and use it to adjust our measure of foreign-born in years where we lack respondents' income information.

The overall correlation between both measures is 0.89. Column ρ of Table A.7 shows country-specific correlations for the years 2009–2012. Both measures are strongly (and significantly) related in all countries.

TABLE A.7 *Relationship between the share of foreign-born and share of low-income foreign-born; first column shows correlation, second column shows average metric distance between both measures*

	ρ	δ
Austria	0.997	0.041
Belgium	0.996	0.089
Denmark	0.940	0.034
Finland	0.850	0.018
France	0.978	0.059
Germany	0.958	0.060
Ireland	0.851	0.021
Portugal	0.969	0.020
Spain	0.928	0.005
Switzerland	0.894	0.118
United Kingdom	0.988	−0.004

Note: Based on EU-LFS subsample, 2009–2012. Low-income foreign-born are defined as those with incomes below the fifth decile of each country's income distribution in each survey year. No information for Sweden, Norway, and the Netherlands.

Appendix

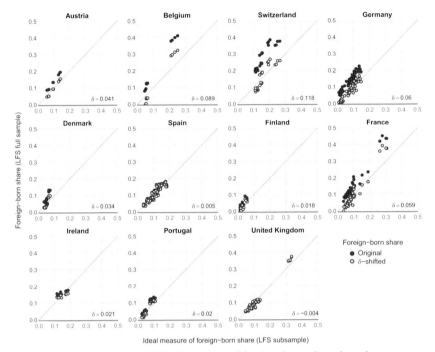

FIGURE A.6 Comparison of ideal measure of foreign-born share based on a subsample of LFS with our full-sample measure of foreign-born share; solid points represent our original measure of foreign-born used in the main text of the book, filled points represent an adjusted version obtained by country-specific difference shifts, δ_c

Their correlation ranges from 0.85 in Finland and Ireland up to 0.99 in Austria, Belgium, and the United Kingdom.

Figure A.6 plots both measures for each country (represented by black points). It again shows the strong linear relation between both measures. But it also reveals that, in some countries, the simple share of foreign-born is consistently above the share of lower income foreign-born. Thus, we calculate a country-specific shift parameter, δ_c, which is the average difference between both measures, from the 2009–2012 subsample and use it to adjust the share of foreign-born in the full (2002–2012) sample. Each country's δ_c value is shown in the last column of Table A.7. The gray-filled points in Figure A.6 show that this eliminates a sizeable part of the gap between both measures. Of course, the δ_c-shifted share of foreign born relies on the assumption of a constant shift throughout our sample. However, absent further information, it provides a useful robustness test for our main model, and we use it in specification (4) of Table 7.5.

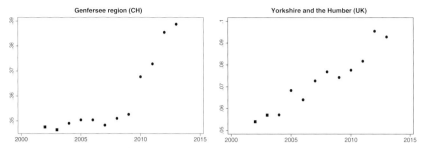

FIGURE A.7 Example of interpolation where linear and quadratic trends are necessary; observed values of heterogeneity are denoted by dots, interpolated values denoted by squares

A.4.2 Interpolation of EU-LFS Time Series

Because we lack EU-LFS data for our first ESS survey year, we impute values for 2002 (and 2003) using interpolation. As Figure A.7 illustrates, we use all available data from ca. 2004 to 2013, which in some cases exhibit a clear linear trend, while other cases suggest a curvilinear pattern. In order to create a generally applicable interpolation strategy, we use a mixture of estimated linear and quadratic fits to interpolate each regions missing values for 2002 and 2003. More precisely, we model heterogeneity in region r and time t, $\hat{h}_{rt}$ by both a linear trend model $\hat{h}_{rt}^{(l)} = \lambda_0 + \lambda_1 t$ as well as a quadratic model $\hat{h}_{rt}^{(q)} = \lambda_0 + \lambda_1 t + \lambda_2 t^2$. Imputed values $\tilde{h}_{rt}$ are a weighted linear combination of these linear and quadratic trend estimates:

$$\tilde{h}_{rt} = \pi \hat{h}_{rt}^{(l)} + (1 - \pi)\hat{h}_{rt}^{(q)} \tag{A.1}$$

Here π is a mixture parameter, which determines if we give more weight to linear or quadratic trend components. After visual inspection of imputation patterns we settled on $\pi = 0.4$, i.e., we weight quadratic trends slightly more. Two examples of resulting interpolated values are shown as black squares in Figure A.7.

A.4.3 Measurement Error Model

We account for measurement error using a Bayesian hierarchical measurement error model (Table A.8). The hierarchical setup is as follows:

$$R_{ijt} \sim N(\mu_{ijt}, \sigma^2) \tag{A.2}$$

$$h_{jt} \sim N(\theta_{jt}, S_{jt}) \tag{A.3}$$

TABLE A.8 *Measurement error model estimates.*

	Est	SD
Income	−0.063	0.011
Black welfare share	−0.153	0.162
Income × Welfare	−0.120	0.036
ω	0.106	0.001
$\text{Var}(\xi_j)$	0.139	0.026
σ^2	3.449	0.035

Note: Posterior means and standard deviations. Based on 18,000 MCMC samples.

$$\theta_{jt} \sim N(0, \omega), \qquad (A.4)$$

with the linear predictor of our regression equation of interest given by:

$$\mu_{ijt} = \alpha\,(v_{it} - \bar{v}t) + \beta\theta_{jt} + \gamma\theta_{jt}(v_{it} - \bar{v}t) + \delta'x_{ijt} + \xi_j + \epsilon_{it}. \qquad (A.5)$$

All regression parameters in equation (A.5) keep their interpretation (with the only difference that latent θ_{jt} is substituted for observed h_{jt}). The new elements in this model are the priors for the measurement error process. Observed BWS is defined as a noisy measure arising from the latent or "true" value θ_{jt}. The amount of noise is determined by S_{jt}, the standard error of the BWS measurement. The latent BWS variable is defined as a normal random variable with mean zero and variance ω. Our Bayesian specification is completed by assigning priors to all parameters. We use vague priors for all regression-type parameters, specified as normal with mean zero and variance 1000. Priors for precision parameters are Gamma: $\sigma_y^{-2} \sim G(a = 0.001, b = 0.001)$, $\sigma_\theta^{-2} \sim G(a = 0.01, b = 0.01)$. Priors for state-specific effects are vague and independent (to mimic the fixed-effects model): $\forall j : \xi_j \sim N(0, 1000)$.

A.4.4 Deindustrialization

We measure the decline in manufacturing by employment numbers in manufacturing as share of total private employment in a state in a given year. Historical data on employment by industrial sector are available from the Bureau of Labor Statistics' State and Area Current Employment Statistics Series (the SM series in BLS's database). The series reaches back to 1990 and continues until today. Thus, we need to construct values for four previous elections, which means extrapolating our series back fourteen years using twenty-five years of observed changes in manufacturing employment. We do so by fitting a flexible model to each state series and calculate backwards predictions based on these model estimates.

Visual inspection of our manufacturing series shows that in most states the rate of change is approximately constant over a large range of years. In order to flexibly capture slow-moving trend structures, we use autoregressive moving average models fit to first differenced manufacturing series in each state. More specifically, the model we use is given by:

$$(1 - \phi_1 \nabla - \cdots - \phi_p \nabla^p)(1 - \nabla) y_t = \alpha + (1 + \theta_1 \nabla + \cdots + \theta_q \nabla^q) e_t$$

$$(A.6)$$

where ∇^b is the backshift operator applied b times. The model allows for an autoregressive structure in observations (the ϕ parameters in the first part of the left-hand side), a moving average structure in residuals (the θ parameters in the right-hand side parenthetical expression), as well as for a constant of change (or "drift"). Not all parameters will be required to describe some state-specific series in sufficient detail. Therefore, we determine lag lengths p and q as well as α empirically. Using a grid search over the space of possible model specifications, we choose the best-fitting model according to the Akaike information criterion. For example, if employment in manufacturing is second-order autoregressive with a drift component (as in Washington), then $q = 0$, and our extrapolation model simplifies to:

$$y'_t = \alpha + \phi_1 y'_{t-1} + \phi_2 y'_{t-2} + e_t \qquad (A.7)$$

where $y'_t = y_t - y_{t-1}$ is the first differenced series. Based on the models so estimated for each state, we extrapolate (predict) past missing observations. Table A.9 shows model estimates for each state, as well as each model's root mean square error and R-squared. The latter show that our ARIMA model captures a substantive part of variation in manufacturing in each state and thus provides a sound basis for backwards extrapolation.

Figure A.8 shows the resulting trends of manufacturing between 1975 and 2010. As expected, one sees a secular decline in manufacturing throughout the United States. However, there are substantial differences between states. Some experienced a rather limited decline starting from low levels, such as Wyoming or North Dakota. Several states (for example Minnesota, Louisiana, or Nebraska) saw modest declines of up to five percentage points in the three decades between 1985 and 2005. A larger

TABLE A.9 *ARIMA extrapolation models for manufacturing share series; parameter estimates, root mean square error and R-squared*

	α	ϕ_1	ϕ_2	θ_1	θ_2	RMSE	Rsq
Alabama	0.005	0.422				0.004	0.992
Alaska		0.400				0.003	0.949
Arizona	0.003	0.488				0.002	0.995
Arkansas	0.005					0.003	0.994
California	0.004			0.544		0.002	0.996
Colorado	0.003	0.624				0.001	0.996
Connecticut	0.004			0.617		0.002	0.997
Delaware	0.004					0.003	0.990
District of Columbia	0.001	0.679				0.000	0.993
Florida	0.003	0.638				0.001	0.998
Georgia	0.004	0.531				0.002	0.997
Hawaii	0.001	0.528				0.001	0.984
Idaho		0.679				0.003	0.986
Illinois	0.004	0.507				0.002	0.995
Indiana		0.003				0.005	0.977
Iowa	0.002					0.004	0.958
Kansas	0.002			0.491		0.003	0.976
Kentucky	0.003	0.514				0.003	0.988
Louisiana	0.002			1.045	0.791	0.001	0.997
Maine	0.004	0.513				0.003	0.995
Maryland	0.003			0.779		0.001	0.999
Massachusetts	0.004			0.588		0.002	0.997
Michigan	0.004	0.407				0.005	0.980
Minnesota	0.002	0.428				0.002	0.989
Mississippi	0.006			0.616		0.004	0.994
Missouri	0.004			0.425		0.002	0.993
Montana	0.001			0.620		0.001	0.988
Nebraska	0.002	0.375				0.002	0.989
Nevada		0.493				0.001	0.932
New Hampshire	0.004	0.330				0.004	0.989
New Jersey	0.004	0.423				0.002	0.998
New Mexico	0.002					0.002	0.989
New York	0.004	0.577				0.001	0.998
North Carolina	0.007	0.684				0.003	0.998
North Dakota				0.731		0.002	0.919
Ohio	0.004			0.329		0.003	0.991
Oklahoma	0.002			0.548		0.003	0.981
Oregon	0.003			0.421		0.003	0.988
Pennsylvania	0.004	0.510				0.002	0.996
Rhode Island	0.005	0.626				0.003	0.997

(continued)

	α	ϕ_1	ϕ_2	θ_1	θ_2	RMSE	Rsq
South Carolina	0.006			0.721		0.003	0.996
South Dakota		0.460				0.004	0.939
Tennessee	0.005	0.457				0.003	0.995
Texas	0.003	0.531				0.002	0.996
Utah	0.003	0.476				0.002	0.993
Vermont	0.003			0.653		0.004	0.982
Virginia		0.910				0.001	0.998
Washington	0.003	0.878	−0.458			0.003	0.988
West Virginia	0.004					0.002	0.995
Wisconsin	0.003	0.403				0.004	0.982
Wyoming		0.628				0.001	0.983

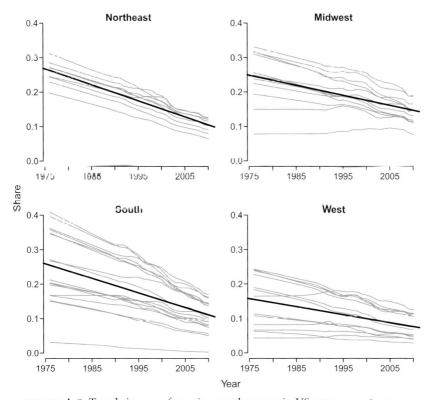

FIGURE A.8 Trends in manufacturing employment in US states, 1976–2010

number (such as Connecticut, Massachusetts, or Pennsylvania) experienced declines of up to ten percentage points in the same period. Nine states saw manufacturing decline by more than ten and up to seventeen percentage points, among them Tennessee, Alabama, and the Carolinas.

A.4.5 Residential Segregation

We measure racial residential segregation in each state in each year using tract-level Census data, similar to Chetty et al. (2014). We create a multi-group segregation index based on a Theil index (Iceland, 2004). Denote by ϕ_r the share of racial group r in a state. We use four groups: whites, Blacks, Hispanics, and others. The level of racial diversity in a state is given by an entropy measure: $E = \sum \phi_r \log_2 1/\phi_r$. When $\phi_r = 0$ then $\phi_r \log_2 1/\phi_r = 0$. Denote by $j = 1, \ldots, N$ census tracts within a state, and by ϕ_{rj} the share of racial group r in tract j. The level of racial diversity within each tract is $E_j = \sum \phi_{rj} \log_2 1/\phi_{rj}$. Finally, denote the total population of tract j by t_j and the total population in the state by T. Then, the level of racial segregation in the state (in each year) is defined as

$$ H = 1 - \left[\sum_j \left(\frac{t_j}{T} E_j \right) \Big/ E \right] \qquad (A.8) $$

This index represents to what extent the racial distribution in each tract deviates from the overall distribution in a state. It ranges from zero to one, where zero represents no segregation (complete heterogeneity), and one represents complete segregation.

Our calculation is based on ca. 65,000 census tracts from the Longitudinal Tract Database (Logan et al., 2014).[1] Using census tracts as areal unit of measurement means employing data from the decennial census conducted in 1980, 1990, 2000, and 2010. Thus, we have state-level segregation measures at four evenly spaced time points. We calculate H for each census and fill in intermediate years using linear interpolation.

A.4.6 Estimates for Additional Individual-Level Models

Table A.10 shows coefficient estimates for our additional individual-level attitude models.

---

[1] In 2010 the average number of census tracts per state was 1,423. We note the valid criticism that census tracts are essentially arbitrary administrative units. However, opting

TABLE A.10 *Attitudes to heterogeneity and redistribution preferences among the poor and rich in Western Europe and the United States; parameter estimates*

	Western Europe[a]		United States[b]	
	(1)	(2)	(3)	(4)
Attitude to heterogeneity	0.019	0.019	0.547	0.542
(immigration, race)	(0.003)	(0.003)	(0.020)	(0.020)
Income distance	−0.075	−0.076	−0.179	−0.179
	(0.005)	(0.005)	(0.012)	(0.012)
Income × Attitude	0.003	0.003	0.043	0.042
	(0.001)	(0.001)	(0.005)	(0.005)
N	61168	61168	17273	17273

[a]European Social Survey data, 2002–2008. Model (1) is a probit model with region random effects, model (2) adds country and year fixed effects. Controls include age, education, indicator variables for being unemployed, self-employed, not in the labor force, and household size. Marginal effects in main text are calculated based on model (2).
[b]General Social Survey data, 1978–2010. Model (3) is a probit model with state random effects, model (4) uses state fixed effects. Controls include age, education, indicator variables for female part-time work, unemployment, self-employment, living in a city. Marginal effects in main text are calculated based on model (4).

A.5 APPENDIX TO CHAPTER 8

Table A.11 lists survey fieldwork periods and associated elections used in the analysis.

A.5.1 Coefficient Estimates of Joint Preferences and Choice Models

Table A.12 shows the full set of estimated coefficients for our joint preference and choice models.

A.5.2 Sensitivity Analysis

In addition to the usual assumptions of basic regression models, decomposing direct and indirect effects requires additional assumptions. These are clearly laid out in Imai et al. (2010; see also Sobel, 2008). Intuitively, the following assumptions are needed: (1) no omitted confounding of

for more detailed spatial resolution (while at the same time maintaining comparability over time) is beyond the scope of this booki.

TABLE A.11 *Survey fieldwork periods and corresponding elections used in the analysis*

Country	Survey fieldwork periods (dd.mm.yy)	Election dates (dd.mm.yy)
Austria	02.02.03–30.09.03; 18.07.07–05.11.07	24.11.02; 01.10.06
Belgium	01.10.02–30.04.03; 04.10.04–31.01.05	13.06.99; 18.05.03
Denmark	28.10.02–19.06.03; 19.09.06–02.05.07	20.11.01; 8.02.05
Finland	20.09.04–20.12.04	16.03.03
France	15.09.03–15.12.03; 28.09.08–31.01.09	09./16.06.02; 10./17.06.07
Germany	20.11.02–16.05.03; 01.09.06–15.01.07	22.09.02; 18.09.05
Great Britain	24.09.02–04.02.03; 05.09.06–14.01.07	07.06.01; 05.05.05
Ireland	11.12.02–12.04.03	17.05.02
Netherlands	01.09.02–24.02.03; 11.09.04–19.02.05	15.05.02; 22.01.03
Norway	16.09.02–17.01.03	10.09.01
Portugal	15.09.02–15.01.03; 19.10.06–25.02.07	17.03.02; 20.02.05
Spain	19.11.02–20.02.03; 27.09.04–31.01.05; 05.09.08–31.01.09	12.03.00; 14.03.04 09.03.08
Sweden	23.09.02–20.12.02	15.09.02
Switzerland	09.09.02–08.02.03; 15.09.04–28.02.05	24.10.99; 19.10.03

Note: Not all ESS waves that corresponded to an election are used, because of unavailable CMP data on party positions.

the treatment–outcome relationship, (2) no omitted confounding of the mediator–outcome relationship, (3) no omitted treatment–mediator confounding, and (4) no mediator–outcome confounder affected by the treatment. These assumptions are often violated, even in randomized studies (Green et al., 2010). With observational data these are highly likely to be violated. The most problematic issue are probably omitted variables that affect both the intermediate variable *and* the outcome. As illustrated in Figure A.9, assume that an omitted variable U influences both preferences and vote choice. While we include a number of controls to reduce the likelihood of substantial omitted confounders, their existence can of course not be ruled out with the data available to us. By not including U in our model a correlation, ρ, between residuals in the preference and vote equation is generated. The direction and size of that correlation cannot be estimated (as including it renders the model unidentified). Thus Imai et al. (2010) and VanderWeele (2010) propose sensitivity analyses to study the impact omitted mediator-outcome confounders have on the resulting estimates. The basic idea is to calculate the indirect effect estimates at given (fixed) levels of ρ. Repeating this calculation over a range of values yields information on how sensitive our results are to omitting unobserved confounders. Following this idea we calculate indirect effects while varying the value of ρ from −0.6 to 0.6. The resulting estimates are plotted in Figures A.11 and A.10 for the United States and Western Europe,

TABLE A.12 *Coefficient estimates for United States and Western European samples*

| | United States[a] | | Western Europe[b] | | | |
| | | | Left party | | Redistrib. party | |
	Est.	s.e.	Est.	s.e.	Est.	s.e.
(A) Redistribution equation						
Expected income	−0.129	0.028	−0.134	0.009	−0.131	0.009
Inequality	−0.068	0.031	0.048	0.021	0.050	0.021
Heterogeneity	−0.026	0.030	0.014	0.025	0.015	0.026
Income distance	−0.364	0.029	−0.127	0.007	−0.128	0.007
×Inequality	0.056	0.027	0.012	0.007	0.012	0.007
×Heterogeneity	−0.062	0.029	−0.025	0.007	−0.025	0.007
Var(ξ)	0.039	0.018	0.103	0.012	0.104	0.012
(B) Vote choice equation						
Preferences	0.179	0.010	0.267	0.009	0.257	0.009
Expected income	0.052	0.017	−0.009	0.013	0.031	0.014
Inequality	0.000	0.020	0.010	0.031	0.086	0.046
Heterogeneity	−0.008	0.019	0.018	0.037	0.058	0.056
Income distance	−0.083	0.017	−0.030	0.010	−0.065	0.010
Var(ζ)	0.071	0.021	0.217	0.025	0.547	0.059

Note: Based on 40,000 MCMC samples. Estimates are posterior means, s.e. are posterior standard deviations.
[a] GSS sample. Heterogeneity measure is Black welfare recipiency rate.
[b] ESS sample. Heterogeneity measure is share of foreign-born.

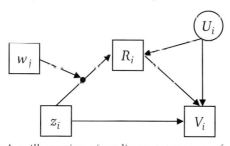

FIGURE A.9 Illustration of mediator–outcome confounding

respectively. They plot indirect effect estimates (expressed as differences in the probability of voting Democrat or for a redistributive party) for expected income, income at low and high levels of heterogeneity and at low and high levels of inequality at varying levels of mediator-outcome confounding. To gain a sense of the magnitude of the confounding correlation, consider that the correlation between education and income is 0.31.

Figure A.10 shows that the indirect effect estimates for our European sample are most sensitive to unobservables that affect both preferences

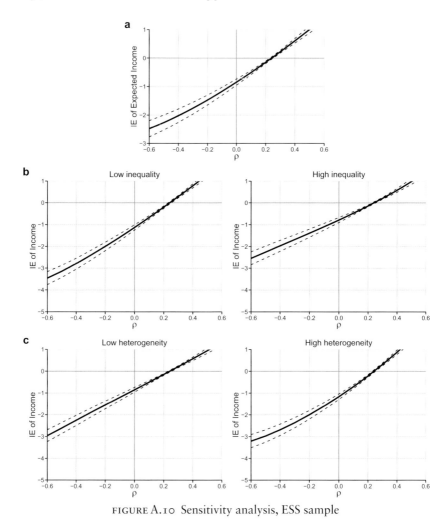

FIGURE A.10 Sensitivity analysis, ESS sample

and choices positively (think of an unmeasured character trait that increases ones preferences for redistribution and the likelihood of voting ''left'). When the induced correlation is larger than ≈0.2 it becomes difficult to statistically distinguish the indirect effect from zero. If the induced residual correlation is negative (think of an unmeasured variable that while increasing redistribution preferences pushes one to more conservative parties) our indirect effect estimates increase in magnitude.

In contrast, Figure A.11 shows that estimates for our US sample are surprisingly more robust. The influence of unobservables follows the

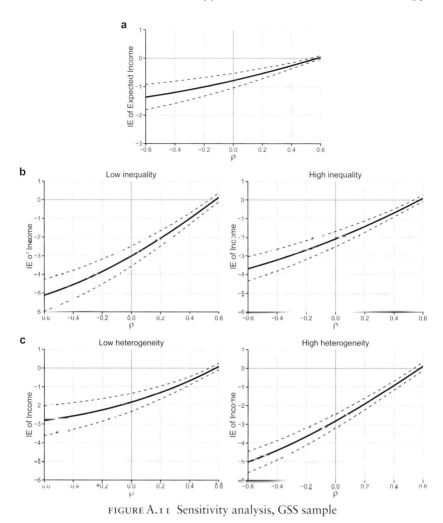

FIGURE A.11 Sensitivity analysis, GSS sample

same directional pattern, but the induced residual correlation would have to be larger than ≈ 0.6 to render the indirect effect estimates insignificant.

A.5.3 Income Imputed

The key variable affected by missing data in large-scale population surveys is often income. Our data is no exception. About 9 percent of cases in our US data lack information on income; the corresponding figure for our

TABLE A.13 *Income imputation; comparison of indirect effect estimates under complete-case analysis and multiple imputation*

	EI	Inequality		Heterogeneity	
		L	H	L	H
A: United States					
Complete-case	−0.614	−2.618	−1.433	−1.549	−2.309
	(0.138)	(0.337)	(0.224)	(0.240)	(0.254)
Imputation	−0.583	−2.466	−1.286	−1.448	−2.109
	(0.135)	(0.331)	(0.218)	(0.234)	(0.247)
B: Western Europe					
Complete-case	−0.985	−1.205	−0.806	−0.864	−1.245
	(0.082)	(0.108)	(0.100)	(0.093)	(0.125)
Imputation	−0.955	−0.961	−0.753	−0.698	−1.110
	(0.078)	(0.101)	(0.097)	(0.089)	(0.117)

Note: Ten imputed datasets. Income imputed using predictive mean matching with five nearest neighbors. EI: expected income. L: low levels of inequality or heterogeneity, H: high levels (refers to tenth and ninetieth percentiles, respectively).

European data is 16 percent. Missing data on income is particularly problematic because the missingness process generating missing observations might be NMAR (not missing at random); i.e., nonreporting of income might be a result of levels of income itself, such as when high income earners refuse to reveal their income. While this issue cannot be solved here, we present later an analysis that imputes missing income assuming that the missingness process is MAR (missing at random) conditional on a vector of observed covariates predictive of income (including age and education, gender, minority status, employment status, and macroeconomic conditions). We create ten imputed data sets using predictive mean matching from five nearest neighbors.

Table A.13 compares complete-case and imputation estimates for the indirect effects of expected income and income conditional on heterogeneity and inequality. Panel (A) displays results for our US sample. We find substantively similar results in the complete-case and imputation analysis. While indirect effect estimates are generally smaller using income-imputed data, the pattern of relative difference (for example, between low- and high-inequality states) is almost unchanged. In the Western European sample, displayed in panel (B), we find a smaller gap in low- and high-inequality regions. In contrast, the difference in low- and high-heterogeneity regions is slightly enhanced.

TABLE A.14 *Indirect effect estimates when respondents' distance to last election is included in vote choice and redistribution preference equations*

	EI	Inequality		Heterogeneity	
		L	H	L	H
A: United States					
Baseline model	−0.614	−2.618	−1.433	−1.549	−2.309
	(0.138)	(0.337)	(0.224)	(0.240)	(0.254)
Election distance	−0.623	−2.647	−1.442	−1.536	−2.357
	(0.139)	(0.341)	(0.224)	(0.239)	(0.257)
Election distance interactions	−0.625	−2.672	−1.498	−1.563	−2.417
	(0.140)	(0.348)	(0.230)	(0.251)	(0.265)
B: Western Europe					
Baseline model	−0.985	−1.205	−0.806	−0.864	−1.245
	(0.082)	(0.108)	(0.100)	(0.093)	(0.125)
Election distance	−1.002	−1.217	−0.799	−0.870	−1.245
	(0.084)	(0.111)	(0.100)	(0.094)	(0.122)
Election distance interactions	−1.000	−1.206	−0.808	−0.870	−1.243
	(0.084)	(0.111)	(0.101)	(0.093)	(0.122)

Note: Based on full models as used in main text (repeated as "baseline model" for comparison). First specification adds election distance (days since last election) variable to preference and choice equations; second specification adds interaction between election distance and covariates. Posterior means with posterior standard deviations in parentheses based on 40,000 MCMC samples.

A.5.4 Misreporting of Vote Choice

In this section we study one aspect of survey misreporting of vote choice: recall error. We account for the possibility that an increase in the distance between survey interview and election increases the likelihood of misreporting (Wright, 1990). The fieldwork period of our surveys usually covers several months, so that within a given country-year there is variation over individuals in the distance between interview and election. We use this variation to account for possible biases in vote recall. Rainey and Jackson (2013) find (using both simulations and an empirical application) that models where election distance is included as covariate perform quite well compared to much more demanding statistical specifications (such as partial observability models). From each survey's paradata we obtain a respondent's day and month of interview and calculate the distance in days to the election that the survey recall question refers to. In our

European sample the median distance is 404 days (the tenth percentile is 140, the ninetieth percentile is 733). In the US sample the median is 507 days (the tenth and ninetieth percentiles are 472 and 571 days).

In Table A.14 we report results when including the days since the last election for each individual. In a more extended specification we allow the effects of expected income, income × heterogeneity and income × inequality to depend on the distance to the last election as well. Comparing indirect effect estimates from these two specifications with the baseline model used in the main text, we find that differences between respondents in the time passed since they cast their vote does not seem to systematically alter our results.

Bibliography

Acemoglu, D. and J. A. Robinson (2005). *Economic Origins of Dictatorship and Democracy*. Cambridge, UK: Cambridge University Press.

Achen, C. H. and L. M. Bartels (2016). *Democracy for Realists: Why Elections Do Not Produce Responsive Government*. Princeton, NJ: Princeton University Press.

Adams, J., M. Clark, L. Ezrow, and G. Glasgow (2004). Understanding change and stability in party ideologies: Do parties respond to public opinion or to past election results? *British Journal of Political Science* 34(4), 589–610.

Adams, J., J. Dow, and S. Merrill (2006). The political consequences of alienation-based and indifference-based voter abstention: Applications to presidential elections. *Political Behavior* 28(1), 65–86.

Adams, J., A. B. Haupt, and H. Stoll (2009). What moves parties? The role of public opinion and global economic conditions in Western Europe. *Comparative Political Studies* 42(5), 611–639.

Adams, J. and Z. Somer-Topcu (2009). Policy adjustment by parties in response to rival parties' policy shifts: Spatial theory and the dynamics of party competition in twenty-five post-war democracies. *British Journal of Political Science* 39(4), 825–846.

Adams, J. S. (1965). Inequity in social exchange. *Advances in Experimental Social Psychology* 2, 267–299.

Adsera, A. and C. Boix (2002). Trade, democracy, and the size of the public sector: The political underpinnings of openness. *International Organization* 56(2), 229–262.

Afonso, A. and L. Rennwald (2018). The changing welfare state agenda of populist radical right parties in Europe. In P. Manow, B. Palier, and H. Schwander (Eds.), *Welfare Democracies and Party Politics: Explaining Electoral Dynamics in Times of Changing Welfare Capitalism*. Oxford, UK: Oxford University Press.

Albert, J. H. and S. Chib (1993). Bayesian analysis of binary and polychotomous response data. *Journal of the American Statistical Association* 88(422), 669–679.

Alesina, A. and G. M. Angeletos (2005). Fairness and redistribution. *American Economic Review* 95(4), 960–980.

Alesina, A., A. Devleeschauwer, W. Easterly, S. Kurlat, and R. Wacziarg (2003). Fractionalization. *Journal of Economic Growth* 8(2), 155–194.

Alesina, A. and N. Fuchs-Schündeln (2007). Good-bye Lenin (or not?): The effect of communism on people's preferences. *American Economic Review* 97(4), 1507–1528.

Alesina, A. and P. Giuliano (2011). Preferences for Redistribution. In J. Benhabib, A. Bisin, and M. O. Jackson (Eds.), *Handbook of Social Economics*, pp. 93–131. San Diego: North-Holland.

Alesina, A., E. Glaeser, and B. Sacerdote (2001). Why doesn't the US have a European-style welfare system? Technical report, National Bureau of Economic Research.

Alesina, A. and E. L. Glaeser (2004). *Fighting Poverty in the US and Europe. A World of Difference*. Oxford, UK: Oxford University Press.

Alesina, A. and E. La Ferrara (2005). Preferences for redistribution in the land of opportunities. *Journal of Public Economics* 89(5–6), 897–931.

Allison, P. D. (2001). *Missing Data*. Thousand Oaks, CA: Sage.

Almlund, M., A. L. Duckworth, J. J. Heckman, and T. Kautz (2011). Personality psychology and economics. In E. A. Hanushek, S. Machin, and L. Woessmann (Eds.), *Handbook of the Economics of Education*, pp. 1–181. Amsterdam: Elsevier.

Almond, G. A. and S. Verba (1965). *The Civic Culture*. Boston: Little, Brown.

Alt, J. (1985). Political parties, world demand, and unemployment. *American Political Science Review* 79, 1016–1040.

Alt, J. and T. Iversen (2017). Inequality, labor market segmentation, and preferences for redistribution. *American Journal of Political Science* 61(1), 21–36.

Alvarez, R. M. and J. Nagler (1995). Voter choice in 1992: Economics, issues and anger. *American Journal of Political Science* 39(3), 714–744.

(1998). Economics, entitlements, and social issues: Voter choice in the 1996 presidential election. *American Journal of Political Science* 42(4), 1349–1363.

Alvarez, R. M., J. Nagler, and J. R. Willette (2000). Measuring the relative impact of issues and the economy in democratic elections. *Electoral Studies* 19(2), 237–253.

Anderson, C. J. and P. Beramendi (2008a). Income inequality and democratic representation. In P. Beramendi and C. J. Anderson (Eds.), *Democracy, Inequality, and Representation: A Comparative Perspective*. New York: Russell Sage Foundation.

(2008b). Income, inequality, and electoral participation. In P. Beramendi and C. J. Anderson (Eds.), *Democracy, Inequality, and Representation. A Comparative Perspective*, pp. 278–311. New York: Russell Sage Foundation.

Anderson, C. J. and M. M. Singer (2008). The sensitive left and the impervious right: Multilevel models and the politics of inequality, ideology, and legitimacy in Europe. *Comparative Political Studies* 41(4/5), 564–599.

Andreoni, J. (1989). Giving with impure altruism: Applications to charity and Ricardian equivalence. *Journal of Political Economy* 97(6), 1447–1458.

(1990). Impure altruism and donations to public goods: A theory of warm-glow giving. *The Economic Journal* 100(401), 464–477.

Ansell, B. (2014). The political economy of ownership: Housing markets and the welfare state. *American Political Science Review* 108(2), 383–402.

Ansell, B. W. (2010). *From the Ballot to the Blackboard: The Redistributive Political Economy of Education*. Cambridge, UK: Cambridge University Press.

Ansell, B. W. and D. J. Samuels (2014). *Inequality and Democratization*. Cambridge, UK: Cambridge University Press.

Ansolabehere, S., J. Rodden, and J. M. J. Snyder (2008). The strength of issues: Using multiple measures to gauge preference stability, ideological constraint, and issue voting. *American Political Science Review* 102(2), 215–232.

Ashok, V., I. Kuziemko, and E. Washington (2015). Support for redistribution in an age of rising inequality: New stylized facts and some tentative explanations. Brookings Papers on Economic Activity, 2015(1), 367–433.

Baker, M. (1997). Growth-rate heterogeneity and the covariance structure of life-cycle earnings. *Journal of Labor Economics* 15(2), 338–375.

Baldwin, P. (1990). *The Politics of Social Solidarity: Class Bases of the European Welfare State, 1875–1975*. Cambridge, UK: Cambridge University Press.

Barnard, J. and D. B. Rubin (1999). Small-sample degrees of freedom with multiple imputation. *Biometrika* 86(4), 948–955.

Barnes, L. (2013). Does median voter income matter? The effects of inequality and turnout on government spending. *Political Studies* 61(1), 82–100.

Barro, R (1973). The control of politicians: An economic model. *Public Choice* 14(1), 19–42.

Bartels, L. M. (2006). What's the matter with what's the matter with Kansas? *Quarterly Journal of Political Science* 1(1), 201–226.

(2009). *Unequal Democracy: The Political Economy of the New Gilded Age*. Princeton, NJ: Princeton University Press.

Bean, C. and E. Papadakis (1998). A comparison of mass attitudes towards the welfare state in different institutional regimes, 1985–1990. *International Journal of Public Opinion Research* 10(3), 211–236.

Becker, G. S. (1968). Crime and punishment: An economic approach. *Journal of Political Economy* 76(2), 169–217.

Becker, G. S. and B. R. Chiswick (1966). Education and the distribution of earnings. *American Economic Review* 56(1/2), 358–369.

Bell, D. A. (1992). *Faces at the Bottom of the Well: The Permanence of Racism*. New York: Basic Books.

Ben-Porath, Y. (1967). The production of human capital and the life cycle of earnings. *Journal of Political Economy* 75(4), 352–365.

Benabou, R. and E. A. Ok (2001). Social mobility and the demand for redistribution: The Poum hypothesis. *The Quarterly Journal of Economics* 116(2), 447–487.

Benabou, R. and J. Tirole (2006). Belief in a just world and redistributive politics. *Quarterly Journal of Economics* 121(2), 699–746.

Benoit, K. and M. Laver (2006). *Party Policy in Modern Democracies*. Oxon: Routledge.

    (2007). Estimating party policy positions: Comparing expert surveys and hand-coded content analysis. *Electoral Studies* 26, 90–107.

Beramendi, P. (2012). *The Political Geography of Inequality. Regions and Redistribution*. Cambridge, UK: Cambridge University Press.

Beramendi, P. and P. Rehm (2016). Who gives, who gains? Progressivity and preferences. *Comparative Political Studies* 49(4), 529–563.

Bernhard, H., U. Fischbacher, and E. Fehr (2006). Parochial altruism in humans. *Nature* 442(7105), 912–915.

Berry, W. D., R. C. Fording, E. J. Ringquist, R. L. Hanson, and C. E. Klarner (2010). Measuring citizen and government ideology in the US states: A re-appraisal. *State Politics & Policy Quarterly* 10(2), 117–135.

Berry, W. D., E. J. Ringquist, R. C. Fording, and R. L. Hanson (1998). Measuring citizen and government ideology in the American states, 1960–93. *American Journal of Political Science* 42(1), 327–348.

Blackwell, M., J. Honaker, and G. King (2012). Multiple overimputation: A unified approach to measurement error and missing data. Working paper.

    (2017). A unified approach to measurement error and missing data: overview and applications. *Sociological Methods & Research* 46(3), 303–341.

Blekesaune, M. and J. Quadagno (2003). Public attitudes toward welfare state policies a comparative analysis of 24 nations. *European Sociological Review* 19(5), 415–427.

Boes, S. and R. Winkelmann (2006). Ordered response models. *Allgemeines Statistisches Archiv* 90(1), 167–181.

Boix, C. (2003). *Democracy and Redistribution*. Cambridge, UK: Cambridge University Press.

Bonoli, G. (2005). The politics of the new social policies: Providing coverage against new social risks in mature welfare states. *Policy & Politics* 33(3), 431–449.

Bourguignon, F. (1999). Crime as a social cost of poverty and inequality: A review focusing on developing countries. *Revista Desarrollo y Sociedad* 44, 61–99.

Boyce, J. K. (1994). Inequality as a cause of environmental degradation. *Ecological Economics* 11(3), 169–178.

Braun, M. and W. Müller (1997). Measurement of education in comparative research. *Comparative Social Research* 16, 163–201.

Brooks, C. and D. Brady (1999). Income, economic voting, and long-term political change in the U.S., 1952–1996. *Social Forces* 77(4), 1339–1374.

Brooks, C. and J. Manza (1997). The social and ideological bases of middle-class political realignment in the United States, 1972 to 1992. *American Sociological Review* 62(2), 191–208.

Brownstone, D. and R. Valletta (2001). The bootstrap and multiple imputations: Harnessing increased computing power for improved statistical tests. *Journal of Economic Perspectives 15*(4), 129–141.

Brynin, M. (2010). Social class as a moving average. ISER Working Paper 2010–06.

Budge, I., H.-D. Klingemann, A. Volkens, J. Bara, E. Tanenbaum, R. C. Fording, D. J. Hearl, H. M. Kim, M. McDonald, and S. Mendez (2001). *Mapping Policy Preferences. Estimates for Parties, Electors, and Governments 1945–1998.* Oxford, UK: Oxford University Press.

Burgoon, B., F. Koster, and M. Van Egmond (2012). Support for redistribution and the paradox of immigration. *Journal of European Social Policy 22*(3), 288–304.

Burke, V. and M. Gish (1999). Welfare reform: Work trigger time limits, exemptions and sanctions under TANF. Congressional Research Service 98-697.

Burns, P. and J. G. Gimpel (2000). Economic insecurity, prejudicial stereotypes, and public opinion on immigration policy. *Political Science Quarterly 115*(2), 201–225.

Butler, J. S. and P. Chatterjee (1997). Tests of the specification of univariate and bivariate ordered probit. *Review of Economics and Statistics 79*(2), 343–347.

Cameron, C. A. and P. K. Trivedi (2005). *Microeconometrics. Methods and Applications.* Cambridge, UK: Cambridge University Press.

Cameron, D. R. (1978). The expansion of the public economy: A comparative analysis. *American Political Science Review 72*(04), 1243–1261.

(1984). Social democracy, corporatism, labour quiescence and the representation of economic interest in advanced capitalist society. In J. H. Goldthorpe (Ed.), *Order and Conflict in Contemporary Capitalism*, pp. 143–178. Oxford, UK: Clarendon Press.

Campbell, A., P. F. Converse, W. E. Miller, and D. E. Stokes (1960). *The American Voter.* New York: Wiley.

Cavaillé, C. and K.-S. Trump (2015). The two facets of social policy preferences. *Journal of Politics 77*(1), 146–160.

CBS (2002). *Demografische kerncijfers per gemeente, 2002.* Voorburg: Centraal Bureau voor de Statistiek.

(2004). *Demografische kerncijfers per gemeente, 2004.* Voorburg: Centraal Bureau voor de Statistiek.

(2006). *Demografische kerncijfers per gemeente, 2006.* Voorburg: Centraal Bureau voor de Statistiek.

(2008). *Demografische kerncijfers per gemeente, 2008.* Voorburg: Centraal Bureau voor de Statistiek.

Chapman, R. G. and K. S. Palda (1983). Electoral turnout in rational voting and consumption perspectives. *Journal of Consumer Research 9*(4), 337–346.

Charness, G. and M. Rabin (2002). Understanding social preferences with simple tests. *The Quarterly Journal of Economics 117*(3), 817–869.

Chesher, A. (1991). The effect of measurement error. *Biometrika 78*(3), 451–462.

Chetty, R., N. Hendren, P. Kline, and E. Saez (2014). Where is the land of opportunity? The geography of intergenerational mobility in the United States. *Quarterly Journal of Economics* 129(4), 1553–1623.

Cho, W. K. T., J. G. Gimpel, and J. J. Dyck (2006). Residential concentration, political socialization, and voter turnout. *Journal of Politics* 68(1), 156–167.

Citrin, J. and D. P. Green (1990). The self-interest motive in American public opinion. *Research in Micropolitics* 3(1), 1–28.

Citrin, J., D. P. Green, C. Muste, and C. Wong (1997). Public opinion toward immigration reform: The role of economic motivations. *Journal of Politics* 59(3), 858–881.

Corneo, G. and H. P. Grüner (2002). Individual preferences for political redistribution. *Journal of Public Economics* 83(1), 83–107.

Covington, J. and R. B. Taylor (1991). Fear of crime in urban residential neighborhoods: Implications of between- and within-neighborhood sources for current models. *Sociological Quarterly* 32(2), 231–249.

Cowell, F. A. (2000). Measurement of inequality. In A. B. Atkinson and F. Bourguignon (Eds.), *Handbook of Income Distribution*, Volume 1, pp. 87–166. Amsterdam: Elsevier.

Cox, G. W. and M. D. McCubbins (1986). Electoral politics as a redistributive game. *Journal of Politics* 48, 370–389.

Cramer, K. J. (2016). *The Politics of Resentment: Rural Consciousness in Wisconsin and the Rise of Scott Walker*. Chicago: University of Chicago Press.

Cusack, T., T. Iversen, and P. Rehm (2006). Risks at work: The demand and supply sides of government redistribution. *Oxford Review of Economic Policy* 22(3), 365–389.

Cusack, T. R. and P. Beramendi (2006). Taxing work. *European Journal of Political Research* 45(1), 43–73.

Cutright, P. (1965). Political structure, economic development, and national social security programs. *American Journal of Sociology* 70, 537–550.

Dahl, R. A. (1973). *Polyarchy: Participation and Opposition*. New Haven, CT: Yale University Press.

Dalton, R. J. (2002). *Citizen Politics: Public Opinion and Political Parties in Advanced Western Democracies*. London: Chatham House Publishers.

Davies, J. B., S. Sandström, A. Shorrocks, and E. N. Wolff (2011). The level and distribution of global household wealth. *The Economic Journal* 121(551), 223–254.

Davis, J. A. and T. W. Smith (1994). General social surveys, 1972–1994. Machine-readable data file. Chicago: Nat. Opinion Res. Center; distributed by Roper Center Public Opinion Research.

Davis, M. L. (1988). Time and punishment: An intertemporal model of crime. *Journal of Political Economy* 96(2), 383–390.

Dawson, M. C. (1995). *Behind the Mule: Race and Class in African-American Politics*. Princeton, NJ: Princeton University Press.

De Koster, W., P. Achterberg, and J. Van der Waal (2013). The new right and the welfare state: The electoral relevance of welfare chauvinism and welfare populism in the Netherlands. *International Political Science Review* 34(1), 3–20.

De La O, A. L. and J. A. Rodden (2008). Does religion distract the poor? Income and issue voting around the world. *Comparative Political Studies* 41(4-5), 437–476.

De Lange, S. L. (2007). A new winning formula? The programmatic appeal of the radical right. *Party Politics* 13(4), 411–435.

DellaVigna, S. (2009). Psychology and economics: Evidence from the field. *Journal of Economic Literature* 47(2), 315–372.

Deltas, G. (2003). The small-sample bias of the Gini coefficient: Results and implications for empirical research. *Review of Economics and Statistics* 85(1), 226–234.

Department of Health and Human Services (2003). Comparison of prior law and the personal responsibility and work opportunity reconciliation act. In G. Mink and R. Solinger (Eds.), *Welfare: A Documentary History of U.S. Policy and Politics*, pp. 663–679. New York: New York University Press.

Dimick, M., D. Rueda, and D. Stegmueller (2016). The altruistic rich? Inequality and other-regarding preferences for redistribution. *Quarterly Journal of Political Science* 11(4), 385–439.

   (2018). Models of other-regarding preferences, inequality, and redistribution. *Annual Review of Political Science* 21(1), 441–460.

Dion, M. (2010). When is it rational to redistribute? A cross-national examination of attitudes toward redistribution. In *Delivery at the 2010 Summer Meeting of the Society of Political Methodology, University of Iowa, Iowa City, IA*, pp. 22–24.

Dion, M. L. and V. Birchfield (2010). Economic development, income inequality, and preferences for redistribution. *International Studies Quarterly* 54(2), 315–334.

Dixit, A. and J. Londregan (1996). The determinants of success of special interests in redistributive politics. *Journal of Politics* 58, 1132–1155.

Donohue, J. and P. Siegleman (1998). Allocating resources among prisons and social programs in the battle against crime. *Journal of Legal Studies* 27(1), 1–43.

Downs, A. (1957). *An Economic Theory of Democracy*. New York: Harper.

Drazen, A. (2000). *Political Economy in Macroeconomics*. Princeton, NJ: Princeton University Press.

DuBow, F., E. McCabe, and G. Kaplan (1980). *Reactions to Crime: A Critical Review of the Literature*. Washington, DC: U.S. Department of Justice.

Duch, R. and R. Stevenson (2008). *The Economic Vote: How Political and Economic Institutions Condition Election Results*. Political Economy of Institutions and Decisions. Cambridge, UK: Cambridge University Press.

Dunne, M. (2003). Education in Europe. Key statistics 2000/01. Technical report, Eurostat, Luxembourg.

Dynan, K. E., J. Skinner, and S. P. Zeldes (2004). Do the rich save more? *Journal of Political Economy* 112(2), 397–444.

Easterly, W. and R. Levine (1997). Africa's growth tragedy: Policies and ethnic divisions. *The Quarterly Journal of Economics* 112(4), 1203–1250.

Ehrlich, I. (1973). Participation in illegitimate activities: A theoretical and empirical investigation. *Journal of Political Economy* 81(3), 521–565.

Ellwood, J. W. and J. Guetzkow (2009). Footing the bill: Causes and budgetary consequences of state spending on corrections. In M. A. S. Steven Raphael (Ed.), *Do Prisons Make Us Safer? The Benefits and Costs of the Prison Boom*. New York: Russell Sage Foundation.

Engels, F. (1993). *The Condition of the Working Class in England*. New York: Oxford University Press.

Erikson, R. and J. H. Goldthorpe (1992). *The Constant Flux: A Study of Class Mobility in Industrial Societies*. Oxford, UK: Claredon Press.

Esping-Andersen, G. (1990). *The Three Worlds of Welfare Capitalism*. Princeton, NJ: Princeton University Press.

Eulau, H. (1986). *Politics, Self, and Society: A Theme and Variations*. Cambridge, MA: Harvard University Press.

Eurostat (2007). *Regions in the European Union. Nomenclature of Territorial Units for Statistics. NUTS 2006*. Luxembourg: Office for Official Publications of the European Communities.

Evans, G. (1999). *The End of Class Politics?: Class Voting in Comparative Context*. Oxford, UK: Oxford University Press.

Evans, G. and N. D. de Graaf (Eds.) (2013). *Political Choice Matters: Explaining the Strength of Class and Religious Cleavages in Cross-National Perspective*. Oxford, UK: Oxford University Press.

Facchini, G. and A. M. Mayda (2012). Individual attitudes towards skilled migration: An empirical analysis across countries. *The World Economy* 35(2), 183–196.

Fair, R. C. (1978). The effect of economic events on votes for president. *The Review of Economics and Statistics* 60(2), 159–173.

Fajnzlber, P., D. Lederman, and N. Loayza (2002). Inequality and violent crime. *Journal of Law and Economics* 45, 1–40.

Fehr, E. and S. Gächter (2000). Fairness and retaliation: The economics of reciprocity. *Journal of Economic Perspectives* 14(3), 159–181.

Fehr, E. and K. M. Schmidt (2006a). The economics of fairness, reciprocity and altruism–experimental evidence and new theories. *Handbook of the Economics of Giving, Altruism and Reciprocity* 1, 615–691.

(2006b). The economics of fairness, reciprocity, and altruism: Experimental evidence and new theories. In S.-C. Kolm and J. M. Ythier (Eds.), *Handbook of the Economics of Giving, Reciprocity, and Altruism*. Amsterdam: Elsevier.

Ferejohn, J. (1986). Incumbent performance and electoral control. *Public Choice* 50(1–3), 5–25.

Finseraas, H. (2008a). Immigration and preferences for redistribution: An empirical analysis of European survey data. *Comparative European Politics* 6(4), 407–431.

Finseraas, H. (2008b). Immigration and preferences for redistribution: An empirical analysis of European survey data. *Comparative European Politics* 6(4), 407–431.

(2009). Income inequality and demand for redistribution: A multilevel analysis of European public opinion. *Scandinavian Political Studies* 32(1), 94–119.

Fiorina, M. P. (1981). *Retrospective Voting in American National Elections*. New Haven, CT: Yale University Press.

Frank, T. (2004). *What's the Matter with Kansas? How Conservatives Won the Heart of America.* New York: Metropolitan Books.

Freedman, D. A. and J. S. Sekhon (2010). Endogeneity in probit response models. *Political Analysis 18*(2), 138–150.

Freeman, G. P. (2009). Immigration, diversity, and welfare chauvinism. *The Forum 7*(3), 1–16.

Freeman, R. (1983). Crime and the labor market. In J. Wilson and J. Petersilia (Eds.), *Crime and Public Policy.* San Francisco: Institute for Contemporary Studies.

Freeman, R. B. and R. Schettkat (2000). The role of wage and skill differences in US–German employment differences. Technical report, National Bureau of Economic Research.

Friedman, M. (1957). *A Theory of the Consumption Function.* Princeton, NJ: Princeton University Press.

(1982). *Capitalism and Freedom.* Chicago: University of Chicago Press.

Garrett, G. (1998). *Partisan Politics in the Global Economy.* Cambridge, UK: Cambridge University Press.

Gelman, A. (2006). Prior distributions for variance parameters in hierarchical models. *Bayesian Analysis 1*(3), 515–534.

Gelman, A. and J. Hill (2007). *Data Analysis Using Regression and Multilevel/Hierarchical Models.* Cambridge, UK: Cambridge University Press.

Gelman, A., D. K. Park, B. Shor, J. Bafumi, and J. Cortina (2008). *Red State, Blue State, Rich State, Poor State: Why Americans Vote the Way They Do.* Princeton, NJ: Princeton University Press.

Gelman, A. and H. Stern (2006). The difference between "significant" and "not significant" is not itself statistically significant. *The American Statistician 60*(4), 328–331.

Gilens, M. (2005). Inequality and democratic responsiveness. *Public Opinion Quarterly 69*(5), 778–796.

(2009). *Why Americans Hate Welfare: Race, Media, and the Politics of Antipoverty Policy.* Chicago: University of Chicago Press.

Gilens, M. and B. I. Page (2014). Testing theories of American politics: Elites, interest groups, and average citizens. *Perspectives on Politics 12*(3), 564–581.

Gill, J. (2008). Is partial-dimension convergence a problem for inferences from MCMC algorithms? *Political Analysis 16*(2), 153–178.

Gottschalk, P. (1997). Inequality, income growth, and mobility: The basic facts. *Journal of Economic Perspectives 11*(2), 21–40.

Gouveia, M. and N. A. Masia (1998). Does the median voter model explain the size of government? Evidence from the states. *Public Choice 97*(1-2), 159–177.

Green, D. P., S. E. Ha, and J. G. Bullock (2010). Enough already about "black box" experiments: Studying mediation is more difficult than most scholars suppose. *The Annals of the American Academy of Political and Social Science 628*(1), 200–208.

Green, D. P., B. Palmquist, and E. Schickler (2004). *Partisan Hearts and Minds: Political Parties and the Social Identities of Voters.* New Haven, CT: Yale University Press.

Greenberg, D. (2010). Introduction. In D. Greenberg (Ed.), *Crime and Capitalism: Readings in Marxist Criminology*. Philadelphia: Temple University Press.

Greene, W. (2004). The behaviour of the maximum likelihood estimator of limited dependent variable models in the presence of fixed effects. *Econometrics Journal 7*, 98–119.

Greene, W. and D. Hensher (2010). *Modeling Ordered Choices: A Primer*. Cambridge, UK: Cambridge University Press.

Greene, W. H. (2002). *Econometric Analysis*. Upper Saddle River, NJ: Prentice Hall.

Gronke, P. (1992). Overreporting the vote in the 1988 senate election study: A response to Wright. *Legislative Studies Quarterly 17*(1), 113–129.

Habyarimana, J., M. Humphreys, D. N. Posner, and J. M. Weinstein (2007, 11). Why does ethnic diversity undermine public goods provision? *American Political Science Review Null*, 709–725.

Hacker, J. S. and P. Pierson (2011). *Winner-Take-All Politics: How Washington Made the Rich Richer – and Turned Its Back on the Middle Class*. New York: Simon and Schuster.

Haider, S. and G. Solon (2006). Life-cycle variation in the association between current and lifetime earnings. *American Economic Review 96*(4), 1308–1320.

Hainmueller, J. and M. J. Hiscox (2007). Educated preferences: Explaining attitudes toward immigration in Europe. *International Organization 61*(2), 399–442.

(2010). Attitudes toward highly skilled and low-skilled immigration: Evidence from a survey experiment. *American Political Science Review 104*(1), 61–84.

Haisken-DeNew, J. P. and J. R. Frick (2005). Desktop companion to the German Socio-Economic Panel Study (GSOEP). www.diw.de/deutsch/sop/service/dtc/dtc.pdf.

Hale, C. (1996). Fear of crime: A review of the literature. *International Review of Victimology 4*(2), 79–150.

Hall, P. A. and D. Soskice (2001). An introduction to varieties of capitalism. In P. A. Hall and D. Soskice (Eds.), *Varieties of Capitalism: The Institutional Foundations of Comparative Advantage*. Oxford, UK: Oxford University Press.

Hanmer, M. J. and K. O. Kalkan (2013). Behind the curve: Clarifying the best approach to calculating predicted probabilities and marginal effects from limited dependent variable models. *American Journal of Political Science 57*(1), 263–277.

Hanson, G. H., K. Scheve, and M. J. Slaughter (2007). Public finance and individual preferences over globalization strategies. *Economics & Politics 19*(1), 1–33.

Hausman, J. A. and D. A. Wise (1979). Attrition bias in experimental and panel data: The Gary income maintenance experiment. *Econometrica 47*(2), 455–473.

Heckman, J. J. (1981a). Heterogeneity and state dependence. In S. Rosen (Ed.), *Studies in Labor Markets*, pp. 91–140. Chicago: University of Chicago Press.

(1981b). The incidental parameters problem and the problem of initial conditions in estimating a discrete time-discrete data stochastic process. In C. F.

Manski and D. McFadden (Eds.), *Structural Analysis of Discrete Data with Econometric Applications*, pp. 179–195. Cambridge, MA: MIT Press.

Heckman, J. J., L. J. Lochner, and P. E. Todd (2006). Earnings functions, rates of return and treatment effects: The Mincer equation and beyond. In E. A. Hanushek and F. Welch (Eds.), *Handbook of the Economics of Education*, Volume 1, pp. 307–458. Amsterdam: Elsevier.

Hersh, E. D. and C. Nall (2016). The primacy of race in the geography of income-based voting: New evidence from public voting records. *American Journal of Political Science* 60(2), 289–303.

Hibbs, D. (1977). Political parties and macroeconomic policy. *American Political Science Review* 71(4), 1467–1487.

Hopkins, D. J. (2010). Politicized places: Explaining where and when immigrants provoke local opposition. *American Political Science Review* 104(1), 40–60.

Hout, M. (2004). Getting the most out of the GSS income measures. GSS Methodological Report 101.

Huber, J. D. (2017). *Exclusion by Elections. Inequality, Ethnic Identity, and Democracy*. Cambridge, UK: Cambridge University Press.

Huber, J. D. and P. Stanig (2008). Voting polarization on redistribution across democracies. Manuscript.

(2011). Church-state separation and redistribution. *Journal of Public Economics* 95(7-8), 828–836.

Iceland, J. (2004). Beyond black and white: Metropolitan residential segregation in multi ethnic America. *Social Science Research* 33(2), 248–271.

Imai, K., L. Keele, D. Tingley, and T. Yamamoto (2011). Unpacking the black box of causality: Learning about causal mechanisms from experimental and observational studies. *American Political Science Review* 105(4), 765–789.

Imai, K., L. Keele, and T. Yamamoto (2010). Identification, inference and sensitivity analysis for causal mediation effects. *Statistical Science* 25(1), 51–71.

Ivarsflaten, E. (2005). The vulnerable populist right parties: No economic realignment fuelling their electoral success. *European Journal of Political Research* 44(3), 465–492.

Iversen, T. (2005). *Capitalism, Democracy, and Welfare*. Cambridge, UK: Cambridge University Press.

Iversen, T. and T. R. Cusack (2000). The causes of welfare state expansion: Deindustrialization or globalization? *World Politics* 52(3), 313–349.

Iversen, T. and F. M. Rosenbluth (2010). *Women, Work, and Politics: The Political Economy of Gender Inequality*. New Haven, CT: Yale University Press.

Iversen, T. and D. Soskice (2001). An asset theory of social policy preferences. *American Political Science Review* 95(4), 875–893.

(2009). Distribution and redistribution: The shadow of the nineteenth century. *World Politics* 61(3), 438.

(2010). Real exchange rates and competitiveness: The political economy of skill formation, wage compression, and electoral systems. *American Political Science Review* 104(03), 601–623.

Iversen, T. and J. D. Stephens (2008). Partisan politics, the welfare state, and three worlds of human capital formation. *Comparative Political Studies* 41(4–5), 600–637.

Jarvis, S. and S. P. Jenkins (1995). *Do the poor stay poor? New evidence about income dynamics from the British Household Panel Survey.* Occasional Paper No. 95–2. Colchester: Institute for Social and Economic Research, University of Essex.

Jenkins, S. P. (2010). The British Household Panel Survey and its income data. IZA Discussion Paper No. 5242.

Jurado, E., G. Brochmann, and J. E. Dølvik (2013). Introduction. Immigration, work and welfare: Towards an integrated approach. In E. Jurado and G. Brochmann (Eds.), *Europe's Immigration Challenge: Reconciling Work, Welfare and Mobility.* New York: IB Tauris.

Karagiannis, E. and M. Kovacevic (2000). A method to calculate the jackknife variance estimator for the Gini coefficient. *Oxford Bulletin of Economics and Statistics* 62(1), 119–122.

Katz, L., S. D. Levitt, and E. Shustorovich (2003). Prison conditions, capital punishment, and deterrenc. *American Law and Economics Review* 5(2), 318–343.

Katzenstein, P. J. (1985). *Small States in World Markets: Industrial Policy in Europe.* Ithaca, NY: Cornell University Press.

Kedar, O. and W. P. Shively (2005). Introduction to the special issue. *Political Analysis* 13(4), 297–300.

Kenworthy, L. and J. Pontusson (2005). Rising inequality and the politics of redistribution in affluent countries. *Perspectives on Politics* 3(3), 449–471.

Kerckhoff, A. C. and M. Dylan (1999). Problems with international measures of education. *Journal of Socio-Economics* 28(6), 759–775.

Key, V. O. (1966). *The Responsible Electorate.* New York: Vintage Books.

Kinder, D. R. and D. O. Sears (1981). Prejudice and politics: Symbolic racism versus racial threats to the good life. *Journal of Personality and Social Psychology* 40(3), 414.

King, D. S. and R. M. Smith (2011). *Still a House Divided: Race and Politics in Obama's America.* Princeton, NJ: Princeton University Press.

King, G., J. Honaker, J. Anne, and S. Kenneth (2001). Analyzing incomplete political science data: An alternative algorithm for multiple imputation. *American Political Science Review* 95(1), 49–69.

King, G., R. O. Keohane, and S. Verba (1994). *Designing Social Inquiry.* Princeton, NJ: Princeton University Press.

Kitschelt, H. and A. J. McGann (1995). *The Radical Right in Western Europe: A Comparative Analysis.* Ann Arbor: University of Michigan Press.

Kitschelt, H. and P. Rehm (2014). Occupations as a site of political preference formation. *Comparative Political Studies* 47(12), 1670–1706.

Kopczuk, W., E. Saez, and J. Song (2010). Earnings inequality and mobility in the United States: Evidence from social security data since 1937. *The Quarterly Journal of Economics* 125(1), 91–128.

Korpi, W. (1983). *The Democratic Class Struggle.* London: Routledge and Kegan Paul.

Korpi, W. and J. Palme (2003). New politics and class politics in the context of austerity and globalization: Welfare state regress in 18 countries, 1975–95. *American Political Science Review* 97(3), 425–446.

Kramer, G. H. (1971). Short-term fluctuations in U.S. voting behavior, 1896–1964. *American Political Science Review* 65(3), 131–143.

Kumlin, S. and S. Svallfors (2007). Social stratification and political articulation: Why attitudinal class differences vary across countries. In S. Mau and B. Veghte (Eds.), *Social Justice, Legitimacy and the Welfare State*, pp. 19–46. Aldershot, UK: Ashgate.

Kymlicka, W. (2015). Solidarity in diverse societies: Beyond neoliberal multiculturalism and welfare chauvinism. *Comparative Migration Studies* 3(1), 17.

Lasswell, H. D. (1950). *Politics: Who Gets What, When, How*. New York: P. Smith.

Lawrance, E. C. (1991). Poverty and the rate of time preference: Evidence from panel data. *Journal of Political Economy* 99, 54–77.

Lawrence, R. Z. (1984). Is deindustrialization a myth? *Annals of the American Academy of Political and Social Science* 475, 39–51.

Lee, D. S. and J. McCrary (2005). Crime, punishment, and myopia. Technical report, National Bureau of Economic Research.

Lee, D. S., E. Moretti, and M. J. Butler (2002). Are politicians accountable to voters?: Evidence from US House roll call voting records. Center for Labor Economics, University of California.

Leighley, J. E. (1995). Attitudes, opportunities and incentives: A field essay on political participation. *Political Research Quarterly* 48(1), 181–209.

Lerman, R. I. and S. Yitzhaki (1989). Improving the accuracy of estimates of Gini coefficients. *Journal of Econometrics* 42(1), 43–47.

Levitt, S. D. and J. A. List (2007). What do laboratory experiments measuring social preferences reveal about the real world? *Journal of Economic Perspectives* 21(2), 153–174.

Levy, F. and R. J. Murnane (1992). US earnings levels and earnings inequality: A review of recent trends and proposed explanations. *Journal of Economic Literature* 30(3), 1333–1381.

Levy, H. and S. P. Jenkins (2008). Documentation for derived current and annual net household income variables, BHPS waves 1–16. Institute for Social and Economic Research, University of Essex.

Lewis-Beck, M. S. (2009). *The American Voter Revisited*. Ann Arbor: University of Michigan Press.

Lindert, P. H. (1996). What limits social spending? *Explorations in Economic History* 33, 1–34.

  (2004). *Growing Public: Volume 1, The Story: Social Spending and Economic Growth since the Eighteenth Century*. Cambridge, UK: Cambridge University Press.

Lipset, S. M. (1983). *Political Man. The Social Bases of Politics*. London: Heinemann.

Lipset, S. M. and S. Rokkan (1967). Cleavage structures, party systems, and voter alignments: An introduction. In *Party Systems and Voter Alignments. Cross-National Perspectives*, pp. 1–64. New York: Free Press.

Little, R. J. A. and D. B. Rubin (2002). *Statistical Analysis with Missing Data*. Hoboken, NJ: Wiley.

Logan, J. R., Z. Xu, and B. Stults (2014). Interpolating US decennial census tract data from as early as 1970 to 2010: A longitudinal tract database. *The Professional Geographer 66*(3), 412–420.

Lowe, W., K. Benoit, S. Mikhaylov, and M. Laver (2011). Scaling policy preferences from coded political texts. *Legislative Studies Quarterly 36*(1), 123–155.

Lü, X., K. F. Scheve, and M. J. Slaughter (2010). Envy, altruism, and the international distribution of trade protection. Working Paper 15700, National Bureau of Economic Research.

Lupu, N. and J. Pontusson (2011). The structure of inequality and the politics of redistribution. *American Political Science Review 105*(2), 316–336.

Luttmer, E. F. (1999). *Group Loyalty and the Taste for Redistribution*. Working paper No. 61. Chicago: University of Chicago.

  (2001). Group loyalty and the taste for redistribution. *Journal of Political Economy 109*(3), 500–528.

Lynn, P. (2006). Quality profile: British Household Panel Survey version 2.0: Waves 1 to 13: 1991–2003. Colchester: Institute for Social and Economic Research, University of Essex.

Mahler, V. A. and D. K. Jesuit (2006). Fiscal redistribution in the developed countries: New insights from the Luxembourg income study. *Socio-Economic Review 4*(3), 483–511.

Mair, P. and C. Mudde (1998). The party family and its study. *Annual Review of Political Science 1*(1), 211–229.

Malhotra, N., Y. Margalit, and C. H. Mo (2013). Economic explanations for opposition to immigration: Distinguishing between prevalence and conditional impact. *American Journal of Political Science 57*(2), 391–410.

Manza, J. and C. Brooks (1999). *Social Cleavages and Political Change: Voter Alignments and U.S. Party Coalitions*. Oxford, UK: Oxford University Press.

Mares, I. (2003). *The Politics of Social Risk*. New York: Cambridge University Press.

Margalit, Y. (2013). Explaining social policy preferences: Evidence from the great recession. *American Political Science Review 107*(1), 80–103.

Mayda, A. M. (2006). Who is against immigration? A cross-country investigation of individual attitudes toward immigrants. *The Review of Economics and Statistics 88*(3), 510–530.

McCarty, N. and J. Pontusson (2009). The political economy of inequality and redistribution. In W. Salverda, B. Nolan, and T. M. Smeeding (Eds.), *The Oxford Handbook of Economic Inequality*, pp. 665–692. Oxford, UK: Oxford University Press.

McCarty, N., K. T. Poole, and H. Rosenthal (2008). *Polarized America: The Dance of Ideology and Unequal Riches*. Cambridge, MA: MIT Press.

McKelvey, R. D. and W. Zavoina (1975). A statistical model for the analysis of ordinal level dependent variables. *Journal of Mathematical Sociology 4*, 103–120.

Mehlum, H., K. Moene, and R. Torvik (2005). Crime induced poverty traps. *Journal of Development Economics 77*(2), 325–340.

Meltzer, A. H. and S. F. Richard (1981). A rational theory of the size of government. *Journal of Political Economy* 89(5), 914–927.

Milanovic, B. (2000). The median-voter hypothesis, income inequality, and income redistribution: An empirical test with the required data. *European Journal of Political Economy* 16(3), 367–410.

Mincer, J. (1958). Investment in human capital and personal income distribution. *Journal of Political Economy* 66(4), 281–302.

(1974). *Schooling, Experience, and Earnings*. New York: Columbia University Press.

Moene, K. O. and M. Wallerstein (2001). Inequality, social insurance and redistribution. *American Political Science Review* 95(4), 859–874.

(2003). Earnings inequality and welfare spending: A disaggregated analysis. *World Politics* 55(4), 485–516.

Moulton, B. R. (1990). An illustration of a pitfall in estimating the effects of aggregate variables on micro units. *The Review of Economics and Statistics* 72(2), 334–338.

Mudde, C. (2007). *Populist Radical Right Parties in Europe*. Cambridge, UK: Cambridge University Press.

Mueller, D. C. (2003). *Public Choice III*. Cambridge, UK: Cambridge University Press.

Muthén, B. and T. Asparouhov (2015). Causal effects in mediation modeling: An introduction with applications to latent variables. *Structural Equation Modeling: A Multidisciplinary Journal* 22(1), 12–23.

Nelson, P. (1999). Redistribution and the income of the median voter. *Public Choice* 98(1/2), 187–194.

Nelson, R. R. and E. S. Phelps (1966). Investment in humans, technological diffusion, and economic growth. *The American Economic Review* 56(2), 69–75.

Openshaw, S. (1983). *The Modifiable Areal Unit Problem*. Norwick, UK: Geo Books.

O'Rand, A. and R. A. Ellis (1974). Social class and social time perspective. *Social Forces* 53(1), 53–62.

O'Rourke, K. H. and R. Sinnott (2006). The determinants of individual attitudes towards immigration. *European Journal of Political Economy* 22(4), 838–861.

Ortega, F. and J. G. Polavieja (2012). Labor-market exposure as a determinant of attitudes toward immigration. *Labour Economics* 19(3), 298–311.

Pacheco, J. (2011). Using national surveys to measure state public opinion over time: A guideline for scholars and applications. *State Politics & Policy Quarterly* 11(4), 415–439.

Page, B. I. and L. Jacobs (2009). *Class War? What Americans Really Think about Economic Inequality*. Chicago: University of Chicago Press.

Paulus, A., M. Čok, F. Figari, P. Hegedüs, N. Kump, O. Lelkes, H. Levy, C. Lietz, S. Lüpsik, D. Mantovani, et al. (2009). The effects of taxes and benefits on income distribution in the enlarged EU. Technical report, EUROMOD Working Paper EM8/09.

Pearl, J. (2001). Direct and indirect effects. *Proceedings of the Seventeenth Conference on Uncertainty in Artificial Intelligence*. San Francisco, CA: Morgan Kaufmann Publishers.

Pepper, J. V. (2002). Robust inferences from random clustered samples: An application using data from the panel study of income dynamics. *Economics Letters* 75(3), 341–345.

Pergament, K. (1997). *The Psychology of Religion and Coping: Theory, Research, Practice*. New York: Guilford Press.

Perotti, R. (1996). Growth, income distribution, and democracy: What the data say. *Journal of Economic Growth* 1(2), 149–187.

Persson, T. and G. Tabellini (2000). *Political Economics. Explaining Economic Policy*. Cambridge, MA: MIT Press.

Piketty, T. (1995). Social mobility and redistributive politics. *The Quarterly Journal of Economics* 110(3), 551–584.

Piketty, T. and E. Saez (2003). Income inequality in the United States, 1913–1998. *Quarterly Journal of Economics* 118(1), 1–41.

Pontusson, J. and D. Rueda (2010). The politics of inequality: Voter mobilization and left parties in advanced industrial states. *Comparative Political Studies* 43(6), 675–705.

Pontusson, J., D. Rueda, and C. R. Way (2002). Comparative political economy of wage distribution: The role of partisanship and labour market institutions. *British Journal of Political Science* 32(2), 281–308.

Powell, G. B. (1982). *Contemporary Democracies*. Cambridge, MA: Harvard University Press.

Przeworski, A. and M. Wallerstein (1988). Structural dependence of the state on capital. *American Political Science Review* 82(1), 11–29.

Psacharopoulos, G. and H. A. Patrinos (2004). Returns to investment in education: A further update. *Education Economics* 12(2), 111–134.

Quinn, K. M. (2004). Bayesian factor analysis for mixed ordinal and continuous responses. *Political Analysis* 12, 338–353.

Quinn, K. M. and A. D. Martin (2002). An integrated computational model of multiparty electoral competition. *Statistical Science* 17(4), 405–419.

Rabinowitz, G., P.-H. Gurian, and S. E. Macdonald (1984). The structure of presidential elections and the process of realignment, 1944 to 1980. *American Journal of Political Science* 27, 611–635.

Rainey, C. and R. A. Jackson (2013). Modeling misreports in self-reported vote choice data. Paper presented at the annual meeting of the Southern Political Science Association, Orlando, FL.

Rector, R. E. and S. E. Youssef (1999). The determinants of welfare caseload decline. Heritage Foundation CDA99-04.

Rehm, P. (2005). Citizen support for the welfare state. WZB discussion paper 2005-02.

(2009). Risks and redistribution: An individual-level analysis. *Comparative Political Studies* 42(7), 855–881.

(2011). Risk inequality and the polarized American electorate. *British Journal of Political Science* 41(2), 363–387.

(2016). *Risk Inequality and Welfare States: Social Policy Preferences, Development, and Dynamics*. Cambridge, UK: Cambridge University Press.

Robins, J. M. (2003). Semantics of causal DAG models and the identification of direct and indirect effects. In P. Green, N. Hjort, and S. Richardson (Eds.), *Highly Structured Stochastic Systems*, pp. 70–81. New York: Oxford University Press.

Rodden, J. (2010). The geographic distribution of political preferences. *Annual Review of Political Science 13*(1), 321–340.

Rodrigiuez, F. C. (1999). Does distributional skewness lead to redistribution? Evidence from the United States. *Economics & Politics 11*, 171–199.

Rodrik, D. (1998). Why do more open economies have bigger governments? *Journal of Political Economy 106*(5), 997–1032.

Romer, P. (1990). Endogenous technological change. *Journal of Political Economy 98*(5), S71–S102.

Romer, T. (1975). Individual welfare, majority voting and the properties of a linear income tax. *Journal of Public Economics 7*, 163–188.

Rothstein, B. (1998). *Just Institutions Matter: The Moral and Political Logic of the Universal Welfare State*. Cambridge, UK: Cambridge University Press.

Rovny, J. (2013). Where do radical right parties stand? Position blurring in multidimensional competition. *European Political Science Review 5*(1), 1–26.

Rubin, D. (1987). *Multiple Imputation for Nonresponse in Surveys*. Hoboken, NJ: Wiley.

(1996). Multiple imputation after 18+ years. *Journal of the American Statistical Association 91*(434), 473–489.

Rubin, D. B. (1986). Statistical matching using file concatenation with adjusted weights and multiple imputations. *Journal of Business & Economic Statistics 4*(1), 87–94.

Rueda, D. (2005). Insider–outsider politics in industrialized democracies: The challenge to Social Democratic parties. *American Political Science Review 99*(1), 61–74.

(2006). Social democracy and active labour-market policies: Insiders, outsiders and the politics of employment promotion. *British Journal of Political Science 36*(3), 385–406.

(2007). *Social Democracy Inside Out: Partisanship and Labor Market Policy in Industrialized Democracies*. Oxford, UK: Oxford University Press.

(2018). Food comes first, then morals: Redistribution preferences, parochial altruism, and immigration in Western Europe. *The Journal of Politics 80*(1), 225–239.

Rueda, D. and J. Pontusson (2000). Wage inequality and varieties of capitalism. *World Politics 52*(03), 350–383.

Rueda, D. and D. Stegmueller (2016). The externalities of inequality: Fear of crime and preferences for redistribution in Western Europe. *American Journal of Political Science 60*(2), 472–489.

Runciman, W. G. (1966). *Relative Deprivation and Social Justice: A Study of Attitudes to Social Inequality in 20th Century England*. Berkeley: University of California Press.

Rushton, P. J., R. D. Chrisjohn, and G. Cynthia Fekken (1981). The altruistic personality and the self-report altruism scale. *Personality and Individual Differences* 2(4), 293–302.

Schattschneider, E. E. (1960). *The Semisovereign People*. New York: Holt, Rinehart and Winston.

Schenker, N. and J. M. Taylor (1996). Partially parametric techniques for multiple imputation. *Computational Statistics & Data Analysis* 22(4), 425–446.

Scheve, K. and D. Stasavage (2006). Religion and preferences for social insurance. *Quarterly Journal of Political Science* 1(3), 255–286.

Scheve, K. F. and M. J. Slaughter (2001). Labor market competition and individual preferences over immigration policy. *Review of Economics and Statistics* 83(1), 133–145.

Schlozman, K. L. (1984). What accent the heavenly chorus? Political equality and the American pressure system. *The Journal of Politics* 46(4), 1006–1032.

Schlozman, K. L., S. Verba, and H. E. Brady (2012). *The Unheavenly Chorus: Unequal Political Voice and the Broken Promise of American Democracy*. Princeton, NJ: Princeton University Press.

Schneider, S. L. and I. Kogan (2008). The international standard classification of education 1997: Challenges in the application to national data and the implementation in cross-national surveys. *The International Standard Classification of Education (ISCED-97). An Evaluation of Content and Criterion Validity for 15 European Countries*. Mannheim: MZES.

Selb, P. and S. Munzert (2013). Voter overrepresentation, vote misreporting, and turnout bias in postelection surveys. *Electoral Studies* 32(1), 186–196.

Shalev, M. (1983). The social democratic model and beyond: Two generations of comparative research on the welfare state. *Comparative Social Research* 3(6), 315–551.

Shayo, M. (2009). A model of social identity with an application to political economy: Nation, class, and redistribution. *American Political Science Review* 103(2), 147–174.

Sinn, H.-W. (1995). A theory of the welfare state. *Scandinavian Journal of Economics* 97(4), 495–526.

Skrondal, A. and S. Rabe-Hesketh (2004). *Generalized Latent Variable Modeling: Multilevel, Longitudinal and Structural Equation Models*. Boca Raton, FL: Chapman & Hall.

Sniderman, P. M. and P. E. Tetlock (1986). Reflections on American racism. *Journal of Social Issues* 42(2), 173–187.

Sobel, M. E. (2008). Identification of causal parameters in randomized studies with mediating variables. *Journal of Educational and Behavioral Statistics* 33(2), 230–251.

Solt, F. (2016). The standardized world income inequality database. *Social Science Quarterly* 97(5), 1267–1281.

Soss, J., S. F. Schram, T. P. Vartanian, and E. O'Brien (2001). Setting the terms of relief: Explaining state policy choices in the devolution revolution. *American Journal of Political Science* 45(2), 378–395.

Spence, A. M. (1974). *Market Signaling: Informational Transfer in Hiring and Related Screening Processes*. Cambridge, MA: Harvard University Press.

Stabe, M. and H. Maier-Borst (2017). German election: AfD's advance in six charts. How the populist party could upend the country's politics on Sunday. *Financial Times*, September 20 2017, http://tinyurl.com/yaknalbg.

Stegmueller, D. (2013a). Modeling dynamic preferences: A Bayesian robust dynamic latent ordered probit model. *Political Analysis* 21(3), 314–333.

(2013b). Religion and redistributive voting in Western Europe. *Journal of Politics* 75(4), 1064–1076.

Stegmueller, D. (2014). Bayesian hierarchical age-period-cohort models with time-structured effects: An application to religious voting in the US, 1972–2008. *Electoral Studies* 33, 52–62.

Stegmueller, D., P. Scheepers, S. Rossteutscher, and E. de Jong (2012). Support for redistribution in Western Europe: Assessing the role of religion. *European Sociological Review* 28(4), 482–497.

Stephens, J. D. (1979). *The Transition from Capitalism to Socialism*. London: Macmillan.

Stigler, G. J. (1973). General economic conditions and national elections. *The American Economic Review* 63(2), 160–167.

Stimson, J. A., M. B. MacKuen, and R. S. Erikson (1995). Dynamic representation. *American Political Science Review* 89(03), 543–565.

Stoop, I., J. Billiet, A. Koch, and R. Fitzgerald (2010). *Improving survey response: Lessons learned from the European Social Survey*. Chichester, UK: John Wiley & Sons.

Svallfors, S. (2010). Policy feedback, generational replacement, and attitudes to state intervention: Eastern and Western Germany, 1990–2006. *European Political Science Review* 2(01), 119.

Swamy, P. A. (1970). Efficient inference in a random coefficient regression model. *Econometrica* 38(2), 311–323.

Tanzi, V. and L. Schuhknecht (2000). *Public Spending in the 20th Century: A Global Perspective*. Cambridge, UK: Cambridge University Press.

Tricomi, E., A. Rangel, C. F. Camerer, and J. P. O'Doherty (2010). Neural evidence for inequality-averse social preferences. *Nature* 463(7284), 1089–1091.

UNESCO (1999). *Operational Manual for ISCED 1997 (International Standard Classification of Education)*. UNESCO.

Van der Meer, T., M. Te Grotenhuis, and B. Pelzer (2010). Influential cases in multilevel modeling: A methodological comment. *American Sociological Review* 75(1), 173–178.

VanderWeele, T. and S. Vansteelandt (2009). Conceptual issues concerning mediation, interventions and composition. *Statistics and Its Interface* 2, 457–468.

VanderWeele, T. J. (2010). Bias formulas for sensitivity analysis for direct and indirect effects. *Epidemiology* 21(4), 540.

Van Oorschot, W. (2008). Solidarity towards immigrants in European welfare states. *International Journal of Social Welfare* 17(1), 3–14.

Van Oorschot, W. and W. Uunk (2007). Welfare spending and the public's concern for immigrants: Multilevel evidence for eighteen European countries. *Comparative Politics* 40(1), 63–82.

Van Ourti, T. and P. Clarke (2011). A simple correction to remove the bias of the
    Gini coefficient due to grouping. *Review of Economics and Statistics* 93(3),
    982–994.

Varian, H. R. (1980). Redistributive taxation as social insurance. *Journal of Public
    Economics 14*, 49–68.

Verba, S., K. L. Schlozman, and H. E. Brady (1995). *Voice and Equality: Civic
    Voluntarism in American Politics*. New York: Cambridge University Press.

Vining, A. and D. L. Weimer (2010). An assessment of important issues concerning
    the application of benefit-cost analysis to social policy. *Journal of Benefit-
    Cost Analysis 1*(1), 1–40.

Volkens, A., P. Lehmann, T. Matthiess, N. Merz, and S. Regel (2016). *The Man-
    ifesto Data Collection. Manifesto Project (MRG/CMP/MARPOR)*. Berlin:
    Wissenschaftszentrum Berlin für Sozialforschung (WZB).

Wagner, G. G., J. R. Frick, and J. Schupp (2007). The German Socio-Economic
    Panel Study (SOEP)–scope, evolution and enhancements. *Schmollers
    Jahrbuch 127*(1), 139–169.

Wansbeek, T. and E. Meijer (2000). *Measurement Error and Latent Variables in
    Econometrics*. Amsterdam: North Holland.

Warr, M. (2000). Fear of crime in the United States: Avenues for research and
    policy. *Criminal Justice 4*(4), 451–489.

Weil, A. and K. Finegold (2002). Introduction. In A. Weil and K. Finegold (Eds.),
    Welfare Reform: The Next Act, pp. xi–xxxi. Lanham, MD: The Urban
    Institute Press.

Western, B. (2006). *Punishment and Inequality in America*. New York: Russell
    Sage Foundation.

Wilensky, H. (1975). *The Welfare State and Equality: Structural and Ideological
    Roots of Public Expenditures*. Berkeley, CA: University of California Press.

Wilson, J. Q. and R. Herrnstein (1985). *Crime and Human Nature*. New York:
    Simon & Shuster.

Wong, C., J. Bowers, T. Williams, and K. D. Simmons (2012). Bringing the person
    back in: Boundaries, perceptions, and the measurement of racial context. *The
    Journal of Politics 74*(4), 1153–1170.

Wong, C. J. (2010). *Boundaries of Obligation in American Politics: Geographic,
    National, and Racial Communities*. Cambridge, UK: Cambridge University
    Press.

Wooldridge, J. M. (2003). Cluster-sample methods in applied econometrics. *The
    American Economic Review 93*(2), 133–138.

Wright, G. C. (1990). Misreports of vote choice in the 1988 NES senate election
    study. *Legislative Studies Quarterly 15*(4), 543–563.

    (1992). Reported versus actual vote: There is a difference and it matters.
    Legislative Studies Quarterly 17(1), 131–142.

Wu, C. F. J. (1986). Jackknife, bootstrap and other resampling methods in
    regression analysis. *The Annals of Statistics 14*(4), 1261–1295.

Yatchew, A. and Z. Griliches (1985). Specification error in probit models. *The
    Review of Economics and Statistics 67*(1), 134–139.

Index

Other Books in the Series

John D. Huber and Charles R. Shipan, *Deliberate Discretion? The Institutional Foundations of Bureaucratic Autonomy*

Ellen Immergut, *Health Politics: Interests and Institutions in Western Europe*

Torben Iversen, *Capitalism, Democracy, and Welfare*

Torben Iversen, *Contested Economic Institutions*

Torben Iversen, Jonas Pontussen, and David Soskice, eds., *Unions, Employers, and Central Banks: Macroeconomic Coordination and Institutional Change in Social Market Economics*

Thomas Janoski and Alexander M. Hicks, eds., *The Comparative Political Economy of the Welfare State*

Joseph Jupille, *Procedural Politics: Issues, Influence, and Institutional Choice in the European Union*

Karen Jusko, *Who Speaks for the Poor? Electoral Geography, Party Entry, and Representation*

Stathis Kalyvas, *The Logic of Violence in Civil War*

Stephen B. Kaplan, *Globalization and Austerity Politics in Latin America*

David C. Kang, *Crony Capitalism: Corruption and Capitalism in South Korea and the Philippines*

Junko Kato, *Regressive Taxation and the Welfare State*

Orit Kedar, *Voting for Policy, Not Parties: How Voters Compensate for Power Sharing*

Robert O. Keohane and Helen B. Milner, eds., *Internationalization and Domestic Politics*

Herbert Kitschelt, *The Transformation of European Social Democracy*

Herbert Kitschelt, Kirk A. Hawkins, Juan Pablo Luna, Guillermo Rosas, and Elizabeth J. Zechmeister, *Latin American Party Systems*

Herbert Kitschelt, Peter Lange, Gary Marks, and John D. Stephens, eds., *Continuity and Change in Contemporary Capitalism*

Herbert Kitschelt, Zdenka Mansfeldova, Radek Markowski, and Gabor Toka, *Post-Communist Party Systems*

David Knoke, Franz Urban Pappi, Jeffrey Broadbent, and Yutaka Tsujinaka, eds., *Comparing Policy Networks*

Ken Kollman, *Perils of Centralization: Lessons from Church, State, and Corporation*

Allan Kornberg and Harold D. Clarke, *Citizens and Community: Political Support in a Representative Democracy*

Amie Kreppel, *The European Parliament and the Supranational Party System*

David D. Laitin, *Language Repertoires and State Construction in Africa*

Fabrice E. Lehoucq and Ivan Molina, *Stuffing the Ballot Box: Fraud, Electoral Reform, and Democratization in Costa Rica*

Benjamin Lessing *Making Peace in Drug Wars: Crackdowns and Cartels in Latin America*

Mark Irving Lichbach and Alan S. Zuckerman, eds., *Comparative Politics: Rationality, Culture, and Structure, 2nd edition*

Evan Lieberman, *Race and Regionalism in the Politics of Taxation in Brazil and South Africa*

Richard M. Locke, *The Promise and Limits of Private Power: Promoting Labor Standards in a Global Economy*

Julia Lynch, *Age in the Welfare State: The Origins of Social Spending on Pensioner's Workers and Children*

Richard A. Nielsen, *Deadly Clerics: Blocked Ambition and the Paths to Jihad*

Aníbal Pérez-Liñán, *Presidential Impeachment and the New Political Instability in Latin America*

Roger D. Petersen, *Understanding Ethnic Violence: Fear, Hatred, and Resentment in 20th Century Eastern Europe*

Roger D. Petersen, *Western Intervention in the Balkans: The Strategic Use of Emotion in Conflict*

Simona Piattoni, ed., *Clientelism, Interests, and Democratic Representation*

Paul Pierson, *Dismantling the Welfare State?: Reagan, Thatcher, and the Politics of Retrenchment*

Marino Regini, *Uncertain Boundaries: The Social and Political Construction of European Economies*

Kenneth M. Roberts, *Changing Course in Latin America: Party Systems in the Neoliberal Era*

Marc Howard Ross, *Cultural Contestation in Ethnic Conflict*

Roger Schoenman, *Networks and Institutions in Europe's Emerging Markets*

Ben Ross Schneider, *Hierarchical Capitalism in Latin America: Business, Labor, and the Challenges of Equitable Development*

Lyle Scruggs, *Sustaining Abundance: Environmental Performance in Industrial Democracies*

Jefferey M. Sellers, *Governing from Below: Urban Regions and the Global Economy*

Yossi Shain and Juan Linz, eds., *Interim Governments and Democratic Transitions*

Beverly Silver, *Forces of Labor: Workers' Movements and Globalization since 1870*

Theda Skocpol, *Social Revolutions in the Modern World*

Prerna Singh, *How Solidarity Works for Welfare: Subnationalism and Social Development in India*

Austin Smith et al, *Selected Works of Michael Wallerstein*

Regina Smyth, *Candidate Strategies and Electoral Competition in the Russian Federation: Democracy without Foundation*

Richard Snyder, *Politics after Neoliberalism: Reregulation in Mexico*

David Stark and Laszló Bruszt, *Postsocialist Pathways: Transforming Politics and Property in East Central Europe*

Sven Steinmo, *The Evolution of Modern States: Sweden, Japan, and the United States*

Sven Steinmo, Kathleen Thelen, and Frank Longstreth, eds., *Structuring Politics: Historical Institutionalism in Comparative Analysis*

Susan C. Stokes, *Mandates and Democracy: Neoliberalism by Surprise in Latin America*

Susan C. Stokes, ed., *Public Support for Market Reforms in New Democracies*

Susan C. Stokes, Thad Dunning, Marcelo Nazareno, and Valeria Brusco, *Brokers, Voters, and Clientelism: The Puzzle of Distributive Politics*

Milan W. Svolik, *The Politics of Authoritarian Rule*

Duane Swank, *Global Capital, Political Institutions, and Policy Change in Developed Welfare States*

Sidney Tarrow, *Power in Movement: Social Movements and Contentious Politics*

Sidney Tarrow, *Power in Movement: Social Movements and Contentious Politics, Revised and Updated Third Edition*

Tariq Thachil, *Elite Parties, Poor Voters: How Social Services Win Votes in India*

Kathleen Thelen, *How Institutions Evolve: The Political Economy of Skills in Germany, Britain, the United States, and Japan*

Kathleen Thelen, *Varieties of Liberalization and the New Politics of Social Solidarity*

Charles Tilly, *Trust and Rule*

Daniel Treisman, *The Architecture of Government: Rethinking Political Decentralization*

Guillermo Trejo, *Popular Movements in Autocracies: Religion, Repression, and Indigenous Collective Action in Mexico*

Rory Truex, *Making Autocracy Work: Representation and Responsiveness in Modern China*

Lily Lee Tsai, *Accountability without Democracy: How Solidary Groups Provide Public Goods in Rural China*

Joshua Tucker, *Regional Economic Voting: Russia, Poland, Hungary, Slovakia and the Czech Republic, 1990–1999*

Ashutosh Varshney, *Democracy, Development, and the Countryside*

Yuhua Wang, *Tying the Autocrat's Hand: The Rise of the Rule of Law in China*

Jeremy M. Weinstein, *Inside Rebellion: The Politics of Insurgent Violence*

Stephen I. Wilkinson, *Votes and Violence: Electoral Competition and Ethnic Riots in India*

Andreas Wimmer, *Waves of War: Nationalism, State Formation, and Ethnic Exclusion in the Modern World*

Jason Wittenberg, *Crucibles of Political Loyalty: Church Institutions and Electoral Continuity in Hungary*

Elisabeth J. Wood, *Forging Democracy from Below: Insurgent Transitions in South Africa and El Salvador*

Elisabeth J. Wood, *Insurgent Collective Action and Civil War in El Salvador*

Deborah J. Yashar, *Homicidal Ecologies: Illicit Economies and Complicit States in Latin America*

Daniel Ziblatt, *Conservative Parties and the Birth of Democracy*